M000200165

WILEY SECURITIES INDUSTRY ESSENTIALS EXAM REVIEW STUDY GUIDE 2020

WILEY SECURITIES INDUSTRY ESSENTIALS EXAM REVIEW STUDY GUIDE 2020

The Securities Institute of America, Inc.

Wiley Efficient Learning™

Cover image: © Jumpeestudio/iStock.com
Cover design: Wiley

Copyright © 2020 by John Wiley & Sons, Inc. All rights reserved.

Published by John Wiley & Sons, Inc., Hoboken, New Jersey.
Published simultaneously in Canada.

No part of this publication may be reproduced, stored in a retrieval system, or transmitted in any form or by any means, electronic, mechanical, photocopying, recording, scanning, or otherwise, except as permitted under Section 107 or 108 of the 1976 United States Copyright Act, without either the prior written permission of the Publisher, or authorization through payment of the appropriate per-copy fee to the Copyright Clearance Center, Inc., 222 Rosewood Drive, Danvers, MA 01923, (978) 750-8400, fax (978) 646-8600, or on the Web at www.copyright.com. Requests to the Publisher for permission should be addressed to the Permissions Department, John Wiley & Sons, Inc., 111 River Street, Hoboken, NJ 07030, (201) 748-6011, fax (201) 748-6008, or online at http://www.wiley.com/go/permissions.

Limit of Liability/Disclaimer of Warranty: While the publisher and author have used their best efforts in preparing this book, they make no representations or warranties with respect to the accuracy or completeness of the contents of this book and specifically disclaim any implied warranties of merchantability or fitness for a particular purpose. No warranty may be created or extended by sales representatives or written sales materials. The advice and strategies contained herein may not be suitable for your situation. You should consult with a professional where appropriate. Neither the publisher nor author shall be liable for any loss of profit or any other commercial damages, including but not limited to special, incidental, consequential, or other damages.

For general information on our other products and services or for technical support, please contact our Customer Care Department within the United States at (800) 762-2974, outside the United States at (317) 572-3993 or fax (317) 572-4002.

Wiley publishes in a variety of print and electronic formats and by print-on-demand. Some material included with standard print versions of this book may not be included in e-books or in print-on-demand. If this book refers to media such as a CD or DVD that is not included in the version you purchased, you may download this material at http://booksupport.wiley.com. For more information about Wiley products, visit www.wiley.com.

ISBN 978-1-119-70371-6 (Paperback)
       978-1-119-70349-5
       978-1-119-70347-1

Printed in the United States of America

V10019545_062920

Contents

Options, Investment Companies, Variable Annuities, and Retirement Plans

Customer Accounts, Client Recommendations, Professional Conduct, and Industry Regulations

Equity and Debt Securities

Introduction to Equity Securities

INTRODUCTION

Learning Objective Statements

Detail how common stock is created.

List stockholders' rights.

Detail the trade date, settlement date, payment date, and violations.

Explain stockholders' relationship with the issuer.

This first lesson will build the foundation upon which the rest of this course is built. Equity securities are divided into two types: common and preferred stock. We examine the features of common stock and preferred stock, as well as the benefits and risks associated with their ownership, but first we must define exactly what meets the definition of a security.

WHAT IS A SECURITY?

A security is any investment product that can be exchanged for value and involves risk. In order for an investment to be considered a security, it must be readily transferable between two parties and the owner must be subject to the loss of some, or all, of the invested principal. If the product is not transferable or does not contain risk, it is not a security.

Types of Securities	Types of Nonsecurities
Common stock	Whole life insurance
Preferred stock	Term life insurance
Bonds	IRAs
Mutual funds	Retirement plans
Variable annuities	Fixed annuities
Variable life insurance	Prospectus
Options	Confirmations
Rights	
Warrants	
ETFs/ETNs	
Real estate investment trusts	
CMOs	

EQUITY = STOCK

The term equity is synonymous with the term stock. Throughout your preparation for this exam and on the exam itself, you will find many terms that are used interchangeably. Equity or stock creates an ownership relationship with the issuing company. Once an investor has purchased stock in a corporation, they become an owner of that corporation. The corporation sells off pieces of itself to investors in the form of shares in an effort to raise working capital. Equity is perpetual, meaning there is no maturity date for the shares and the investor may own the shares until they decide to sell them. Most corporations use the sale of equity as their main source of business capital.

COMMON STOCK

Each share of common represents an ownership interest

There are thousands of companies whose stock trades publicly and who have used the sale of equity as a source of raising business capital. All publicly traded companies must issue common stock before they may issue any other type of equity security. There are two types of equity securities: common stock and preferred stock. While all publicly traded companies must have sold or issued common stock, not all companies may want to issue or sell preferred stock. Let's take a look at the creation of a company and how common stock is created.

CORPORATE TIME LINE

The following is a representation of the steps that corporations must take in order to sell their common stock to the public, as well as what may happen to that stock once it has been sold to the public.

AUTHORIZED STOCK

(handwritten margin note: max. # of shares comp. can issue)

Authorized stock is the maximum number of shares that a company may sell to the investing public in an effort to raise cash to meet the organization's goals. The number of authorized shares is arbitrarily determined and is set at the time of incorporation. A corporation may sell all or part of its authorized stock. If the corporation wants to sell more shares than it's authorized to sell, the shareholders must approve an increase in the number of authorized shares.

ISSUED STOCK

(handwritten margin note: what the comp. has issued, which is less than the Authorized stock)

Issued stock is stock that has been authorized for sale and that has actually been sold to the investing public. The total number of authorized shares typically exceeds the total number of issued shares so that the corporation may sell additional shares in the future to meet its needs. Once shares have been sold to the investing public, they will always be counted as issued shares, regardless of their ownership or subsequent repurchase by the corporation. It's important to note that the total number of issued shares may never exceed the total number of authorized shares.

Additional authorized shares may be issued in the future for any of the following reasons:

- Pay a stock dividend
- Expand current operations
- Exchange common shares for convertible preferred or convertible bonds
- Satisfy obligations under employee stock options or purchase plans

OUTSTANDING STOCK

Outstanding stock is stock that has been sold or issued to the investing public and that actually remains in the hands of the investing public.

EXAMPLE

XYZ corporation has 10,000,000 shares authorized and has sold 5,000,000 shares to the public during its initial public offering. In this case, there would be 5,000,000 shares of stock issued and 5,000,000 shares outstanding.

TREASURY STOCK

Treasury stock is stock that has been sold to the investing public, which has subsequently been repurchased by the corporation. The corporation may elect to reissue the shares or it may retire the shares that it holds in treasury stock. Treasury stock does not receive dividends, nor does it vote.

A corporation may elect to repurchase its own shares for any of the following reasons:

- To maintain control of the company
- To increase earnings per share
- To fund employee stock purchase plans
- To use shares to pay for a merger or acquisition

To determine the amount of treasury stock, use the following formula:

issued stock – outstanding stock = treasury stock

Smill - 2M = 3M Treasury

EXAMPLE

If, in the case of XYZ, the company decides to repurchase 3,000,000 of its own shares, then XYZ would have 5,000,000 shares issued: 2,000,000 shares, and 3,000,000 shares of treasury stock.

It's important to note that once the shares have been issued, they will always be counted as issued shares. The only thing that changes is the number of outstanding shares and the number of treasury shares.

VALUES OF COMMON STOCK

A common stock's market value is determined by supply and demand and may or may not have any real relationship to what the shares are actually worth. The market value of common stock is affected by the current and future expectations for the company.

BOOK VALUE

A corporation's book value is the theoretical liquidation value of the company. The book value is found by taking all of the company's tangible assets and subtracting all of its liabilities. This will give you the total book value. To determine the book values per share, divide the total book value by the total number of outstanding common shares.

PAR VALUE

Par value, in a discussion regarding common stock, is only important if you are an accountant looking at the balance sheet. An accountant uses the par value as a way to credit the money received by the corporation from the initial sale of the stock to the balance sheet. For investors, it has no relationship to any measure of value, which may otherwise be employed.

RIGHTS OF COMMON STOCKHOLDERS

As an owner of common stock, investors are owners of the corporation. As such, investors have certain rights that are granted to all common stock holders.

PREEMPTIVE RIGHTS

As a stockholder, an investor has the right to maintain his or her percentage interest in the company. This is known as a preemptive right. Should the company wish to sell additional shares to raise new capital, they must first offer the new shares to existing shareholders. If the existing shareholders decide not to purchase the new shares, then the shares may be offered to the general public. When a corporation decides to conduct a rights offering, the board of directors must approve the issuance of the additional shares. If the number of shares to be issued under the rights offering would cause the total number of outstanding shares to exceed the total number of authorized shares, then shareholder approval will be required. Existing shareholders will have to approve an increase in the number of authorized shares before the rights offering can proceed.

Number of Existing Shares	Number of New Shares	Total Shares after Offering
100,000	100,000	200,000
10,000 10% ownership	10,000 10% of offering	20,000 10% ownership

In this example, the company has 100,000 shares of stock outstanding and an investor has purchased 10,000 of those original shares. As a result, the investor owns 10% of the corporation. The company wishing to sell 100,000 new shares to raise new capital must first offer 10% of the new shares to the current investor (10,000 shares), before the shares may be offered to the general public. This means that if the investor decides to purchase the additional shares, as is the case in the example, the investor will have maintained his or her 10% interest in the company.

A shareholder's preemptive right is ensured through a rights offering. The existing shareholders have the right to purchase the new shares at a discount to the current market value for up to 45 days. This is known as the subscription price. Once the subscription price is set, it remains constant for the 45 days, while the price of the stock is moving up and down in the market place.

There are three possible outcomes for a right. They are:

1. **Exercised:** The investor decides to purchase the additional shares and sends in the money, along with the rights to receive the additional shares.

2. **Sold:** The rights have value and if the investor does not want to purchase the additional shares, they may be sold to another investor who would like to purchase the shares.

3. **Expire:** The rights will expire when no one wants to purchase the stock. This will only occur when the market price of the share has fallen below the subscription price of the right and the 45 days has elapsed.

CHARACTERISTICS OF A RIGHTS OFFERING

Once a rights offering has been declared, the company's common stock will trade with the rights attached. The stock in this situation is said to be trading cum rights. The company's stock, which is the subject of the rights offering, will trade cum rights between the declaration date and the ex date. After the ex date, the stock will trade without the rights attached or will trade ex rights. The value of the common stock will be adjusted down by the value of the right on the ex-rights date. During a rights offering, each share will be issued one right. The subscription price and the number of rights required to purchase one additional share will be detailed in the terms of the offering on the rights certificate. During a rights offering, the issuer will retain an investment bank to act as a standby underwriter and the investment bank will stand by, ready to purchase any shares that are not purchased by the rights holders.

VOTING

As a common stockholder, you have the right to vote on the major issues facing the corporation. You are a part owner of the company and, as a result, you have a right to say how the company is run. The biggest emphasis is placed on the election of the board of directors.

Common stockholders may also vote on:

• Issuance of bonds or additional common shares.

• Stock splits.

• Mergers and acquisitions.

• Major changes in corporate policy.

METHODS OF VOTING

There are two methods by which the voting process may be conducted: statutory and cumulative. A stockholder may cast one vote for each share of stock owned and the statutory or cumulative methods will determine how those votes are cast. The test focuses on the election of the board of directors, so we will use that in our example.

 FOCUSPOINT

An investor own a 200 shares of XYZ. There are two board members to be elected and there are four people running in the election. Under both the statutory and cumulative methods of voting, take the number of shares owned and multiply them by the number of people to be elected to determine how many votes the shareholder has; in this case, 200 shares × 2 = 400 votes. The cumulative or statutory methods dictate how those votes may be cast.

Candidate	Statutory	Cumulative
1	200 votes	400 votes
2		
3		
4	200 votes	

The statutory method requires that the votes be distributed evenly among the candidates for whom the investor wishes to vote.

The cumulative method allows shareholders to cast all of their votes in favor of one candidate, if they so choose. The cumulative method is said to favor smaller investors for this reason.

LIMITED LIABILITY

A stockholder's liability is limited to the amount of money invested in the stock. Stockholders cannot be held liable for any amount past their invested capital.

FREELY TRANSFERABLE

Common stock and most other securities are freely transferable. That is to say that one investor may sell their shares to another investor without limitation and without requiring the approval of the issuer. The transfer of a security's ownership, in most cases, is facilitated through a broker dealer. The transfer of ownership is executed in the secondary market on either an exchange or in the over-the-counter market. Ownership of common stock is evidenced by a stock certificate which identifies the:

- Name of the issuing company.
- Number of shares owned.
- Name of the owner of record.
- CUSIP number.

In order to transfer or sell the shares, the owner must endorse the stock certificate or sign a power of substitution known as a stock or bond power. Signing the certificate or a stock or bond power makes the securities transferable into the new buyer's name.

THE TRANSFER AGENT

The transfer agent is the company that is in charge of transferring the record of ownership from one party to another. The transfer agent:

- Cancels old certificates registered to the seller.
- Issues new certificates to the buyer.
- Maintains and records a list of stockholders.
- Ensures that shares are issued to the correct owner.
- Locates lost or stolen certificates.
- Issues new certificates in the event of destruction.
- May authenticate a mutilated certificate.

THE REGISTRAR

The registrar is the company responsible for auditing the transfer agent to ensure that the transfer agent does not erroneously issue more shares than are authorized by the company. In the case of a bond issue, the registrar will certify that the bond is a legally binding debt of the company. The function of the transfer agent and the registrar may not be performed by a single department of any one company. A bank or a trust company usually performs the functions of the transfer agent and the registrar.

CUSIP NUMBERS

The Committee on Uniform Securities Identification Procedures issues CUSIP numbers that are printed on the stock or bond certificates to help identify the security. CUSIP numbers must also appear on trade confirmations.

INSPECTION OF BOOKS AND RECORDS

All stockholders have the right to inspect the company's books and records. For most shareholders, this right is ensured through the company's filing of quarterly and annual reports. Stockholders also have the right to obtain a list of shareholders, but they do not have the right to review other corporate financial data that the corporation may deem confidential.

RESIDUAL CLAIM TO ASSETS

In the event of a company's bankruptcy or liquidation, common stockholders have the right to receive their proportional interest in residual assets. After all the other security holders have been paid (along with all creditors of the corporation), common stockholders may claim the residual assets. For this reason, common stock is the most junior security.

Pretest

INTRODUCTION TO EQUITY SECURITIES

la.finra.intro.eq.sec.001_1811

1. Authorized stock is all of the following, except:

   a. It is the maximum number of shares a company may sell.

   b. It is arbitrarily determined at the time of incorporation and may not be changed.

   c. It may be sold in total or in part when the company goes public.

   d. It may be sold to investors to raise operating capital for the company.

la.finra.intro.eq.sec.002_1811

2. Common stockholders do not have the right to vote on which of the following issues?

   a. Election of the board of directors.

   b. Stock splits.

   c. Issuance of additional common shares.

   d. Bankruptcy.

la.finra.intro.eq.sec.003_1811

3. It may be necessary for a company to repurchase some of its stock, to increase its treasury stock, for which one of the following reasons:

   a. To maintain control of the company.

   b. To allow the company to pay out smaller dividends.

   c. To increase the funding in the company's treasury.

   d. To reassure its investors that all is well.

sa.finra.intro.eq.sec.001_1811

4. A company you own common stock in has just filed for bankruptcy. As a shareholder, you will have the right to receive:

   a. The par value of the common shares.

   b. New common shares in the reorganized company.

   c. A percentage of your original investment.

   d. Your proportional percentage of residual assets.

sa.finra.intro.eq.sec.002_1811

5. All of the following are rights of common stockholders, except:

   a. Right to elect the board of directors.

   b. Right to vote for executive compensation.

   c. Right to vote for a stock split.

   d. Right to maintain their percentage of ownership in the company.

Why Do People Buy Stock?

INTRODUCTION

Learning Objective Statements

Analyze the different features and investment objectives for purchasing both common and preferred stock.

Compare the investment objectives for purchasing common and preferred stock.

Explain the different features of preferred stock.

This lesson explores why people want to invest in common stock, as well as some risks that come with owning it. Preferred stock is also discussed at length to prepare you thoroughly for the exam.

The main reason people invest in common stock is for capital appreciation. They want their money to grow in value over time. An investor in common stock hopes to buy the stock at a low price and sell it at a higher price at some point in the future.

EXAMPLE

An investor purchases 100 shares of XYZ at $20 per share on March 15, 2014. On April 20 of 2015, the investor sells 100 shares of XYZ for $30 per share, realizing a profit of $10 per share or $1,000 on the 100 shares.

INCOME

Many corporations distribute a portion of their earnings to their investors in the form of dividends. This distribution of earnings creates income for the investor, and investors in common stock generally receive dividends quarterly. The amount of income that an investor receives each year is measured relative to what the investor has paid—or will pay—for the stock, and is known as the dividend yield or the current yield.

EXAMPLE   ABC pays a $.50 quarterly dividend to its shareholders. The stock is currently trading at $20 per share. What is its current yield (also known as dividend yield)?

$$\text{current yield} = \text{annual income}/\text{current market price}$$

$$\$.50 \times 4 = \$2.00 \qquad \$2/\$20 = 10\%$$

The investor in this example is receiving 10% of the purchase price of the stock each year in the form of dividends, which, by itself, would be a nice return for the investor.

Some investors may elect to have their shares enrolled in a corporation's dividend reinvestment program (DRIP). The dividends received by the investor will be used to purchase additional shares of the corporation. The investor will be liable for taxes on the dividend and the amount of the dividends reinvested will be added to the cost base for tax purposes. So long as the corporation pays a dividend, the investor will have more shares of the company at the end of each year.

WHAT ARE THE RISKS OF OWNING COMMON STOCK?

The major risk in owning common stock is that the stock may fall in value. There are no sure things in the stock market and, even if you own stock in a great company, you may end up losing money.

DIVIDENDS MAY BE STOPPED OR REDUCED

Common stockholders are not entitled to receive dividends just because they own part of the company. It is up to the company to elect to pay a dividend. The corporation is in no way obligated to pay a dividend to common shareholders.

JUNIOR CLAIM ON CORPORATE ASSETS

A common stockholder is the last person to get paid if the company is liquidated. It is very possible that after all creditors and other investors are paid, there will be little or nothing left for the common stockholder.

HOW DOES SOMEONE BECOME A STOCKHOLDER?

We have reviewed some of the reasons why an investor would want to become a stockholder. Now we need to review how someone becomes a stockholder. Although some people purchase the shares directly from the corporation when the stock is offered to the public directly, most investors purchase the shares from other investors. These investor-to-investor transactions take place in the secondary market on the exchange or in the over-the-counter market. Although the transaction in many cases only take seconds to execute, trades actually take several days to fully complete. Let's review the important dates regarding transactions, which are done for a "regular-way" settlement.

TRADE DATE

The trade date is the day when your order is actually executed. Although an order has been placed with a broker, it may not be executed on the same day. There are certain types of orders that may take several days or even longer to execute, depending on the type of order. A market order will be executed immediately (as soon as it is presented to the market), making the trade date the same day the order was entered.

SETTLEMENT DATE

The buyer of a security actually becomes the owner of record on the settlement date. When an investor buys a security from another investor, the selling investor's name is removed from the security and the buyer's name is recorded as the new owner. Settlement date is 2 business days after the trade date. This is known as T+2 for all regular-way transactions in common stock, preferred stock, corporate bonds, and municipal bonds. Government bonds and options all settle the next business day following the trade date.

PAYMENT DATE

The payment date is the day when the buyer of the security has to have the money in to the brokerage firm to pay for the purchase. Under industry rules, the payment date for common and preferred stock and corporate and municipal bonds is 4 business days after the trade date or T+4. Payment dates are regulated by the Federal Reserve Board under Regulation T of the Securities Exchange Act of 1934. Although many brokerage firms require their customers to have their money in to pay for their purchases sooner than the rules state, the customer has up to 4 business days to pay for the trade.

VIOLATION

If the customer fails to pay for the purchase within the 4 business days allowed, the customer is in violation of Regulation T. As a result, the brokerage firm will "sell out" and freeze the customer's account. On the 5th business day following the trade date, the brokerage firm will sell out the securities for which the customer failed to pay. The customer is responsible for any loss that may occur as a result of the sell out and the brokerage firm may sell out shares of another security in the investor's account in order to cover the loss. The brokerage firm will then freeze the customer's account, which means the customer must deposit money up front for any purchases they want to make in the next 90 days. After the 90 days have expired, the customer is considered to have reestablished good credit and may then conduct business in the regular way and take up to 4 business days to pay for his or her trades.

PREFERRED STOCK

Preferred stock is an equity security with a fixed income component. Like a common stockholder, the preferred stockholder is an owner of the company. However the preferred stockholder is investing in the stock for the fixed income that the preferred shares generate through their semiannual dividends. Preferred stock has a stated dividend rate or a fixed rate that the corporation must pay to its preferred shareholders. Growth is generally not achieved through investing in preferred shares.

TAKENOTE!

While not the norm, some companies issue adjustable rate preferred shares. The dividend rate on these shares will be adjusted based on a benchmark such as Treasury bill rates. Because the dividend rate adjusts with market interest rates the price of the shares tends to be stable.

FEATURES OF ALL PREFERRED STOCK

There are a number of different types of preferred stock but all preferred stock has the same basic features.

PAR VALUE

Par value on preferred stock is very important because that's what the dividend is based on. Par value for all preferred shares is $100 unless otherwise stated. Companies generally express the dividend as a percentage of par value for preferred stock.

EXAMPLE

How much would the following investor receive in annual income from the investment in the following preferred stock?

An investor buys 100 shares of TWT 9% preferred.
$100 × 9% = $9 per share × 100 = $900

PAYMENT OF DIVIDENDS

The dividend on preferred shares must be paid before any dividends are paid to common shareholders. This gives the preferred shareholder a priority claim on the corporation's distribution of earnings.

DISTRIBUTION OF ASSETS

If a corporation liquidates or declares bankruptcy, the preferred shareholders are paid prior to any common shareholder, giving the preferred shareholder a higher claim on the corporation's assets.

PERPETUAL

Preferred stock, unlike bonds, is perpetual with no maturity date. Investors may hold shares for as long as they wish or until the shares are called in by the company under a call feature.

NONVOTING

Most preferred stock is nonvoting. Occasionally the holder of a cumulative preferred stock may receive voting rights in the event the corporation misses several dividend payments.

INTEREST RATE SENSITIVE

Because of the fixed income generated by preferred shares, their price will be more sensitive to changes in interest rates than the price of their common stock counterparts. As interest rates decline, the value of preferred shares tends to increase, and when interest rates rise, the value of the preferred shares tends to fall. This is known as an inverse relationship.

TYPES OF PREFERRED STOCK

Preferred stock, unlike common stock, may have different features associated with it. Most of the features are designed to make the issue more attractive to investors and, therefore, benefit the owners of preferred stock.

STRAIGHT/NONCUMULATIVE

The straight preferred stock has no additional features. The holder is entitled to the stated dividend rate and nothing else. If the corporation is unable to pay the dividend, it is not owed to the investor.

CUMULATIVE PREFERRED

A cumulative feature protects the investor in cases when a corporation is having financial difficulties and cannot pay the dividend. Dividends on cumulative preferred stock accumulate in arrears until the corporation is able to pay them. If the dividend on a cumulative preferred stock is missed, it is still owed to the holder. Dividends in arrears on cumulative issues are always the first dividends to be paid. If the company wants to pay a dividend to common shareholders, they must first pay the dividends in arrears, as well as the stated preferred dividend, before common holders receive anything.

 FOCUSPOINT

GNR has an 8% cumulative preferred stock outstanding. It has not paid the dividend this year or for the prior 3 years. How much must the holders of GNR cumulative preferred be paid per share before the common stockholders are paid a dividend?

The dividend has not been paid this year nor for the previous 3 years, so the holders are owed 4 years' worth of dividends or:

4 × \$8 = \$32 per share

PARTICIPATING PREFERRED

Holders of participating preferred stock are entitled to receive the stated preferred rate as well as additional common dividends. The holder of participating preferred receives the dividend payable to the common stockholders over and above the stated preferred dividend.

CONVERTIBLE PREFERRED

A convertible feature allows the preferred stockholder to convert or exchange their preferred shares for common shares at a fixed price known as the conversion price.

EXAMPLE TRW has issued a 4% convertible preferred stock, which may be converted into TRW common stock at $20 per share. How many shares may the preferred stockholder receive upon conversion?

number of shares = par/conversion price (CVP)
$100/$20 = 5

The investor may receive five common shares for every preferred share.

These are some additional concepts regarding convertible securities that will be addressed in the convertible bond section.

CALLABLE PREFERRED

A call feature is the only feature that benefits the company and not the investor. A call feature allows the corporation to call in or redeem the preferred shares at their discretion or after some period of time has expired. Most callable preferred stock may not be called in during the first few years after its issuance. This feature, which does not allow the stock to be called in its early years, is known as call protection. Many callable preferred shares will be called at a premium price above par. For example, a $100 par preferred stock may be called at $103. The main reasons a company would call in their preferred shares would be to eliminate the fixed dividend payment or to sell a new preferred stock with a lower dividend rate when interest rates decline. Preferred stock is more likely to be called by the corporation when interest rates decline.

Pretest

WHY DO PEOPLE BUY STOCK?

la.finra.ppl.buy.stock.001_1811

1. ABC common stock declined dramatically in value over the last quarter but the dividend it declared for payment this quarter has remained the same. The dividend yield on the stock has:

    a. Not changed because the board has to declare the dividend amount.

    b. Gone down because the yield is a stated rate.

    c. Gone up as the price of ABC has fallen.

    d. Been fixed at the time of issuance.

la.finra.ppl.buy.stock.002_1811

2. An investor owns 100 shares of XYZ 8% participating preferred stock. XYZ's common stock pays a quarterly dividend of $.25. How much will the investor earn each year in dividends?

    a. $825.

    b. $90.

    c. $180.

    d. $900.

Handwritten notes: 100 x .08% = $8   8 x 100 = $800   .25 x 4 = $1.00   1.00 x 100 = $100   800 + 100 = 900

la.finra.ppl.buy.stock.003_1811

3. An investor who buys a 7% cumulative preferred stock will receive semiannual dividends of:

    a. $7 per share.

    b. 7% of the corporate profits.

    c. $3.50 per share.

    d. 3.5% of the corporate profits.

la.finra.ppl.buy.stock.004_1811

4. As the owner of a cumulative preferred stock, an investor would have all of the following rights, except:

     a. Voting if dividends are missed for a significant period of time.

     b. The right to receive past dividends not paid by the corporation.

     c. The right to exchange the preferred for the underlying common shares.

     d. The right to receive the past dividends before common holders receive a dividend.

sa.finra.ppl.buy.stock.001_1811

5. An investor buys a 10% preferred stock at 110. What is its current yield?

     a. 10.4%.

     b. 9.1%. $10/100 = 9.1$

     c. 10%.

     d. 9.5%.

sa.finra.ppl.buy.stock.002_1811

6. An investor buys 100 shares of XYZ 7% convertible preferred stock which are convertible into XYZ common stock at $20 per share. How many shares of common stock are there upon conversion?

     a. 5.

     b. 400.

     c. 500.

     d. 5,000.

par / conversion price = 100/20 = 5

mult by prefered shares

$5 \times 100 = 500$

Dividends, Rights, Warrants, and ADRs

INTRODUCTION

Learning Objective Statements

Calculate the impact of taxation of dividends.

Evaluate the impact of dividends and detail the dividend process.

Compare the characteristics of rights warrants, ADRS, REITS, and DPPs.

Why are dividends, rights, warrants, and ADRs important to financial securities? What do they have in common? How are they different? These are just a few of the questions this lesson examines. A detailed explanation of each, followed by relevant examples, will help you build your knowledge in this area.

TYPES OF DIVIDENDS

There are a number of ways in which a corporation may pay a dividend to its shareholders. The type of dividend declared for payment may vary between corporation and economic circumstances.

CASH

A cash dividend is the most common form of dividend and it is one that the test focuses on. A corporation will send out a cash payment (in the form of a check) directly to the stockholders. For those stockholders who have their stock held in the name of the brokerage firm, a check will be sent to the brokerage firm and the money will be credited to the investor's account. Securities held in the name of the brokerage firm are said to be held in street name. To determine the amount that an investor will receive, simply multiply the amount of the dividend to be paid by the number of shares.

EXAMPLE

JPF pays a $.10 dividend to shareholders. An investor who owns 1,000 shares of JPF will receive $100.

1,000 shares × $.10 = $100

Stock dividend = ↙#shares
↓value of share b/c ↑# of shares

STOCK

A corporation that wants to reward its shareholders—but also wants to conserve cash for other business purposes—may elect to pay a stock dividend to their shareholders. Each investor will receive an additional number of shares based on the number of shares that they own. The market price of the stock will decline after the stock dividend has been distributed to reflect the fact that there are now more shares outstanding, but the total market value of the company will remain the same.

EXAMPLE

If HRT pays a 5% stock dividend to its shareholders, an investor with 500 shares will receive an additional 25 shares. This is determined by multiplying the number of shares owned by the amount of the stock dividend to be paid.

500 × 5% = 25

PROPERTY/PRODUCT

This is the least likely way in which a corporation would pay a dividend, but it is a permissible dividend distribution. A corporation may send out to its shareholders samples of its products or portions of its property.

DIVIDEND DISTRIBUTION

If a corporation decides to pay a dividend to its common stockholders, they may not discriminate as to who receives the dividend. The dividend must be paid to all common stockholders of record. An investor who already owns the stock does not need to notify the company that they are entitled to receive the pending dividend, because it will be sent to them automatically. However, new purchasers of the stock may or may not be entitled to receive the dividend, depending on when they purchased the stock relative to when the dividend is going to be distributed. We now examine the dividend distribution process.

DECLARATION DATE

The declaration date is the day that the board of directors decides to pay a dividend to common stockholders of record. The declaration date is the starting point for the entire dividend process. The company must notify the regulators at the exchange or FINRA (depending where the stock trades), at least 10 business days prior to the record date.

EX-DIVIDEND DATE

The ex-dividend date or the ex date is the first day when purchasers of the security are no longer entitled to receive the dividend that the company has declared for payment. Stated another way, the ex date is the first day when the stock trades without (ex) the dividend attached. The exchange or FINRA set the ex date for the stock, based on the record date determined and announced by the corporation's board of directors. Because it takes 2 business days for a trade to settle, the ex date is always 1 business day prior to the record date.

RECORD DATE

This is the day when investors must have their name recorded on the stock certificate in order to be entitled to receive the dividend that was declared by the board of directors. Any stockholder whose name is on the stock certificate (owners of record) will be entitled to receive the dividend. The investor would have had to have purchased the stock before the ex-dividend date in order to be an owner of record on the record date. The record date is determined by the corporation's board of directors and is used to determine the shareholders that will receive the dividend.

PAYMENT DATE

This is the day when the corporation actually distributes the dividend to shareholders and it completes the dividend process. The payment date is controlled and set by the board of directors of the corporation and is usually four weeks following the record date.

STOCK PRICE AND THE EX-DIVIDEND DATE

It is important to note that the value of the stock prior to the ex-dividend date reflects the value of the stock with the dividend. On the ex-dividend date, the stock is now trading without the dividend attached and new purchasers will not receive the dividend that had been declared for payment. As a result, the stock price will be adjusted down on the ex-dividend date in an amount equal to the dividend.

 FOCUSPOINT

TRY declares a $.20 dividend payable to shareholders of record as of Thursday, August 22. The ex-dividend date will be 1 business day prior to the record date. In this case, the ex date will be Wednesday, August 21. If TRY closed on Tuesday, August 20, at $24 per share, the stock would open at $23.80 on Wednesday.

Sunday	Monday	Tuesday	Wednesday	Thursday	Friday	Saturday
				1	2	3
4	5	6	7	8	9	10
11	12	13	14	15	16	17
18	19	20	21	22	23	24
25	26	27	28	29	30	31

TAXATION OF DIVIDENDS

All qualified dividends received by investors are taxed at a rate of 15% for ordinary income earners and at a set rate of 20% for high-income earners. A key to determine which rate applies will be the investor's marginal tax rate. If a question asks you about an investor who is in a high tax bracket such as 39%, the 20% rate will apply for the year the dividend is received. The tax rate for dividends is a hotly debated topic and may be subject to change.

SELLING DIVIDENDS

Selling dividends is a violation! An investment adviser may not use the pending dividend payment as the sole basis of their recommendation to purchase the stock. Additionally, using the pending dividend as a means to create urgency on the part of the investor to purchase the stock is a prime example of this type of violation. If the investor were to purchase the shares just prior to the ex-dividend date simply to receive the dividend, the investor—in many cases—would end up worse off. The dividend in this case would actually be a return of the money that the investor used to purchase the stock and then the investor would have a tax liability when he or she received the dividend.

DIVIDEND DISBURSEMENT PROCESS

The corporation's dividend disbursement agent is responsible for the distribution of dividends and will send the dividends to the shareholders of record on the record date. For convenience, most investors have their securities held in the name of the broker dealer, also known as street name. As a result, the dividend disbursement agent will send the dividends directly to the broker dealer. The broker dealer's dividend department will collect the dividends and distribute them to the beneficial owners.

WARRANTS

A warrant is a security that gives the holder the opportunity to purchase common stock. Like a right, the warrant has a subscription price. However, the subscription price on a warrant is always above the current market value of the common stock when the warrant is originally issued. A warrant has a much longer life than a right and the holder of a warrant may have up to 10 years to purchase the stock at the subscription price. The long life is what makes the warrant valuable, even though the subscription price is higher than the market price of the common stock when the warrant is issued.

HOW DO PEOPLE GET WARRANTS?

UNITS

Many times, companies will issue warrants to people who have purchased their common stock when it was originally sold to the public during its initial public offering (IPO). A common share that comes with a warrant attached to purchase an additional common share is known as a unit.

ATTACHED TO BONDS

Many times, companies will attach warrants to their bond offerings as a "sweetener" to help market the bond offering. The warrant to purchase the common stock makes the bond more attractive to the investor and may allow the company to issue the bonds with a lower coupon rate.

SECONDARY MARKET

Warrants will often trade in the secondary market just like the common stock. An investor who wishes to participate in the potential price appreciation of the common stock may elect to purchase the corporation's warrant instead of its common shares.

POSSIBLE OUTCOMES OF A WARRANT

A warrant, like a right, may be exercised or sold by the investor. A warrant may also expire if the stock price is below the warrant's subscription price at its expiration.

Rights vs. Warrants

Rights		Warrants
Up to 45 days	**Term**	Up to 10 years
Below the market	**Subscription Price**	Above the market
May trade with or without common stock	**Trading**	May trade with or without common stock or bonds
Issued to existing shareholders to ensure preemptive rights	**Who**	Offered as a sweetener to make securities more attractive

AMERICAN DEPOSITARY RECEIPTS (ADRs)/
AMERICAN DEPOSITARY SHARES (ADSs)

American depositary receipts facilitate the trading of foreign securities in U.S. markets. An ADR is a receipt that represents the ownership of foreign shares that are being held abroad in a branch of a U.S. bank. Each ADR represents ownership of between one to 10 shares of the foreign stock and the holder of the ADR may request delivery of the foreign shares. Holders of ADRs also have the right to vote and the right to receive dividends that the foreign corporation declares for payment to shareholders.

CURRENCY RISKS

Foreign currency
vs
U.S dollar risk

The owner of an ADR has currency risk along with the normal risks associated with the ownership of the stock. Should the currency of the country decline relative to the U.S. dollar, the holder of the ADR will receive fewer U.S. dollars when a dividend is paid and less in U.S. dollars when the security is sold. It's important to note that the dividend on the ADR is paid by the corporation to the custodian bank, in the foreign currency. The custodian bank will convert the dividend to U.S. dollars for distribution to the holders of the ADRs.

FUNCTIONS OF THE CUSTODIAN BANK ISSUING ADRs

ADRs are actually issued and guaranteed by the bank that holds the foreign securities on deposit. The custodian bank is the registered owner of the foreign shares and must guarantee that the foreign shares remain in the bank as long as the ADRs remain outstanding. Foreign corporations will often use ADRs as a way of generating U.S. interest in their company. The issuance of the ADR allows them to avoid the long and costly registration process for their securities.

REAL ESTATE INVESTMENT TRUSTS/REITs

A real estate investment trust, or a REIT, is a special type of equity security. REITs are organized for the specific purpose of buying, developing, or managing a portfolio of real estate. REITs are organized as a corporation or as a trust and publicly traded REITs will trade on the exchanges or in the over-the-counter market just like other stocks. A real estate investment trust is organized as a conduit for the investment income generated by the portfolio of real estate. REITs are entitled to special tax treatment under Internal Revenue Code Subchapter M. A REIT will not pay taxes at the corporate level as long as:

- It receives 75% of its income from real estate.

- It distributes at least 90% of its taxable income to shareholders.

As long as the REIT meets these requirements, the income will be allowed to flow through to the shareholders and will be taxed at their rate. Dividends received by REIT shareholders will continue to be taxed as ordinary income.

It is important to note that REITs do not pass through losses or expenses to shareholders, only income. REIT investors own an undivided share of the underlying real estate portfolio. An investor may elect to invest in a REIT rather than directly in real estate ownership because of the greater liquidity provided by the REIT and the quality of the property manager.

NONTRADED REITs

Nontraded real estate investment trusts or REITs lack liquidity, have high fees, and can be difficult to value. The fees for investing in a nontraded REIT may be as much as 15% of the per shares price. These fees include commissions and expenses which cannot exceed 10% of the offering price. Investors are often attracted to the high yields offered by these investments. Firms who conduct business in these products must conduct ongoing suitability determination on the REITs they recommend. Firms must react to red flags in the financial statements and from the REIT's management and adjust the recommendation process accordingly or stop recommending if material changes take place that would make the REIT unsuitable. Holding periods can be 8 years or more and the opportunities to liquidate the investments may be very limited. Furthermore, distributions from the REITs themselves may be based on the use of borrowed funds and may include a return of principal which may be adversely impacted and cause the distributions to be vulnerable to being significantly reduced or stopped altogether. Distributions may exceed cash flow and the amount of the distributions, if any, are at the discretion of the Board of Directors. Nontraded REITs like exchange traded REITs must distribute 90% of the income to shareholders and must file annual reports (10-Ks) and quarterly reporrs (10-Qs) with the SEC. Broker dealers who sell nontraded REITs must provide investors with a valuation of the REIT within 18 months of the closing of the offering of shares.

DIRECT PARTICIPATION PROGRAMS AND LIMITED PARTNERSHIPS

Direct participation programs and limited partnerships are entities that allow income, expenses, gains, losses, and tax benefits to be passed through to investors. There is generally no active secondary market for these investments, so it's important that investors understand and can afford the risks associated with direct participation programs and limited partnerships. Series 65 candidates can expect to see several questions on this material on their exam.

LIMITED PARTNERSHIPS

A limited partnership is an entity that allows all of the economic events of the partnership to flow through to the partners. These economic events are:

- Income
- Gains
- Losses
- Tax credits
- Deductions

There are two types of partners in a limited partnership. They are the limited partners and the general partner. The limited partners:

- Put up the investment capital.
- Losses are limited to their investment.

- Receive the benefits from the operation.

- May not exercise management over the operation.

- May vote to change the objective of the partnership.

- May vote to switch or remove the general partner.

- May sue the general partner, if the general partner does not act in the best interest of the partnership.

Limited partners may never exercise any management or control over the limited partnership. Doing so would jeopardize their limited status and they may be considered a general partner.

The general partner is the person or corporation that manages the business and has unlimited liability for the obligations of the partnership business. The general partner may also:

- Buy and sell property for the partnership.

- Receive compensation for managing the partnership.

- Enter into legally binding contracts for the partnership.

The general partner must also maintain a financial interest in the partnership of at least 1%. The general partner may not:

- Commingle funds of the general partner with the funds of the partnership.

- Compete against the partnership.

- Borrow from the partnership.

It is important to note that there are no tax consequences at the partnership level. In order to qualify for the preferential tax treatment, a DPP or LP must avoid at least two of the six characteristics of a corporation. These characteristics are:

- Continuity of life

- Profit motive

- Central management

- Limited liability

- Associates
- Freely transferable interest

Several of the characteristics cannot be avoided, such as associates and a profit motive. The easiest two characteristics of a corporation to avoid are continuity of life and freely transferable interest. The LP can put a termination date on the partnership and substitute limited partners may not be accepted or may only be accepted once the general partner has agreed.

STRUCTURING AND OFFERING LIMITED PARTNERSHIPS

The foundation of every limited partnership is the partnership agreement. All limited partners must be given a copy of the partnership agreement. The partnership agreement will spell out all of the terms and conditions, as well as the business purpose for the partnership. The powers and limitations of the general partner's authority will be one of the main points detailed in the partnership agreement. Prior to forming a limited partnership, the general partner will have to file a certificate of limited partnership in the state in which the partnership is formed. The certificate will include:

- Name and address of the partnership
- A description of the partnership's business
- The life of the partnership
- Size of limited partner's investments (if any)
- Conditions for assignment of interest by limited partners
- Conditions for dissolving the partnership
- Conditions for admitting new limited partners
- The projected date for the return of capital if one is set

A material change to any of these conditions must be updated on the certificate within 30 days.

Most limited partnerships will be offered to investors through a private placement. All investors who purchase a limited partnership through a private placement must receive a private placement memorandum. Private placements, with very limited exceptions, may only be offered to accredited investors. However, a few limited partnerships will be offered to the public through a standard public offering. All investors who purchase a limited partnership though a public offering must receive a prospectus. If the partnership is sold through a syndicator, the syndicator is responsible for filing the partnership documents. The maximum fee that may be received by the syndicator is limited to 10% of the offering. If a secondary market develops for a partnership, the partnership will be known as a master limited partnership or MLP. All investors wishing to become a limited partner must complete the partnership's subscription agreement. The subscription agreement will include:

- A power of attorney appointing the general partner

- A statement of the prospective limited partner's net worth

- A statement regarding the prospective limited partner's income

- A statement from the prospective limited partner that he or she understands and can afford the risks related to the partnership

TYPES OF LIMITED PARTNERSHIPS

A limited partnership may be organized for any lawful purpose. The limited partnerships that are most common are set up to:

- Invest in real estate.

- Invest in oil and gas wells.

- Engage in equipment leasing.

There are several types of real estate partnerships. They are:

- Existing property

- New construction

- Raw land

- Government-assisted housing

- Historic rehabilitation

Type of LP	Risk	Advantages	Disadvantages	Tax Benefits
Existing property Purchase income property	Low	Immediate predictable cash flow	Rental problems and repairs	Deductions for mortgage interest and depreciation
New construction Build units for appreciation or rental	Higher	Potential capital gains and low maintenance	No deduction for current expenses and no promise of rental or sale	Deduction of expenses and depreciation only after completion
Raw land Purchase land for appreciation	Highest	Only appreciation potential	No tax deductions or income	No tax benefits
Government-assisted housing Low-income housing	Low	Government rent subsidies and tax credits	High maintenance costs and risk of a change in government programs	Tax credits and any losses on the property
Historic Rehabilitation Restore sites for use	Higher	Tax credits	Financing trouble; no rental history	Tax credits deductions and depreciation

TAX REPORTING FOR DIRECT PARTICIPATION PROGRAMS

Direct participation programs are organized as either limited partnerships or as Subchapter S corporations. These entities allow for the flow-through of income and losses and the DPP has no tax consequences. The DPP will only report the results of its operation to the IRS. The responsibility for paying any taxes due rests with the partners or shareholders. DPPs allow the losses to flow through to the investors. Losses from DPPs can only be used to offset the investor's passive income. Investors may not use the losses to shelter or offset ordinary income. Investors should not purchase DPPs simply for the tax benefits; they should purchase them to earn a return. Any DPP that is found to have been formed simply to create tax benefits may subject the investors to strict penalties. Investors could owe back taxes, fines, or be prosecuted for fraud.

LIMITED PARTNERSHIP ANALYSIS

Before investing in a limited partnership, investors should analyze the key features of the partnership to ensure that the partnership's objectives meet their investment objectives. The investor should review:

- Economic viability of the program
- Tax considerations
- Management's ability
- Lack of liquidity
- Time horizon
- Whether it is a blind pool or a specified program
- Internal rate of return

A blind pool is a partnership in which less than 75% of the assets that the partnership is going to acquire have been identified. In a specified program, more than 75% of the assets that the partnership is going to acquire have been identified.

A partnership's internal rate of return is the discounted present value of its projected future cash flow.

TAX DEDUCTIONS VS. TAX CREDITS

Tax deductions that are generated by partnerships are used to lower the investor's taxable income. A tax credit results in a dollar-for-dollar reduction in the amount of taxes due from the investor.

OTHER TAX CONSIDERATIONS

If a limited partnership has used up all of its deductions and has a gain on the sale of a depreciated asset, the sale above the asset's depreciated cost basis may subject the limited partners to a taxable recapture. There are two types of loans that a partnership may take out: a nonrecourse loan and a recourse loan. With a nonrecourse loan, if the partnership defaults, the lender has no recourse to the limited partners. With a recourse loan, in the event of the partnership's default, the lender can go after the limited partners for payment. A recourse loan can increase the investor's cost base. Partners must monitor their cost base and adjust it for:

- Cash or property contributions to the partnership.

- Recourse loans.

- Any cash or property received from the partnership.

Investors are responsible for any gain on the sale of their partnership interest in excess of their cost basis.

DISSOLVING A PARTNERSHIP

A partnership will terminate on the date set forth in the partnership agreement, unless earlier terminated. A partnership may dissolve if a majority of the limited partners vote for its dissolution. If the partnership terminates its activities, the general partner must cancel the certificate of limited partnership and liquidate the partnership assets. The priority of payments will be as follows:

- Secured lenders
- General creditors
- Limited partners' profits first, then return of investment
- General partner for fees first, then profits, then return of capital

 TAKENOTE!

An investor in a limited partnership is subject to both liquidity risk and legislative risk. Investors may not be able to liquidate their interest when they need to and the government may change tax laws relating to their investment. As a result, an investor should not have more than 10% of their portfolio in limited partnerships.

Pretest

DIVIDENDS, RIGHTS, WARRANTS, AND ADRS

la.finra.div.war.adrs.001_1811

1. A corporation may pay a dividend in which of the following ways? Choose the most complete response.

   a. Stock.

   b. Cash.

   c. Stock of another company.

   d. All of the above.

la.finra.div.war.adrs.002_1811

2. All qualified dividends for ordinary income earners are:

   a. Taxed as ordinary income each year.

   b. Tax-free income.

   c. Taxed as special interest-free income.

   d. Taxed at a set rate of 15%.

la.finra.div.war.adrs.003_1811

3. Which of the following is not true regarding American Depositary Receipts (ADRs)?

   a. They are receipts of ownership of foreign shares being held abroad in a U.S. bank.

   b. Each ADR represents 100 shares of foreign stock, and the ADR holder may request delivery of the foreign shares.

   c. ADR holders have the right to vote and to receive dividends that the foreign corporation declares for shareholders.

   d. The foreign country may issue restrictions on the foreign ownership of stock.

la.finra.div.war.adrs.004_1811

4. If a 5% stock dividend is paid to an investor who owns 800 shares of stock already, the investor will receive how many shares?

   a. 4 shares.

   b. 8 shares.

   c 40 shares.

   d. 80 shares.

sa.finra.div.war.adrs.001_1811

5. An investor has purchased shares of a foreign company through an ADR. Which of the following is not true?

   a. The ADR may represent one or more shares of the company's common stock.

   b The dividend will be paid in U.S. dollars.

   c. The investor may elect to exchange the ADR for the underlying common shares.

   d. The investor is subject to currency risk.

sa.finra.div.war.adrs.002_1811

6. Common dividends are all of the following except:

   a. A portion of the earnings of the company.

   b. A source of income for the investor.

   c. Generally paid quarterly.

   d A figure determined by subtracting the current yield from the current market price.

Dividend yield (current yield) found by dividing annual income by current market price.

% DY = AI / CMP

Introduction to Debt Securities

INTRODUCTION

Learning Objective Statements

Comprehend bond pricing.

Compare and contrast bond yields.

Understand how the bond market functions.

Analyze the refunding and redemption process.

Explain how bond maturities impact pricing and yields.

Many different types of entities issue bonds in an effort to raise working capital. Corporations and municipalities, along with the U.S. government and U.S. government agencies, all issue bonds in order to meet their capital needs. A bond represents a loan to the issuer in exchange for its promise to repay the face amount of the bond, known as the principal amount at maturity. On most bonds, the investor receives semiannual interest payments during the bond's term. These semiannual interest payments, along with any capital appreciation or depreciation at maturity, represent the investor's return. A bondholder invests primarily for the interest income that will be generated during the bond's term.

CORPORATE BONDS

Corporations will issue bonds in an effort to raise working capital to build and expand their businesses. Corporate bondholders are not owners of the corporation; they are creditors of the company. Corporate debt financing is known as leverage financing because the company pays interest only on the loan until maturity. Bondholders do not have voting rights as long as the company pays the interest and principal payments in a timely fashion. If the company defaults, the bondholders may be able to use their position as creditors to gain a voice in the company's management. Bondholders will always be paid before preferred and common stockholders in the event of liquidation. Interest income received by investors on corporate bonds is taxable at all levels, federal, state, and local.

TYPES OF BOND ISSUANCE

BEARER BONDS

Bonds that are issued in coupon or bearer form do not record the owner's information with the issuer and the bond certificate does not have the legal owner's name printed on it. As a result, anyone who possesses the bond is entitled to receive the interest payments by clipping the coupons attached to the bond and depositing them in a bank or trust company for payment. Additionally, the bearer is entitled to receive the principal payment at the bond's maturity. Bearer bonds are no longer issued within the United States; however, they are still issued outside the country.

REGISTERED BONDS

Most bonds now are issued in registered form. Bonds that have been issued in registered form have the owner's name recorded on the books of the issuer and the buyer's name will appear on the bond certificate.

PRINCIPAL-ONLY REGISTRATION

recorded w/ issuer but must clip coupons to receive interest pay.

Bonds that have been registered as to principal only have the owner's name printed on the bond certificate. The issuer knows who owns the bond and who is entitled to receive the principal payment at maturity. However, the bondholder will still be required to clip coupons to receive the semiannual interest payments.

FULLY REGISTERED

Bonds that have been issued in fully registered form have the owner's name recorded for both the interest and principal payments. The owner is not required to clip coupons and the issuer will send out the interest payments directly to the holder on a semiannual basis. The issuer will also send the principal payment along with the last semiannual interest payment directly to the owner at maturity. Most bonds in the United States are issued in fully registered form.

registered + recorded. No clipping

BOOK ENTRY/JOURNAL ENTRY

Bonds that have been issued in book entry or journal entry form have no physical certificate issued to the holder as evidence of ownership. The bonds are fully registered and the issuer knows who is entitled to receive the semiannual interest payments and the principal payment at maturity. The investor's only evidence of ownership is the trade confirmation, which is generated by the brokerage firm when the purchase order has been executed.

No physical bond but recorded w/ issues

BOND CERTIFICATE

If a bond certificate is issued, it must include:

- Name of issuer
- Principal amount
- Issuing date
- Maturity date
- Interest payment dates
- Place where interest is payable (paying agent)
- Type of bond
- Interest rate
- Call feature (if any or noncallable)
- Reference to the trust indenture

BOND PRICING

Once issued, corporate bonds trade in the secondary market between investors similar to the way equity securities do. The price of bonds in the secondary market depends on all of the following:

- Rating
- Interest rates
- Term
- Coupon rate
- Type of bond
- Issuer
- Supply and demand
- Other features, that is, callable, convertible

Corporate bonds are always priced as a percentage of par and par value for all bonds is always $1,000, unless otherwise stated.

PAR VALUE

Par value of a bond is equal to the amount that the investor has loaned to the issuer. The terms par value, face value, and principal amount are synonymous and are always equal to $1,000. The principal amount is the amount that will be received by the investor at maturity, regardless of the price the investor paid for the bond. An investor who purchases a bond in the secondary market for $1,000 is said to have paid par for the bond.

DISCOUNT

In the secondary market, many different factors affect the price of the bond. It is not at all unusual for an investor to purchase a bond at a price that is below the bond's par value. Anytime an investor buys a bond at a price that is below the par value, they are said to be buying the bond at a discount.

PREMIUM

Often market conditions will cause the price of existing bonds to rise and make them attractive for investors to purchase a bond at a price that is greater than its par value. Anytime an investor buys a bond at a price that exceeds its par value, the investor is said to have paid a premium.

CORPORATE BOND PRICING

All corporate bonds are priced as a percentage of par into fractions of a percent. For example, a quote for a corporate bond reading 95 actually translates into:

95% × $1,000 = $950

A quote for a corporate bond of 97¼ translates into:

97.25% × $1,000 = $972.50

BOND YIELDS

A bond's yield is the investor's return for holding the bond. Many factors affect the yield that an investor will receive from a bond such as:

- Current interest rates
- Term of the bond
- Credit quality of the issuer
- Type of collateral
- Convertible or callable
- Purchase price

An investor who is considering investing in a bond needs to be familiar with the bond's nominal yield, current yield, and yield to maturity.

NOMINAL YIELD

A bond's nominal yield is the interest rate that is printed or "named" on the bond. The nominal yield is always stated as a percentage of par. It is fixed at the time of the bond's issuance and never changes. The nominal yield may also be called the coupon rate. For example, a corporate bond with a coupon rate of 8% will pay the holder $80.00 per year in interest.

8% × $1,000 = $80. The nominal yield is 8%.

CURRENT YIELD

The current yield is a relationship between the annual interest generated by the bond and the bond's current market price. To find any investment's current yield, use the following formula:

annual income/current market price

For example, let's take the same 8% corporate bond used in the previous example on nominal yield and see what its current yield would be if we paid $1,100 for the bond.

annual income = 8% × $1,000 = $80

current market price = 110% × $1,000 = $1,100

current yield = $80/$1,100 = 7.27%

In this example, we have purchased the bond at a premium or a price that is higher than par and we see that the current yield on the bond is lower than the nominal yield.

Let's take a look at the current yield on the same bond if we were to purchase the bond at a discount or a price which is lower than par. Let's see what the current yield for the bond would be if we pay $900 for the bond.

annual income = 8% × $1,000 = $80

current market price = 90% × $1,000 = $900

current yield = $80/$900 = 8.89%

In this example we see that the current yield is higher than the nominal yield. By showing examples calculating the current yield for the same bond purchased at both a premium and a discount, we have demonstrated the inverse relationship between prices and yields. That is to say, prices and yields on income-producing investments move in the opposite direction. As the price of an investment rises, the investment's yield falls. Conversely, as the price of the investment falls, the investment's yield will rise.

YIELD TO MATURITY

A bond's yield to maturity is the investor's total annualized return for investing in the bond. A bond's yield to maturity takes into consideration the annual income received by the investor along with any difference between the price the investor paid for the bond and the par value that will be received at maturity. It also assumes that the investor is reinvesting the semiannual interest payments at the same rate. The yield to maturity is the most important yield for an investor who purchases the bond.

YIELD TO MATURITY: PREMIUM BOND

The yield to maturity for a bond purchased at a premium will be the lowest of all the investor's yields. Although an investor may purchase a bond at a price that exceeds the par value of the bond, the issuer is only obligated to pay the bondholder the par value upon maturity. For example: An investor who purchases a bond at 110 or for $1,100 will receive only $1,000 at maturity and, therefore, will lose the difference of $100. This loss is what causes the yield to maturity to be the lowest of the three yields for an investor who purchases a bond at a premium.

YIELD TO MATURITY: DISCOUNT BOND

The yield to maturity for a bond purchased at a discount will be the highest of all of the investor's yields. In this case, the investor has purchased the bond at a price that is less than the par value of the bond. In this example, even though the investor paid less than the par value for the bond, the issuer is still obligated to pay him or her the full par value of the bond at maturity or the full $1,000. For example: An investor who purchases a bond at 90 or for $900 will still be entitled to receive the full par amount of $1,000 at maturity, therefore, gaining $100. This gain is what causes the yield to maturity to be the highest of the three yields for an investor who purchases a bond at a discount.

CALCULATING THE YIELD TO CALL

In the event that the bond may be called in or redeemed by the issuer under a call feature, an investor may calculate the approximate yield to call by using the approximate number of years left until the bond may be called.

 TAKENOTE!

The yield to call will always extend past the yield to maturity. The yield to call will always be the highest yield on a bond purchased at a discount and it will always be the lowest yield for a bond purchased at a premium.

YIELD SPREADS

Investors must look at the competing yields that are offered by a wide variety of bonds. The difference in the yields offered by two bonds is known as the yield spread. Many bonds are measured by the relationship between the bond's yield and the yield offered by similar term Treasury securities. This is known as the spread over Treasuries. As perceptions about the issuer and the economy change, yield spreads will change. During times of uncertainty, investors will be less likely to hold more risky debt securities. As a result, the yield spread between Treasuries and more risky corporate debt will widen. An increase in the spread can be seen as an indication that the economy is going to go into a recession and that the issuers of lower quality debt will likely default. Alternatively, a decrease in the spread will be seen as a predictor of an improving economy.

THE REAL INTEREST RATE

Investors must calculate the effect inflation will have on the interest they receive on fixed-income securities. The interest rate received by an investor, before the effects of inflation are considered, is known as the nominal interest rate. The real interest rate is what the investor will receive after inflation is factored in. For example, if an investor is receiving an 8%

interest rate on a corporate bond when inflation is running at 2%, the investor's real interest rate would be 6%. The investor's nominal interest rate consists of the real interest rate plus an inflation premium. The inflation premium factors in the expected rate of inflation during various bond maturities.

BOND MATURITIES

When a bond matures, the principal payment and the last semiannual interest payment are due. Corporations will select to issue bonds with the maturity type that best fits their needs, based on the interest rate environment and marketability.

TERM MATURITY

A term bond is the most common type of corporate bond issue. With a term bond, the entire principal amount becomes due on a specific date. For example, if XYZ corporation issued $100,000,000 worth of 8% bonds due June 1, 2025, the entire $100,000,000 would be due to bondholders on June 1, 2025. On June 1, bondholders would also receive their last semiannual interest payment and their principal payment.

SERIAL MATURITY

A serial bond issue is one that has a portion of the issue maturing over a series of years. Traditionally, serial bonds have larger portions of the principal maturing in later years. The portion of the bonds maturing in later years will carry a higher yield to maturity because investors who have their money at risk longer will demand a higher interest rate.

BALLOON MATURITY

A balloon issue contains a maturity schedule that repays a portion of the issue's principal over a number of years, just like a serial issue. However, with a balloon maturity, the largest portion of the principal amount is due on the last date.

SERIES ISSUE

With a series issue, corporations may elect to spread the issuance of the bonds over a period of several years. This will give the corporation the flexibility to borrow money to meet its goals as its needs change.

Pretest

INTRODUCTION TO DEBT SECURITIES

la.finra.intro.debt.sec.001_1811

1. An investor holding an 8% subordinated debenture will receive how much at maturity?

   a. $1,000.

   b. $1,080.

   c. $1,040.

   d. Depends on the purchase price.

la.finra.intro.debt.sec.002_1811

2. An investor buys $10,000 of 10% corporate bonds with 5 years left to maturity. The investor pays 120 for the bonds. What is the investor's current yield?

   a. 8.33%.

   b. 11.1%.

   c. 6%.

   d. 9.2%.

   $10\%/1,000 \overset{\$}{=} 100$

   ~~100~~ $\$100 / \$1,200 = 8.33\%$

la.finra.intro.debt.sec.003_1811

3. An investor would expect to realize the largest capital gain by buying bonds that are:

   a. Long-term when rates are high.

   b. Short-term when rates are low.

   c. Short-term when rates are high.

   d. Long-term when rates are low.

sa.finra.intro.debt.sec.001_1811

4. An investor has purchased 10 corporate bonds at a price of 135. At the end of the day, the bonds are quoted at 136.25. How much have the bonds risen in dollars?

1 Bond = $10.00, 1.25 points

12.50 x 10 bonds = 125

   (a.) $125.

   b. $12.50.

   c. $1.25.

   d. $.125.

sa.finra.intro.debt.sec.002_1811

5. In response to a customer's request for information on how inflation will affect their return realized from their semiannual coupon payments, you would look at the:

   (a.) Real interest rate. *will determine the return after inflation*

   b. Adjusted interest rate.

   c. Interest conversion rate.

   d. Current interest rate.

Types of Corporate Bonds

INTRODUCTION

Learning Objective Statements

Explain the different types of bond issuance and collateral.

Calculate conversion and parity price for convertible bonds.

Detail the impact of bond ratings on prices, yield, and risk.

Do you know the difference between secured and unsecured bonds? If not, don't worry! This lesson will make things crystal clear. We explore different types of bonds, including: mortgage bonds, subordinated debentures, and zero-coupon bonds. Other topics discussed include The Trust Indenture Act of 1939, Euro and Yankee Bonds, and how to retire corporate bonds.

A corporation will issue or sell bonds as a means to borrow money to help the organization meet its goals. Corporate bonds are divided into two main categories: secured and unsecured.

SECURED BONDS

A secured bond is one that is backed by a specific pledge of assets. The assets that have been pledged become known as collateral for the bond issue or the loan. A trustee will hold the title to the collateral and, in the event of default, the bondholders may claim the assets that have been pledged. The trustee will then attempt to sell off the assets in an effort to pay off the bondholders.

MORTGAGE BONDS

A mortgage bond is a bond that has been backed by a pledge of real property. The corporation will issue bonds to investors and the corporation will pledge real estate, owned by the company, as collateral. A mortgage bond works in a similar fashion to a residential mortgage. In the event of default, the bondholders take the property.

EQUIPMENT TRUST CERTIFICATES

An equipment trust certificate is backed by a pledge of large equipment that the corporation owns. Airlines, railroads, and large shipping companies often borrow money to purchase the equipment they need through the sale of equipment trust certificates. Airplanes, railroad cars, and ships are all good examples of the types of assets that might be pledged as collateral. In the event of default, the equipment is liquidated by the trustee in an effort to pay off the bondholders.

COLLATERAL TRUST CERTIFICATES

A collateral trust certificate is a bond that has been backed by a pledge of securities that the issuer has purchased for investment purposes or they could be backed by shares of a wholly owned subsidiary. Both stocks and bonds are acceptable forms of collateral as long as another issuer has issued them. Securities that have been pledged as collateral are generally required to be held by the trustee for safekeeping. In the event of a default, the trustee will attempt to liquidate the securities, which have been pledged as collateral, and divide the proceeds among the bondholders.

It's important to note that while having a specific claim against an asset that has been pledged as collateral benefits the bondholder, bondholders do not want to take title to the collateral. Bondholders invest for the semiannual interest payments and the return of their principal at maturity.

Bearer Bonds: A bearer bond is a bond or debt security issued by a business entity such as a corporation, or a government. As a bearer instrument, it differs from the more common types of investment securities in that it is unregistered—no records are kept of the owner, or the transactions involving ownership. Whoever physically holds the paper on which the bond is issued is the presumptive owner of the instrument. This is useful for investors who wish to retain anonymity. Recovery of the value of a bearer bond in the event of its loss, theft, or destruction is usually impossible.

UNSECURED BONDS

Unsecured bonds are known as debentures and have no specific asset pledged as collateral for the loan. Debentures are only backed by the good faith and credit of the issuer. In the event of a default, the holder of a debenture is treated like a general creditor.

SUBORDINATED DEBENTURES

A subordinated debenture is an unsecured loan to the issuer that has a junior claim on the issuer in the event of default relative to straight debenture. Should the issuer default, the holders of the debentures and other general creditors will be paid before the holders of the subordinate debentures will be paid anything.

INCOME/ADJUSTMENT BONDS

Corporations that are in severe financial difficulty usually issue income or adjustment bonds. The bond is unsecured and the investor is only promised to be paid interest if the corporation has enough income to do so. As a result of the large risk that the investor is taking, the interest rate is very high and the bonds are issued at a deep discount to par. An income bond is never an appropriate recommendation for an investor seeking income or safety of principal.

ZERO-COUPON BONDS

A zero-coupon bond is a bond that pays no semiannual interest. It is issued at a deep discount from the par value and appreciates up to par at maturity. This appreciation represents the investor's interest for purchasing the bond. Corporations, the U.S. government, and municipalities will all issue zero-coupon bonds in an effort to finance their activities. An investor might be able to purchase the $1,000 principal payment in 20 years for as little as $300 today. Because zero-coupon bonds pay no semiannual interest and the price is so deeply discounted from par, the price of the bond will be the most sensitive to a change in the interest rates. Both corporate and U.S. government zero-coupon bonds subject the investor to federal income taxes on the annual appreciation of the bond. This is known as phantom income.

GUARANTEED BONDS

A guaranteed bond is a bond whose interest and principal payments are guaranteed by a third party such as a parent company. The higher the credit rating of the company who is guaranteeing the bonds, the better the guarantee.

CONVERTIBLE BONDS

A convertible bond is a corporate bond that may be converted or exchanged for common shares of the corporation at a predetermined price known as the conversion price. Convertible bonds have benefits to both the issuer and the investor. Because the bond is convertible, it will usually pay a lower rate of interest than nonconvertible bonds. This lower interest rate can save the corporation an enormous amount of money in interest expense over the life of the issue. The convertible feature also benefits the investor if the common stock does well. If the shares of the underlying common stock appreciate, the investor could realize significant capital appreciation in the price of the bond and may also elect to convert the bond into common stock in the hopes of realizing additional appreciation. An investor in the bond maintains a senior position as a creditor while enjoying the potential for capital appreciation.

CONVERTING BONDS INTO COMMON STOCK

All Series 65 candidates must be able to perform the conversion calculations for both convertible bonds and preferred stock. It is essential that prospective representatives are able to determine the following:

Number of shares: To determine the number of shares that can be received upon conversion, use the following formula:

par value/conversion price

FOCUSPOINT

XYZ has a 7% subordinated debenture trading in the market place at 120. The bonds are convertible into XYZ common stock at $25 per share. How many shares can the investor receive upon conversion?

$1,000/$25 = 40 shares
par conv

The investor is entitled to receive 40 shares of XYZ common stock for each bond that he or she owns.

PARITY PRICE

A stock's parity price determines the value at which the stock must be priced in order for the value of the common stock to be equal to the value of the bond that the investor already owns. The value of the stock that can be received by the investor upon conversion must be equal to, or at parity with, the value of the bond. Otherwise, converting the bonds into common stock would not make economic sense. Determining parity price is a two-step process. First, determine the number of shares that can be received by using the formula: par value/conversion price. Then it is necessary to calculate the price of each share at the parity price.

To determine parity price, use the following formula:

$$\frac{\textbf{current market value of the convertible bond}}{\textbf{number of shares to be recceived}}$$

In this example, the convertible bond was quoted at 120, which equals a dollar price of $1,200. We determined that the investor could receive 40 shares of stock for each bond so the parity price equals:

$1,200/40 = $30

If the question is looking for the number of shares or the parity price for a convertible preferred stock, the formulas are the same and the only thing that changes is the par value. Par value for all preferred stocks is $100, instead of the $1,000 par value for bonds.

ADVANTAGES OF ISSUING CONVERTIBLE BONDS

Only corporations may issue convertible bonds. Some of the advantages of issuing convertible bonds to the company are:

- Makes the issue more marketable
- Can offer a lower interest rate
- If the bonds are converted, the debt obligation is eliminated.
- The issuance of the convertible bonds does not immediately dilute ownership or earnings per share.

DISADVANTAGES OF ISSUING CONVERTIBLE BONDS

There are some disadvantages to issuing convertible bonds for the company such as:

- Reduced leverage upon conversion
- Conversion causes the loss of tax-deductible interest payments
- Conversion dilutes shareholder's equity
- Conversion by a large holder may shift control of the company

CONVERTIBLE BONDS AND STOCK SPLITS

If a corporation declares a stock split or a stock dividend, the conversion price of the bond will be adjusted accordingly. The trust indenture of a convertible bond will state the maximum number of shares that the corporation may issue while the bonds are outstanding, as well as the minimum price at which the additional shares may be issued.

THE TRUST INDENTURE ACT OF 1939

The Trust Indenture Act of 1939 requires that corporate bond issues in excess of $5,000,000, that are to be repaid during a term in excess of 1 year, issue a trust indenture for the issue. The trust indenture is a contract between the issuer and the trustee. The trustee acts on behalf of all bondholders and ensures that the issuer is in compliance with all promises and covenants made to the bondholders. The trustee is appointed by the corporation and is usually a bank or a trust company. The Trust Indenture Act of 1939 only applies to corporate issuers. Both federal and municipal issuers are exempt.

BOND INDENTURE

Corporate bonds may be issued with either an open-end or closed-end indenture. Bonds issued with an open-end indenture allow the corporation to issue additional bonds secured by the same collateral and whose claim on the collateral is equal to the original issue. A closed-end indenture does not allow the corporation to issue additional bonds having an equal claim on the collateral. If the corporation wants to issue new bonds, their claim must be subordinate to the claim of the original issue or secured by other collateral.

RATINGS CONSIDERATIONS

When the rating agencies assign a rating to a debt issue, they must look at many factors concerning the issuer's financial condition such as:

- Cash flow
- Total amount and type of debt outstanding
- Ability to meet interest and principal payments
- Collateral
- Industry and economic trends
- Management

S&P and Moody's are the two biggest ratings agencies. In order for a corporation to have their debt rated by one of these agencies, the issuer must request it and pay for the service. One of the main reasons a corporation would want to have their debt rated is because many investors will not purchase bonds that have not been rated. Additionally, if the issuer receives a higher rating, they will be able to sell the bonds with a lower interest rate.

FOCUSPOINT

Standard & Poor's	Moody's
AAA	Aaa
Investment grade or high grade	
BBB	Baa
Speculative high-yield junk bonds	

EXCHANGE TRADED NOTES (ETNs)

Exchange-traded notes, sometimes known as equity-linked notes or index-linked notes, are debt securities that base a maturity payment on the performance of an underlying security or group of securities such as an index. ETNs do not make coupon or interest payments to investors during the time the investor owns the ETN. ETNs may be purchased and sold at any time during the trading day and may be purchased on margin and sold short. One very important risk factor to consider when evaluating an ETN is the fact that ETNs are unsecured and carry the credit risk of the issuing bank or broker dealer. Similarly, principal protected notes (PPNs), which are structured products that guarantee the return of the investor's principal if the note is held until maturity, carry a principal guarantee that is only as good as the issuer's credit rating and, therefore, are never 100% guaranteed.

EURO AND YANKEE BONDS

A Eurobond is a bond issued in the domestic currency of the issuer but sold outside of the issuer's country. For example, if Virgin Plc sold bonds to investors in Japan with the principal and interest payable in British pounds, this would be an example of a Eurobond. A Eurobond carries significant currency risk should the value of the foreign currency fall relative to the domestic currency of the purchaser. If the foreign currency fell, the interest and principal payments to be received in the foreign currency would result in the receipt of fewer units of the domestic currency upon conversion. A Eurodollar bond is a bond issued by a foreign issuer denominated in U.S. dollars and sold to investors outside of the United States and outside of the issuer's country. Eurodollar bonds are issued in barer form by foreign corporations, federal governments, and municipalities. Eurobonds trade with accrued interest and interest is paid annually.

A Yankee bond is similar to a Eurodollar bond, except that Yankee bonds are dollar-denominated bonds issued by a foreign issuer and sold to U.S. investors. If Virgin sold the same bonds to U.S. investors but the bonds' interest and principal were denominated in U.S. dollars rather than in British pounds, the bonds would be a Yankee bond. The advantage of a Yankee bond over a Eurobond for U.S. investors is that the Yankee bond does not have any currency risk.

VARIABLE RATE SECURITIES

The two main types of variable rate securities are Auction Rate Securities and Variable Rate Demand Obligations (VRDO). Auction Rate Securities are long-term securities that are traded as short-term securities. The interest rate paid will be reset at regularly scheduled auctions for the securities every 7, 28, or 35 days. Investors who buy or who elect to hold the securities will have the interest rate paid on the securities reset to the clearing rate until the next auction. Should the auction fail due to a lack of demand, investors who were looking to sell the securities may not have immediate access to their funds. VRDOs have the interest rate reset at set intervals daily, weekly, or monthly. The interest rate set on the VRDO is set by the dealer to a rate that will allow the instruments to be priced at par. Investors may elect to put the securities back to the issuer or a third party on the reset date. Variable rate securities may be issued as debt securities or as preferred stock offerings.

RETIRING CORPORATE BONDS

The retirement of a corporation's debt may occur under any of the following methods:

- Redemption
- Refunding
- Prerefunding
- Exercise of a call feature by the company
- Exercise of a put feature by the investor
- Tender offering
- Open market purchases

REDEMPTION

Bonds are redeemed upon maturity and the principal amount is repaid to investors. At maturity, investors will also receive their last semiannual interest payment.

REFUNDING

Many times corporations will use the sale of new bonds to pay off the principal of their outstanding bonds. Corporations will issue new bonds to refund their maturing bonds or call the outstanding issue in whole or in part under a call feature. This is known as refunding corporate debt. Refunding corporate debt is very similar to refinancing a home mortgage.

PREREFUNDING

A corporation may seek to take advantage of a low interest rate environment by prerefunding their outstanding bonds prior to being able to retire them under a call feature. The proceeds from the new issue of bonds are placed in an escrow account and invested in government securities. The interest generated in the escrow account is used to pay the debt service of the outstanding or prerefunded issue. The prerefunded issue will be called in by the company on the first call date. Because the prerefunded bonds are now backed by the government securities held in the escrow account, they are automatically rated AAA. Once an issue has been prerefunded (or advance refunded), the issuer's obligations under the indenture are terminated. This is known as defeasance.

CALLING IN BONDS

Many times corporations will attach a call feature to their bonds that will allow them to call in and retire the bonds, either at their discretion or on a set schedule. The call feature gives the corporation the ability to manage the amount of debt outstanding, as well as the ability to take advantage of favorable interest rate environments. Most bonds are not callable in the first several years after issuance. This is known as call protection. A call feature on a bond benefits the company, not the investor.

PUTTING BONDS TO THE COMPANY

As a way to make a bond issue more attractive to investors, a company may attach a put feature or put option on their bonds. Under a put option, the holder of the bonds may tender the bonds to the company for redemption. Some put features will allow the bondholders to put the bonds to the company for redemption if their rating falls to low or if interest rates rise significantly. A put option on a bond benefits the bondholder.

TENDER OFFERS

A company may make a tender offer in an effort to reduce its outstanding debt or as a way to take advantage of low interest rates. Tender offers may be made for both callable and noncallable bonds. Companies usually offer a premium for the bonds in order to make the offer attractive to bondholders.

OPEN-MARKET PURCHASES

Issuers, in an effort to reduce the amount of their outstanding debt, may simply repurchase the bonds in the marketplace.

Pretest

TYPES OF CORPORATE BONDS

la.finra.typ.corp.bond.001_1811

1. Which type of bonds require the investor to deposit coupons to receive their interest payments but have the owner's name recorded on the books of the issuer?

    a. Registered bonds.

    b. ~~Bearer bond~~s.

    c. ~~Book entry/journal entry bon~~ds.

    d. Principal-only bonds.

la.finra.typ.corp.bond.002_1811

2. The type of bond that is secured by real estate is called a:

    a. Real estate trust certificate.

    b. Mortgage bond.

    c. Equipment trust certificate.

    d. Collateral trust certificate.

la.finra.typ.corp.bond.003_1811

3. Collateral trust certificates use which of the following as collateral?

    a. Real estate.

    b. Mortgage.

    c. Stocks and bonds issued by the same company.

    d. Stocks and bonds issued by another company.

    pledged securities they own, issued by a different company @ collateral for the issue

la.finra.typ.corp.bond.004_1811

4. An ABC corporate bond is quoted at 110 and is convertible into ABC common at 20 per share parity. Price for the stock is:

    a. 21.

    (b) 22.

    c. 23.

    d. 24.

[handwritten: no. of shares = par/common value price = 50 ; 1,000/20]

[handwritten: parity price = CMV /#of shares = 22 ; 1,100 /50]

la.finra.typ.corp.bond.005_1811

5. XYZ has 8% subordinated debentures trading in the market place at $120. They are convertible into XYZ common stock at $25 per share. What is the parity price of the common stock?

    a. 29.

    b. 31.

    (c.) 30.

    d. 28.

[handwritten: 1,000/25 = 40 ; 1200/40 = 30]

sa.finra.typ.corp.bond.001_1811

6. Which bonds are issued as a physical certificate without the owner's name on them and require whoever possesses these bonds to clip the coupons to receive their interest payments as well as surrender the bond at maturity in order to receive the principal payment?

    a. Registered bonds.

    b. Book entry/journal entry bonds.

    c. Principal-only registered bonds.

    (d.) Bearer bonds.

sa.finra.typ.corp.bond.002_1811

7. All of the following are reasons a corporation would attach a warrant to their bond, except to:

    a. Save money.

    b. Make the bond more attractive.

    (c.) Increase the number of shares outstanding when the warrants are exercised.

    d. Lower the coupon.

[handwritten: (-) Sweetener that allows the issuer to offer lower coupon rate. · Can be seperated from bond + sold on the secondary markets before expiration.]

Municipal Bonds

INTRODUCTION

Learning Objective Statements

Describe the key features of general obligation bonds and revenue bonds.

Analyze the various sources of debt service.

Analyze the tax treatment of interest payments.

List the different types of short-term municipal securities.

State and local governments will issue municipal bonds in order to help local governments meet their financial needs. Most municipal bonds are considered to be almost as safe as Treasury securities issued by the federal government. However, unlike the federal government, an issuer of municipal securities does default from time to time. The degree of safety varies from state to state and from municipality to municipality.

Municipal securities may be issued by:

- States.
- Territorial possessions of the United States, such as Puerto Rico.
- Legally constituted taxing authorities and their agencies.
- Public authorities that supervise ports and mass transit.

TYPES OF MUNICIPAL BONDS

GENERAL OBLIGATION BOND

General obligation bonds (also known as GOs) are full faith and credit bonds. The bonds are backed by the full faith and credit of the issuer and by their ability to raise and levy taxes. In essence, tax revenues back the bonds. GOs will often be issued to fund projects that benefit the entire community and the financed projects generally do not produce revenue of any kind. General obligation bonds would be issued, for example, to fund a local park, a new school building, or a new police station. General obligation bonds that have been issued by the state are backed by income and sales taxes while GOs that have been issued by local governments or municipalities are backed by property taxes.

VOTER APPROVAL

General obligation bonds are a drain on the tax revenue of the state or municipality that issues them. The amount of general obligation bonds that may be issued must be within certain debt limits and requires voter approval. The maximum amount of general obligation debt that may be issued is known as the statutory debt limit. State and municipal governments may not issue general obligation debt in excess of their statutory limit.

PROPERTY TAXES

General obligation bonds issued at the local level are mostly supported by property tax revenue received from property owners. A property owner's taxes are based on the assessed value of the property, not on its actual market value. Towns will periodically send an assessor to inspect properties and determine what the properties' assessed values are.

| EXAMPLE | A homeowner whose home has a market value of $100,000 will not be taxed on the entire market value of the home. If the town uses a 75% assessment rate, the home's assessed value would be $75,000. |

OVERLAPPING DEBT

Taxpayers are subject to the taxing authority of various municipal authorities. Municipal debt issued by different municipal authorities that draws revenue from the same base of taxpayers is known as overlapping debt or coterminous debt.

EXAMPLE

The county water authority issued bonds that are supported by the property taxes levied in the county. The water authority's debt overlaps the town's and county's other general obligation debt by drawing support from the same tax revenue. State issues are not included when determining overlapping debt because they are supported by other revenue sources such as state sales taxes and income taxes.

REVENUE BONDS

A revenue bond is a municipal bond that has been issued to finance a revenue-producing project such as a toll bridge. The proceeds from the issuance of the bond will construct or repair the facility, and the debt payments will be supported by revenue generated by the facility. Municipal revenue bonds are exempt from the Trust Indenture Act of 1939, but all revenue bonds must have an indenture that spells out the following:

- Rate covenant

- Maintenance covenant

- Additional bond test

- Catastrophe clause

- Call or put features

- Flow of funds

- Outside audit

- Insurance covenant

- Sinking fund

INDUSTRIAL DEVELOPMENT BONDS/INDUSTRIAL REVENUE BONDS

An industrial revenue bond or an industrial development bond is a municipal bond issued for the benefit of a private corporation. The proceeds from the issuance of the bond will go toward building a facility or toward purchasing equipment for the corporation. The facility or equipment then will be leased back to the corporation and the lease payments will support the debt service on the bonds. Interest earned by some high-income earners on industrial development bonds may be subject to the investor's alternative minimum tax. States are limited as to the amount of industrial revenue bonds that may be issued, based on the population of the state.

LEASE RENTAL BONDS

A lease-back arrangement is created when a municipality issues a municipal bond to build a facility for an authority or agency such as a school district. The proceeds of the issue would be used to build the facility that is then leased to the agency and the lease payments support the bond's debt service.

SPECIAL TAX BONDS

A special tax bond is issued to meet a specific goal. The bond's debt service is paid only by revenue generated from specific taxes. The debt service on special tax bonds is, in many cases, supported by "sin" taxes, such as taxes on alcohol, tobacco, gasoline, hotel and motel fees, and business licenses. Keep in mind that special tax bonds are revenue bonds, not general obligation bonds.

SPECIAL ASSESSMENT BONDS

A special assessment bond will be issued in order to finance a project that benefits a specific geographic area or portion of a municipality. Sidewalks and reservoirs are examples of projects that may be financed through issuance of special assessment bonds. The homeowners in the area that benefit from the project will be subject to a special tax assessment. The assessment will then be used to support the debt service of the bonds. Homeowners that do not benefit from the project are not subject to the tax assessment.

DOUBLE-BARRELED BONDS

Double-barreled bonds are bonds that have been issued to build or maintain a revenue-producing facility such as a bridge or a roadway. The initial debt service is supported by the user fees generated by the facility. However, if the revenue generated by the facility is insufficient to support the bond's interest and principal payments, the payments will be supported by the general tax revenue of the state or municipality. The debt service on double-barreled bonds is backed by two sources of revenue. Because the tax revenue of the state or municipality also backs them, revenue bonds are rated and trade like general obligation bonds.

MORAL OBLIGATION BONDS

A moral obligation bond is issued to build or maintain a revenue-producing facility such as a park that charges an entrance fee or a tunnel that charges a toll. If the revenue generated by the facility is insufficient to cover the debt service, the state legislature may vote to allocate tax revenue to cover the shortfall. A moral obligation bond does not require that the state cover any shortfall; it merely gives them the option to. Some reasons why a state may elect to cover a shortfall are to:

- Keep a high credit rating on all municipal issues
- Ensure that interest rates on their municipal issues do not rise

NEW HOUSING AUTHORITY/PUBLIC HOUSING AUTHORITY

New housing authority (NHA) and public housing authority (PHA) bonds are issued to build low-income housing. The initial debt service for the bonds is the rental income received from the project's tenants. Should the rental income be insufficient to cover the bond's debt service, the U.S. government covers any shortfall. Because the payments are guaranteed by the federal government, NHA/PHA bonds are considered to be the safest type of municipal bond. NHA/PHA bonds are not considered to be double-barreled bonds because any shortfall will be covered by the federal government, not the state or municipal government.

SHORT-TERM MUNICIPAL FINANCING

States and municipalities, like other issuers, need to obtain short-term financing to manage their cash flow and will sell both short-term notes and tax-exempt commercial paper. Short-term notes are sold in anticipation of receiving other revenue and are issued an MIG rating by Moody's investor service. The MIG ratings range from 1 to 4, with a rating of MIG 1 being the highest and a rating of MIG 4 being the lowest. The types of short-term notes a state or municipality may issue are:

- Tax anticipation notes (TANs).

- Revenue anticipation notes (RANs).

- Bond anticipation notes (BANs).

- Tax and revenue anticipation notes (TRANs).

Municipal tax-exempt commercial paper matures in 270 days or less and will usually be backed by a line of credit at a bank.

TAXATION OF MUNICIPAL BONDS

The interest earned by investors from municipal bonds is free from federal income taxes. The doctrine of reciprocal immunity, established by the Supreme Court in 1895, sets forth that the federal government will not tax the interest earned by investors from municipal securities and that the states will not tax interest earned by investors on federal securities. The decision that established this doctrine was repealed in 1986 and allows for the federal taxation of municipal bond interest. This, however, is highly unlikely.

TAX-EQUIVALENT YIELD

It's important for investors to consider the tax implications of investing in municipal bonds. Because the interest earned from municipal bonds is federally tax free, municipal bonds offer a lower rate than other bonds of similar quality. Even though the rate is oftentimes much lower, the investor may still be better off with the lower rate municipal than with a higher rate corporate bond. Investors in a higher tax bracket will realize a greater benefit from the tax exemption than investors in a lower tax bracket. To determine where an investor would be better off after taxes, look to the tax-equivalent yield that is found by using the following formula:

tax-free yield (100% – investor's tax bracket)

For example, take an investor considering purchasing a municipal bond with a coupon rate of 7%. The investor is also considering investing in a corporate bond instead. The investor is in the 30% federal tax bracket and wants to determine which bond is going to give the greatest return after taxes.

tax-equivalent yield = 7%/(100% – 30%) = 7%/.7 = 10%

In this example, if the corporate bond of similar quality does not yield more than 10%, then the investor is better off with the municipal bond. However, if the corporate bond yields more than 10%, the investor is better off with the corporate bond.

PURCHASING A MUNICIPAL BOND ISSUED IN THE STATE IN WHICH THE INVESTOR RESIDES

If an investor purchases a municipal bond issued within the state in which he or she resides, then the interest earned on the bond will be free from federal, state, and local income taxes.

TRIPLE TAX FREE

Municipal bonds that have been issued by a territory such as Puerto Rico or Guam are given tax-free status for the interest payments from federal, state, and local income taxes.

BOND SWAPS

An investor from time to time may wish to sell a bond at a loss for tax purposes. The loss is realized when the investor sells the bond. The investor may not repurchase the bond, or a bond that is substantially the same, for 30 days after the sale is made. The investor may purchase bonds that differ as to the issuer, the coupon, or maturity, thus creating a bond swap and not a wash sale. A wash sale would result in the loss being disallowed by the IRS, because a bond swap does not affect the investor's ability to claim the loss.

ANALYZING MUNICIPAL BONDS

The quality and safety of municipal bonds varies from issuer to issuer. Investors who purchase municipal securities need to be able to determine the risk that may be associated with a particular issuer or with a particular bond.

ANALYZING GENERAL OBLIGATION BONDS

The quality of a general obligation bond is largely determined by the financial health of the issuing state or municipality. General obligation bonds are supported through the tax revenue that has been received by the issuer. The ability of the issuer to levy and collect tax revenue varies from state to state and from municipality to municipality. It is important that the fundamental health of the issuer be examined before investing in municipal bonds. Just as an investor would read a company's financial reports before purchasing their stock or bonds, an investor should read the reports of a state or municipality before purchasing their bonds.

Pretest

MUNICIPAL BONDS

la.finra.muni.bons.001_1811

1. Which of the following municipal issues would most likely have more than one source of revenue?

    a. Bonds issued by the state to cover general working expenses.

    b. Bonds issued by the county to improve the municipal courthouse.

    c. Bonds issued by a town to improve school buildings.

    d. Bonds issued by a turnpike authority to improve roads.

la.finra.muni.bons.002_1811

2. Which of the following is correct regarding general obligation bonds but not true of revenue bonds?

    a. General obligation bonds are subject to voter approval.

    b. General obligation bonds are issued through negotiation.

    c. General obligation bonds are supported by use fees received by the town.

    d. General obligation bonds have term maturities.

la.finra.muni.bons.003_1811

3. Which one of the following debt securities pays interest?

    a. Commercial paper.

    b. T-bill.

    c. Industrial revenue bond.

    d. Banker's acceptance.

sa.finra.muni.bons.001_1811

4. When contrasting a corporate bond to a municipal bond of the same quality and maturity, you would observe which of the following?

    a. The corporate bond is more volatile.

    b. The corporate bond has a lower coupon rate.

    c. The municipal bond is more volatile.

    d. The corporate bond has a higher coupon rate.

sa.finra.muni.bons.002_1811

5. Which of the following municipal bonds issued by a large city could produce taxable income to some investors?

    a. Double-barreled bonds.

    b. Special tax bonds.

    c. Revenue bonds.

    d. Industrial revenue bonds.

Government and Government Agency Issues

INTRODUCTION

Learning Objective Statements

Contrast the features of various Treasury securities.

Detail the purpose of government agencies and analyze the issuance and investment features of CMOs.

The U.S. government is the largest issuer of debt. It is also the issuer with the least amount of default risk. Default risk is also known as credit risk and is the risk that the issuer will not be able to meet its obligations under the terms of the bond in a timely fashion. The U.S. government issues debt securities with maturities ranging from 1 month up to 30 years. The Treasury Department issues the securities on behalf of the federal government and they are a legally binding obligation of the federal government. Interest earned by the investors from U.S. government securities is only taxed at the federal level. State and local governments do not tax the interest income.

SERIES EE BONDS

Series EE bonds are commonly known as savings bonds. They are purchased directly from the U.S. government at a discount from their face value, typically 50%. Series EE bonds pay no semiannual interest and may be redeemed at maturity for the face value. Interest for the investor is earned through the bond's appreciation toward the face value. The interest earned through this appreciation is taxable by the federal government and the investor may pay taxes on this money each year or may wait until the bond matures. The investor may also elect to roll the matured Series EE bonds into Series HH bonds and continue to defer taxes.

SERIES HH BONDS

A Series HH bond may only be purchased by trading in matured Series EE bonds. They may not be purchased for cash. Series HH bonds, unlike EEs, pay semiannual interest and are available in denominations of $500 to $10,000 and mature in 10 years. Series HH bonds may be redeemed at their face value at any time.

TREASURY BILLS, NOTES, AND BONDS

The most widely held U.S. government securities are Treasury bills, notes, and bonds. These direct obligations of the U.S. government range from 1 month up to 30 years.

PURCHASING TREASURY BILLS

Treasury bills range in maturity from 4 to 52 weeks and are auctioned off by the Treasury Department through a weekly competitive auction. Large banks and broker dealers, known as primary dealers, submit competitive bids or tenders for the bills being sold. The Treasury awards the bills to the bidders who submitted the highest bids and work their way down to lower bids until all of the bills are sold. Treasury bills pay no semiannual interest and are issued at a discount from par. The bill appreciates up to par at maturity and the appreciation represents the investor's interest. Because bills are priced at a discount from par, a higher dollar price represents a lower interest rate for the purchaser.

All noncompetitive tenders are filled before any competitive tenders are filled. A bidder who submits a noncompetitive tender agrees to accept the average of all the yields accepted by the Treasury and does not try to get the best yield. All competitive tenders are limited to a maximum amount of

$500,000. All bids accepted and filled by the Treasury are settled in fed funds. Treasury bills range in denominations from $100 up to $1,000,000.

 TAKENOTE!

A quote for a Treasury bill has a bid that appears to be higher than the offer, but remember that the bills are quoted on a discounted yield basis. The higher bid actually represents a lower dollar price than the offer.

Example

Bid	Ask
2.91	2.75

TREASURY NOTES

Treasury notes are the U.S. government's intermediate-term security and range in term from 1 year up to 10 years. Treasury notes pay semiannual interest and are auctioned off by the Treasury every 4 weeks. Treasury notes are issued in denominations ranging from $100 up to $1,000,000 and may be refunded by the government. If a Treasury note is refunded, the government will offer the investor a new Treasury note with a new interest rate and maturity. The investor may always elect to receive their principal payment instead of accepting the new note.

TREASURY BONDS

Treasury bonds are the U.S. government's long-term bonds. Maturities on Treasury bonds range from 10 years up to 30 years. Treasury bonds, like Treasury notes, pay semiannual interest and are issued in denominations ranging from $100 up to $1,000,000. Some Treasury bonds may be called in at par by the treasury. If the Treasury Department calls in a bond issue, they must give holders 4 months' notice before calling the bonds.

TREASURY BOND AND NOTE PRICING

Treasury notes and bonds are quoted as a percentage of par. However, unlike their corporate counterparts, Treasury notes and bonds are quoted as a percentage of par down to 32nds of 1%. For example, a Treasury bond quote of 92.02 translates into:

92-2/32% × $1,000 = $920.625

A quote of 98.04 translates into:

98.125% × $1,000 = $981.25

It is important to remember that the number after the decimal point represents 32nds of a percent.

Treasury Security	Type of Interest	Term	Priced
Bill	None	4, 13, 26, 52 weeks 1, 3, 6, 12 months	At a discount from par
Note	Semiannual	1–10 years	As a percentage of par to 32nds of 1%
Bond	Semiannual	10–30 years	As a percentage of par to 32nds of 1%

The minimum denomination for purchasing a Treasury bill, note, or bond from TreasuryDirect.gov is $100. All quotes in the secondary market are based on $1,000 par value.

 TAKENOTE!

The Treasury does not currently sell 1-year bills. However, this is a policy decision and the Treasury may at any time elect to issue 1-year bills, just as it recently decided to reissue 30-year bonds.

TREASURY STRIPS

The term Treasury STRIPS actually stands for separate trading of registered interest and principal securities. The Treasury securities are separated into two parts: a principal payment and semiannual interest payments. Treasury

STRIPS are zero-coupon bonds that are backed by U.S. government securities. An investor may purchase the principal payment component of $1,000, due on a future date at a discount. An investor seeking some current income may wish to purchase the semiannual coupon payments due over the term of the Treasury securities.

STRIPS may be purchased by an investor who needs to have a certain amount available on a known date in the future (like the time when a child is going to college). By purchasing STRIPS, the investor is guaranteed to have $1,000 on that date in the future for each security purchased.

TREASURY RECEIPTS

Treasury receipts are similar to Treasury STRIPS, except that broker dealers and banks create them. Broker dealers and banks will purchase large amounts of Treasury securities, place them in a trust, and sell off the interest and principal payments to different investors.

TREASURY INFLATION PROTECTED SECURITIES (TIPS)

Treasury inflation protected securities, or TIPS, offer the investor protection from inflation. The TIPS are sold with a fixed interest rate and their principal is adjusted semiannually to reflect changes in the consumer price index. During times of inflation, the principal amount of TIPS will be increased and the investor's interest payments will rise, while during times of falling prices, the principal amount of the bond will be adjusted down and the investor will receive a lower interest payment.

EXAMPLE

A conservative investor purchases TIPS with a coupon rate of 4%. Prior to taking inflation into consideration, the investor will receive 4% × $1,000 or $40 per year, paid as $20 or 2% every 6 months. TIPS pay interest every 6 months based on the adjusted principal amount. If Inflation is running at 6% per year over the next 2 years the investor's principal and interest payments will be as follows:

Year	Semiannual Adjustment	Adjusted Principal	Adjusted Payment
1	Number 1	$1,030	$20.60
1	Number 1	$1,60.90	$21.22
2	Number 2	$1,092.73	$21.85
2	Number 2	$1,125.51	$22.51

Because inflation was running at 6% per year the principal was increased by 3% every 6 months. The adjustment to the principal and interests compounds semiannually and results in the continued increase in the principal amount and payment received. To determine the amount of the payment take half of the coupon rate and multiply it by the adjusted principal. In the example, TIPS paid interest at a rate of 2% of the adjusted principal every 6 months. If on your test you cannot remember how to calculate compound interest over time you may approximate it by simply taking the inflation rate over a given period and multiplying it by the principal. In our case, 6% per year for 2 years = 12%. 12% of $1,000 = $120. The adjusted principal would be approximately $1,120. On the exam round up to the next nearest answer. As you can see the approximate method gets you within about $5 of the compounded principal.

 TAKENOTE!

Because the principal amount of TIPS is adjusted every 6 months to account for inflation the real return or the inflation-adjusted return will always be equal to the coupon rate.

AGENCY ISSUES

The federal government has authorized certain agencies and certain quasi agencies to issue debt securities that are collectively referred to as agency issues. Revenues generated through taxes, fees, and interest income back these agency securities. Investors who purchase agency securities are offered interest rates that generally fall in between the rates offered by similar term Treasury and corporate securities. Investors who purchase agency issues in the secondary market will be quoted prices for the agency issues that are based on a percentage of par just like corporate issues.

GOVERNMENT NATIONAL MORTGAGE ASSOCIATION (GNMA)

The Government National Mortgage Association often referred to as Ginnie Mae is a wholly owned government corporation and is the only agency whose securities are backed by the full faith and credit of the U.S. government. The purpose of Ginnie Mae is to provide liquidity to the mortgage markets. Ginnie Mae buys up pools of mortgages that have been insured by the Federal Housing Administration (FHA) and the Department of Veteran Affairs (VA). The ownership in these pools of mortgages is then sold off to private investors in the form of pass-through certificates. Investors in Ginnie Mae pass-through certificates receive monthly interest and principal payments based on their investment. As people pay down their mortgages, part of each payment is interest and part of each payment is principal and both portions flow through to the investor on a monthly basis. The only real risk in owning a Ginnie Mae is the risk of early refinancing. As the interest rates in the marketplace fall, people are more likely to refinance their homes and, as a result, the investor will not receive higher interest rates for as long as they had hoped. Ginnie Mae pass-through certificates are issued with a minimum denomination of $1,000 and the interest earned by investors is taxable at all levels: federal, state, and local. Yield quotes on Ginnie Maes are based on a 12-year prepayment assumption because most mortgages are repaid early as a result of refinancing, moving, or a homeowner simply paying off their mortgage.

FEDERAL NATIONAL MORTGAGE ASSOCIATION (FNM)

The Federal National Mortgage Association, also known as Fannie Mae, is a public for-profit corporation. Fannie Mae's stock trades publicly and is in business to realize a profit by providing mortgage capital. It's called an agency security because Fannie Mae has a credit facility with the government and receives certain favorable tax considerations. Fannie Mae purchases mortgages and, in turn, packages them to create mortgage-backed securities. These mortgage-backed notes are issued in denominations from $5,000 to $1,000,000 and pay interest semiannually. Fannie Mae also issues debentures with a minimum denomination of $10,000 that mature in 3 to 25 years. Interest is paid semiannually and the interest earned by investors from Fannie Mae securities is taxable at all levels: federal, state, and local.

FEDERAL HOME LOAN MORTGAGE CORPORATION (FHLMC)

The Federal Home Loan Mortgage Corporation also known as Freddie Mac is a publicly traded company in business to earn a profit on its loans. Freddie Mac purchases residential mortgages from lenders and, in turn, packages them into pools and sells off interests in those pools to investors. Interest earned by investors from FHLMC-issued securities is taxable at all levels: federal, state, and local.

 TAKENOTE!

Both Fannie Mae and Freddie Mac have been placed in receivership by the U.S. government.

FEDERAL FARM CREDIT SYSTEM

The Federal Farm Credit System is a group of privately owned lenders that provide different types of financing for farmers. The FFCS sells off farm credit securities in order to obtain the funds to provide to farmers. The securities are the obligations of all lenders in the system and are not backed by the U.S. government. The securities pay interest every 6 months and are only available in book-entry form. There are several lenders of which you need to be aware:

- Federal Land Bank provides mortgage money.

- Bank of the Cooperatives provides money for feed and grain.

- Federal Intermediate Credit Bank provides money for tractors and equipment.

COLLATERALIZED MORTGAGE OBLIGATION (CMO)

A collateralized mortgage obligation is a mortgage-backed security issued by private finance companies, as well as by FHLMC and FNMA. The securities are structured much like a pass-through certificate and their term is set into different maturity schedules, known as tranches. Pools of mortgages on one-family to four-family homes collateralize CMOs. Because CMOs are backed by mortgages on real estate, they are considered relatively safe investments and are given a AAA rating. The only real risk that the owner of a CMO faces is the risk of early refinance. CMOs pay interest and principal monthly. However, they pay the principal to only one tranche at a time in $1,000 payments. The CMO pays off each tranche until the final tranche known as a Z tranche is paid off. The Z tranche is the most volatile CMO tranche.

CMOs and interest rates

CMOs, like other interest-bearing investments, will be affected by a change in the interest-rate environment. CMOs may experience the following if interest rates change:

- If interest rates fall, homeowners will refinance more quickly and the holder of the CMO will be paid off more quickly than they hoped.

- The rate of principal payments may vary.

- If interest rates rise, refinancing may slow down and the investors will be paid off more slowly than hoped for.

Most CMOs have an active secondary market and are considered relatively liquid securities. However, the more complex CMOs may not have an active secondary market and may be considered illiquid. Interest earned by investors from CMOs is taxable at all levels: federal, state, and local.

TYPES OF CMOs

Like many other investments there are several different types of CMOs. They are:

- Principal only (PO)

- Interest only (IO)

- Planned amortization class (PAC)

- Targeted amortization class (TAC)

PRINCIPAL-ONLY CMOs

Principal-only CMOs, as the name suggests, receives only the principal payments made on the underlying mortgage. Principal-only CMOs receive both the scheduled principal payments as well as any prepayments made by the homeowners in the pool. Because the principal-only CMO does not receive any interest payments, it is sold at a discount to its face value. The appreciation of the CMO, up to its face value, represents the investor's return. The price of a principal-only CMO is sensitive to a change in interest rates. As interest rates fall, the value of the CMO rises, as prepayments accelerate. A rise in interest rates has the opposite effect.

INTEREST-ONLY CMOs

Interest-only CMOs receive the interest payments made by homeowners in the pool of underlying mortgages. Interest-only CMOs will also sell at a discount to their face value due to the amortization of the underlying mortgages. Interest-only CMOs increase in value as interest rates rise and decrease in value as interest rates fall, as a result of the changes in prepayments on the underlying pool of mortgages. The changes in the prepayments on the underlying mortgages will affect the number of interest payments the holder of the CMO receives. As interest rates rise, prepayments slow, thus increasing the number of interest payments the investor receives. The more interest payments the CMO holder receives, the more valuable the CMO becomes.

PLANNED AMORTIZATION CLASS (PAC) CMO

Planned amortization class CMOs are paid off first and offer the investor the most protection against prepayment risk and extension risk. If prepayments come in too quickly, those principal payments will be deferred to another CMO known as a support class to protect the owner of the PAC from prepayment risk. If principal payments are made more slowly, principal payments will be taken from a support class to protect the investor against extension risk.

TARGETED AMORTIZATION CLASS (TAC) CMOs

Targeted amortization class CMOs only offer the investor protection from prepayment risk. If principal payments are made more quickly, they will be transferred to a support class. However, if principal payments come in more slowly, payments will not be taken from a support class and will be subject to extension risk.

 TAKENOTE!

More complex CMOs are not suitable for all investors and investors should sign a suitability statement before investing. The secondary market for complex CMOs may also be very illiquid.

PRIVATE-LABEL CMOs

Private-label CMOs are issued by investment banks and the payment of interest and principal payments are the responsibility of the issuing investment bank. The payments due to a holder of a private-label CMO are not guaranteed by any government agency. The credit ratings of the private-label CMOs are based on the collateral that backs the CMO and the credit rating of the issuer. If the private-label CMO uses agency issues as collateral for the CMO, those agency issues still carry the guarantee of the issuing government agency.

Pretest

GOVERNMENT AND GOVERNMENT AGENCY ISSUES

la.finra.gov.ag.iss.001_1811

1. When is the interest on an EE savings bond paid?

   a. When redeemed.

   b. Annually.

   c. Quarterly.

   d. Monthly.

la.finra.gov.ag.iss.002_1811

2. All of the following are true regarding the Federal National Mortgage Association (Fannie Mae) except:

   a. It purchases mortgages and packages them to create mortgage-backed securities that pay interest semiannually.

   b. It provides an investment free of federal, state, and local taxes.

   c. It is a public for-profit corporation.

   d. Its purpose is to earn a profit by providing mortgage capital.

la.finra.gov.ag.iss.003_1811

3. An investor purchased a Treasury bond at 95.03. How much did he pay for the bond?

   a. $ 9,530.00.

   b. $ 9,500.9375.

   c. $ 950.9375.

   d. $ 953.00.

sa.finra.gov.ag.iss.001_1811

4. Your customer wants to invest in a conservative income-producing investment and is inquiring about GNMAs. She wants to know the minimum dollar amount required to purchase a pass-through certificate. You should tell her:

   a. $1,000.

   b. $10,000.

   c. There is no minimum; you can invest almost any sum.

   d. $5,000.

sa.finra.gov.ag.iss.002_1811

5. Your customer buys a U.S. T-bond at 103.16. How much did he pay for the bond?

   a. $1,031.60.

   b. $103.16.

   c. 1,035.00.

   d. $10,316.00.

The Money Market

INTRODUCTION

Learning Objective Statements

Identify the various money market instruments.

Indicate the function served through the issuance of the instrument.

Identify the various interest rates.

The money market is a place where issuers go to obtain short-term financing. An issuer who needs funds for a short term, typically under 1 year, will sell short-term instruments known as money market instruments to obtain the necessary funds. Corporations, municipalities, and the U.S. government all use the money market to obtain short-term financing.

MONEY MARKET INSTRUMENTS

Money market instruments are highly liquid fixed-income securities issued by governments and corporations with high credit ratings. Because of the high quality of the issuers and because of the short-term maturities, money market instruments are considered very safe.

CORPORATE MONEY MARKET INSTRUMENTS

Both corporations and banks sell money market instruments to obtain short-term financing. These money market instruments issued will include:

- Bankers' acceptances
- Negotiable certificates of deposit

- Commercial paper
- Federal funds loans
- Repurchase agreements
- Reverse repurchase agreements

BANKERS' ACCEPTANCES

In order to facilitate foreign trade (import/export), corporations use bankers' acceptances (BAs). The BA acts like a line of credit or a postdated check. The BA is a time draft that will be cleared by the issuing bank on the day it comes due to whomever presents it for payment. The maturity dates on BAs range from as little as 1 day to a maximum of 270 days (9 months).

NEGOTIABLE CERTIFICATES OF DEPOSIT

A negotiable certificate of deposit (CD) is a time deposit with a fixed interest rate and a set maturity ranging from 30 days to 10 years or more. A negotiable CD, unlike the traditional CD, may be exchanged or traded between investors. The minimum denomination for a negotiable CD is $100,000. Many negotiable CDs are issued in denominations exceeding $1,000,000, but the FDIC only insures the first $250,000.

COMMERCIAL PAPER

The largest and most creditworthy corporations use commercial paper as a way to obtain short-term funds. Commercial paper is an unsecured promissory note or an IOU issued by the corporation. Corporations sell commercial paper to finance such things as short-term working capital or to meet their cash needs due to seasonal business cycles, with maturities ranging from 1 day to a maximum of 270 days. Commercial paper is issued at a discount to its face value and has an interest rate that is below what a commercial bank would typically charge for the funds and it is typically issued in book entry form. There are two types of commercial paper: direct paper and dealer paper. With direct paper, the issuer sells the paper directly to the public without the use of a dealer. Dealer paper is sold to dealers who then resell the paper to investors.

FEDERAL FUND LOANS

Federal fund loans are loans between two large banks that are typically made for short periods of time in amounts of $1,000,000 or more. These loans may be exchanged in the money market between investors.

REPURCHASE AGREEMENTS

A repurchase agreement is a fully collateralized loan made between a dealer and a large institutional investor. These loans are usually collateralized with U.S. government securities that have been sold to the lender. The borrower (seller) agrees to repurchase the securities from the lender at a slightly higher price. The slightly higher price represents the lender's interest.

REVERSE REPURCHASE AGREEMENT

In a reverse repurchase agreement, the institutional investor initiates the transaction by selling the securities to the dealer and agrees to repurchase them at a later time. In a reverse repurchase agreement, the borrower (seller) is the institution, not the dealer.

FIXED VS. OPEN REPURCHASE AGREEMENTS

With a fixed repurchase agreement, the borrower (seller) agrees to repurchase the securities at a fixed price on a specified date. With an open repurchase agreement, the date of the repurchase is not fixed, and the open repurchase agreement becomes a demand note for the lender and may be called in.

 TAKENOTE!

Corporate issues with less than 1 year remaining to maturity, regardless of the original maturity, may be traded in the money market.

GOVERNMENT MONEY MARKET INSTRUMENTS

The federal government and many of its agencies go to the money market to obtain short-term funds. Government money market instruments include:

- Treasury bills
- Treasury and agency securities with less than 1 year remaining
- Short-term discount notes issued by government agencies

MUNICIPAL MONEY MARKET INSTRUMENTS

State and local government sell securities in the municipal money market to obtain short-term financing. The municipal money market instruments are:

- Bond anticipation notes
- Tax anticipation notes
- Revenue anticipation notes
- Tax and revenue anticipation notes
- Tax-exempt commercial paper

Government and municipal issues with less than 1 year to maturity, regardless of the original maturity, may be traded in the money market.

INTERNATIONAL MONEY MARKET INSTRUMENTS

Often large institutions place U.S. dollars in foreign accounts to earn a higher rate of interest. These dollars being held outside of the United States are known as Eurodollars. A U.S. dollar–denominated account outside of the United States is known as a Eurodollar deposit. These deposits typically have maturities of up to 180 days, and they are traded between large European banks and institutions, much like federal fund loans in the United States.

INTEREST RATES

Interest rates, put simply, are the cost of money. Overall interest rates are determined by the supply and demand for money, along with any upward price movement in the cost of goods and services, known as inflation. There are several key interest rates upon which all other rates depend:

- Discount rate
- Federal funds rate
- Broker call loan rate
- Prime rate

THE DISCOUNT RATE

The discount rate is the interest rate that the Federal Reserve Bank charges on loans to member banks. A bank may borrow money directly from the Federal Reserve by going to the discount window, and the bank will be charged the discount rate. The bank is then free to lend out this money at a higher rate and earn a profit, or it may use these funds to meet a reserve requirement shortfall. Although a bank may borrow money directly from the Federal Reserve, this is discouraged, and the discount rate has become largely symbolic.

FEDERAL FUNDS RATE

The federal funds rate is the rate that member banks charge each other for overnight loans. The federal funds rate is widely watched as an indicator for the direction of short-term interest rates.

BROKER CALL LOAN RATE

The broker call loan rate is the interest rate that banks charge on loans to broker dealers to finance their customers' margin purchases. Many broker dealers will extend credit to their customers to purchase securities on margin. The broker dealers will obtain the money to lend to their customers from the bank, and the loan is callable or payable on demand by the broker dealer.

PRIME RATE

The prime rate is the rate that banks charge their largest and most creditworthy corporate customers on loans. The prime rate has lost a lot of its significance in recent years because mortgage lenders are now basing their rates on other rates, such as the 10-year Treasury note. The prime rate is, however, very important for consumer spending, because most credit card interest rates are based on prime plus a margin.

LONDON INTERBANK OFFERED RATE/LIBOR

LIBOR is the most widely used measure of short-term interest rates around the world. The LIBOR rate is the market-driven interest rate charged by and between financial institutions similar to the fed funds rate in the United States. LIBOR loans range from 1 day to 1 year and the rate is calculated by the British Banker's Association in a variety of currencies including euros, U.S. dollars, and yen.

Pretest

THE MONEY MARKET

la.finra.mon.market.001_1118

1. The money market is a place where issuers go to:

   a. Obtain long-term financing.

   b. Obtain short-term financing.

   c. Offer higher interest rates for a higher yield.

   d. Exchange money market instruments to their mutual benefit.

la.finra.mon.market.002_1118

2. Which of the following could trade in the money market?

   a. Short-term equity.

   b. Newly issued corporate bonds.

   c. Newly issued options contracts.

   d. A Treasury note issued nine years ago.

la.finra.mon.market.003_1118

3. Which of the following may always trade in the money market?

   a. T-bond.

   b. T-note.

   c. ADR.

   d. Bankers' acceptance.

la.finra.mon.market.004_1118

4. The maximum duration for a piece of commercial paper is:

   a. 45 days.

   b. 10 years.

   c. 1 year.

    d. 9 months.

5. A bank with a shortfall meeting their reserve requirement could borrow money from another bank and pay the:

    a. Federal funds rate.

    b. Broker call loan rate.

    c. Prime rate.

    d. Discount rate.

6. Which of the following is NOT a corporate money market instrument?

    a. Negotiable certificates of deposit.

    b. Treasury bills.

    c. Repurchase agreements.

    d. Commercial paper.

7. Which of the following is NOT true of money market instruments?

    a. They are highly liquid fixed-income securities.

    b. They are issued by corporations with high credit ratings, and are thus considered safe.

    c. They are considered risky because of short-term maturities.

    d. They are a method used to obtain short-term financing.

Economics, Corporate Fundamentals, Issuing, and Trading Securities

An Introduction to Economics and Corporate Fundamentals

INTRODUCTION

Learning Objective Statements

Explain the four stages of the business cycle and its impact on the economy as a whole.

Analyze the impact of inflation.

Interpret various indicators to predict the business cycle.

Demonstrate the functions of the Federal Reserve Board.

Contrast monetary and fiscal policy.

Assess the financial condition of a corporation from examining the financial statements.

Economics, put simply, is the study of shortages: supply versus demand. As the demand for a product or service rises, the price of those products or services tends to rise. Alternatively, if the provider of those goods or services tries to flood the market with those goods or services, the price tends to decline as the supply outpaces the demand. The supply and demand model works for all goods and services including stocks, bonds, real estate, and money.

GROSS DOMESTIC PRODUCT

A country's gross domestic product (GDP) measures the overall health of a nation's economy. The GDP is defined as the value of all goods and services produced in a country including consumption, investments, government spending, and exports minus imports during a given year.

Economists chart the health of the economy by measuring the country's GDP and by monitoring supply and demand models, along with the nation's business cycle. A country's economy is always in flux. Periods of increasing output are always followed by periods of falling output. The business cycle has four distinct stages:

1. Expansion

2. Peak

3. Contraction

4. Trough

EXPANSION

During an expansionary phase, an economy will see an increase in overall business activity and output. Corporate sales, manufacturing output, wages, and savings will all increase while the economy is expanding or growing. An economy cannot continue to grow indefinitely and GDP will top out at the peak of the business cycle. An economic expansion is characterized by:

- Increasing GDP

- Rising consumer demand

- Rising stock market

- Rising production

- Rising real estate prices

PEAK

As the economy tops out, the GDP reaches its maximum output for this cycle as wages, manufacturing, and savings all peak.

CONTRACTION

During a contraction, GDP falls, along with productivity, wages, and savings. Unemployment begins to rise, the stock market begins to fall, and corporate profits decline as inventories rise.

TROUGH

The economy bottoms out in the trough as GDP hits its lowest level for the cycle. As GDP bottoms out, unemployment reaches its highest level, wages bottom out, and savings bottom out. The economy is now poised to enter a new expansionary phase and start the cycle all over again.

RECESSION

A recession is defined as a period of declining GDP, which lasts at least 6 months or two quarters. Recessions may vary in degree of severity and in duration. Extended recessions may last up to 18 months and may be accompanied by steep downturns in economic output. In the most severe recessions falling prices erode businesses' pricing power, margins, and profits as deflation takes hold. Recessions are generally triggered by an overall decrease in spending by businesses and consumers. As businesses and consumers pull back spending, overall demand falls. Businesses and consumers will often reduce spending as a cautionary measure in response to an economic event or shock, such as a financial crisis, or the busting of a bubble in an inflated asset class, such as real estate or the stock market.

DEPRESSION

A depression is characterized by a decline in GDP, which lasts at least 18 months or six consecutive quarters. GDP often falls by 10% or more during a depression. A depression is the most severe type of recession and is accompanied by extremely high levels of unemployment and frozen credit markets. The steep fall in demand is more likely to lead to deflation during a depression.

ECONOMIC INDICATORS

There are various economic activities that one can look at to try to identify where the economy is in the business cycle. An individual can also use these economic indicators as a way to try and predict the direction of the economy in the future. The three types of economic indicators are:

1. Leading indicators

2. Coincident indicators

3. Lagging indicators

LEADING INDICATORS

Leading indicators are business conditions that change prior to a change in the overall economy. These indicators can be used as a gauge for the future direction of the economy. Leading indicators include:

- Building permits

- Stock market prices

- Money supply (M2)

- New orders for consumer goods

- Average weekly initial claims in unemployment

- Changes in raw material prices

- Changes in consumer or business borrowing

- Average work week for manufacturing

- Changes in inventories of durable goods

COINCIDENT INDICATORS

Changes in the economy cause an immediate change in the activity level of coincident indicators. As the business cycle changes, the level of activity in coincident indicators can confirm where the economy is. Coincident indicators include:

- GDP

- Industrial production
- Personal income
- Employment
- Average number of hours worked
- Manufacturing and trade sales
- Nonagricultural employment

LAGGING INDICATORS

Lagging indicators will only change after the state of the economy has changed direction. Lagging indicators can be used to confirm the new direction of the economy. Lagging indicators include:

- Average duration of unemployment
- Corporate profits
- Labor costs
- Consumer debt levels
- Commercial and industrial loans
- Business loans

SCHOOLS OF ECONOMIC THOUGHT

The study of economics is a social science with many different schools of thought. Economics has been referred to as the dismal science, as it is largely focused on the study of shortages. Economists generally believe that low inflation and low unemployment are signs of a healthy economy. However, the different schools of economic thought believe that economic prosperity can be restored or maintained through very different approaches.

CLASSICAL ECONOMICS

The classical economic theory also known as supply side economics believes that lower taxes and less government regulation will stimulate growth and increase demand through higher employment. Less regulation of business creates lower barriers to entry for employers and allows employers to produce goods at lower prices and to create more jobs. As a result of the lower prices, lower taxes, and higher employment, aggregate demand in the economy will increase, positively impacting the nation's gross domestic product.

KEYNESIAN ECONOMICS

John Maynard Keynes first published his theories on economics in 1936 during the Great Depression. The Keynesian economic model believes that a mixed economy based on private and public sector efforts will produce desired economic conditions. Keynesians believe that the decisions made in the private sector can lead to supply and demand imbalances and that an active policy response from the public sector in the form of government spending (fiscal policy) and adjustments to the money supply (monetary policy) is required.

THE MONETARISTS

Economists who subscribe to monetary economics believe that the supply of money in the economy can influence the direction of the economy and prices as a whole. During times of low demand and high unemployment the economy can be stimulated by increasing the money supply. As more money enters the system, interest rates fall, increasing demand. As more money enters the system, the value of the currency tends to decline, and during times of expansionary monetary policy, inflation may increase. Milton Friedman, the founder of the monetarist movement, believed that the main focus of central banks should be on price stability.

ECONOMIC POLICY

The government has two tools that it can use to try to influence the direction of the economy. Monetary policy, which is controlled by the Federal Reserve Board, determines the nation's money supply, while fiscal policy is controlled by the president and Congress and determines government spending and taxation.

TOOLS OF THE FEDERAL RESERVE BOARD

The Federal Reserve Board will try to steer the economy through the business cycle by adjusting the level of the money supply and interest rates. The Fed may:

- Change the reserve requirement for member banks.

- Change the discount rate charged to member banks.

- Set target rates for federal fund loans.

- Buy and sell U.S. government securities through open-market operations.

- Change the amount of money in circulation.

- Use moral suasion.

INTEREST RATES

Interest rates, put simply, are the cost of money. Overall interest rates are determined by the supply and demand for money, along with any upward price movement in the cost of goods and services, known as inflation. There are several key interest rates upon which all other rates depend:

- Discount rate

- Federal funds rate

- Broker call loan rate

- Prime rate

THE DISCOUNT RATE

The discount rate is the interest rate that the Federal Reserve Bank charges on loans to member banks. A bank may borrow money directly from the Federal Reserve by going to the discount window, and the bank will be charged the discount rate. The bank is then free to lend out this money at a higher rate and earn a profit, or it may use these funds to meet a reserve requirement shortfall. Although a bank may borrow money directly from the Federal Reserve, this is discouraged, and the discount rate has become largely symbolic.

FEDERAL FUNDS RATE

The federal funds rate is the rate that member banks charge each other for overnight loans. The federal funds rate is widely watched as an indicator for the direction of short-term interest rates.

BROKER CALL LOAN RATE

The broker call loan rate is the interest rate that banks charge on loans to broker dealers to finance their customers' margin purchases. Many broker dealers will extend credit to their customers to purchase securities on margin. The broker dealers will obtain the money to lend to their customers from the bank, and the loan is callable or payable on demand by the broker dealer.

PRIME RATE

The prime rate is the rate that banks charge their largest and most creditworthy corporate customers on loans. The prime rate has lost a lot of its significance in recent years because mortgage lenders are now basing their rates on other rates, such as the 10-year Treasury note. The prime rate is, however, very important for consumer spending, because most credit card interest rates are based on prime plus a margin.

RESERVE REQUIREMENT

Member banks must keep a percentage of their depositors' assets in an account with the Federal Reserve. This is known as the reserve requirement. The reserve requirement is intended to ensure that all banks maintain a certain level of liquidity. Banks are in business to earn a profit by lending money. As the bank accepts accounts from depositors, it pays them interest on their money. The bank, in turn, takes the depositors' money and loans it out at higher rates, earning the difference. If the Fed wanted to stimulate the economy, it might reduce the reserve requirement for banks, which would allow the banks to lend more. By making more money available to borrowers, interest rates will fall and, therefore, demand will increase, helping to stimulate the economy. If the Fed wanted to slow down the economy, it might increase the reserve requirement. The increased requirement would make less money available to borrowers. Interest rates would rise as a result and the demand for goods and services would slow down. Changing the reserve requirement is the least-used Fed tool.

CHANGING THE DISCOUNT RATE

The Federal Reserve Board may change the discount rate in an effort to guide the economy through the business cycle. Remember, the discount rate is the rate that the Fed charges member banks on loans. This rate is highly symbolic, but as the Fed changes the discount rate, all other interest rates change with it. If the Fed wanted to stimulate the economy, it would reduce the discount rate. As the discount rate falls, all other interest rates fall with it, making the cost of money lower. The lower interest rate should encourage borrowing and demand to help stimulate the economy. If the Fed wanted to slow the economy down, it would increase the discount rate. As the discount rate increases, all other rates go up with it, raising the cost of borrowing. As the cost of borrowing increases, demand and the economy slow down.

FEDERAL OPEN MARKET COMMITTEE

The Federal Open Market Committee (FOMC) is the Fed's most flexible tool. The FOMC through open-market operations will buy and sell U.S. government securities in the secondary market in order to control the money supply. If the Fed wants to stimulate the economy and reduce rates, it will buy government securities. When the Fed buys the securities, money is instantly sent into the banking system. As the money flows into the banks, more money is available to lend. Because there is more money available, interest rates go down and borrowing and demand should increase to stimulate the economy. If the Fed wants to slow the economy down it will sell U.S. government securities. When the Fed sells the securities, money flows from the banks and into the Fed, thus reducing the money supply. Because there is less money available to be loaned out, interest rates increase, slowing borrowing and demand. This will have a cooling effect on the economy. The FOMC also issues statements that can "jawbone" investors to take certain actions and sets a benchmark for what it believes the fed funds rate should be. However, the marketplace is the ultimate factor in setting the fed funds rate.

MONEY SUPPLY

Prior to determining an appropriate economic policy, economists must have an idea of the amount of money that is in circulation, along with the amount of other types of assets that will provide access to cash. Economists gauge the money supply using three measures. They are:

- M1
- M2
- M3

M1

M1 is the largest and most liquid measure of the nation's money supply and it includes:

- Cash
- Demand deposits (Checking accounts)

M2

M2 includes all the measures in M1 plus:

- Money market instruments
- Time deposits of less than $100,000
- Negotiable CDs exceeding $100,000
- Overnight repurchase agreements

M3

M3 includes all of the measures in M1 and M2 plus:

- Time deposits greater than $100,000
- Repurchase agreements with maturities greater than 1 day

DISINTERMEDIATION

Disintermediation occurs when people take their money out of low-yielding accounts offered by financial intermediaries or banks and invest money in higher yielding investments.

MORAL SUASION

The Federal Reserve Board will often use moral suasion as a way to influence the economy. The Fed is very powerful and very closely watched. By simply implying or expressing its views on the economy, it can slightly influence the economy.

Monetarists believe that a well-managed money supply, with an increasing bias, will produce price stability and promote the overall health of the economy. Milton Friedman is believed to be the founder of the monetarist movement.

FISCAL POLICY

Fiscal policy is controlled by the president and Congress and determines how they manage the budget and government expenditures to help steer the economy through the business cycle. Fiscal policy may change the levels of:

- Federal spending.

- Federal taxation.

- Creation or use of federal budget deficits or surpluses.

Fiscal policy assumes that the government can influence the economy by adjusting its level of spending and taxation. If the government wants to stimulate the economy, it may increase spending. The assumption here is that as the government spends more, it will increase aggregate demand and, therefore, productivity. Additionally, if the government wants to stimulate the economy, it may reduce the level of taxation. As the government reduces taxes, it leaves a larger portion of earnings for the consumers and businesses to spend. This should also have a positive impact on aggregate demand. Alternatively, if the government wants to slow down the economy, it may reduce spending to lower the level of aggregate demand or raise taxes to reduce demand by taking money out of the hands of the consumers.

John Maynard Keynes believed that it was the duty of the government to be involved with controlling the direction of the economy and the nation's overall economic health.

As both the Federal Reserve Board and the government monitor the overall health of the U.S. economy, they look at various indicators, some of which are:

- Consumer price index
- Inflation/deflation
- Real GDP

CONSUMER PRICE INDEX (CPI)

The consumer price index is made up of a basket of goods and services that consumers use most often in their daily lives. The consumer price index is used to measure the rate of change in overall prices. A CPI that is rising would indicate that prices are going up and that inflation is present. A falling CPI would indicate that prices are falling and deflation is present.

INFLATION/DEFLATION

Inflation is the persistent increase in prices, while deflation is the persistent decrease in prices. Both economic conditions can harm a county's economy. Inflation will eat away at the purchasing power of the dollar and results in higher prices for goods and services. Deflation will erode corporate profits as weak demand in the marketplace drives prices for goods and services lower.

REAL GDP

Real GDP is adjusted for the effects of inflation or deflation over time. GDP is measured in constant dollars so that the gain or loss of the dollar's purchasing power will not show as a change in the overall productivity of the economy.

Both monetary policy and fiscal policy have a major effect on the stock market as a whole.

The following are bullish for the stock market:

- Falling interest rates
- Increasing money supply
- Increase in government spending
- Falling taxes

The following are bearish for the stock market:

- Increasing taxes
- Increasing interest rates
- Falling government spending
- Falling money supply

INTERNATIONAL MONETARY CONSIDERATIONS

The world has become a global marketplace. Each country's economy is affected to some degree by the economies of other countries. Currency values relative to other currencies impact a country's international trade and the balance of payments. The amount of another country's currency that may be received for a country's domestic currency is known as the exchange rate. The balance of payments measures the net inflow (surplus) or outflow (deficit) of money. The largest component of the balance of payments is the balance of trade. As the exchange rates fluctuate, one country's goods may become more expensive, while another county's goods become less expensive. A weak currency benefits exporters, while a strong currency benefits importers.

LONDON INTERBANK OFFERED RATE / LIBOR

LIBOR is the most widely used measure of short-term interest rates around the world. The LIBOR rate is the market-driven interest rate charged by and between financial institutions, similar to the fed funds rate in the United States. LIBOR loans range from 1 day to 1 year and the rate is calculated by the British Banker's Association in a variety of currencies including euros, U.S. dollars, and yen.

YIELD CURVE ANALYSIS

Economists and investors may analyze both the cost of borrowed funds given various maturities and the general health of the economy by looking at the shape of the yield curve. With a normal, ascending, positive, or upward sloping yield curve, the level of interest rates increases as the term of the maturity increases. Simply put, lenders are going to demand higher interest rates on longer-term loans. The longer the lenders have to wait to be repaid and the longer their money is at risk, the higher the level of compensation (interest) required to make the loan. Higher interest rates also compensate the lenders for the time value of money. The dollars received in 10, 20, or 30 years will be worth less than the value of the dollars loaned to borrowers today. An upward sloping curve is present during times of economic prosperity and depicts the expectation of increased interest rates in the future. The yield curve will also graphically demonstrate investors' expectations about inflation. The higher the expectations are for inflation, the higher the level of corresponding interest rates for the period of high inflation. Occasionally the yield curve may become inverted, negative, or downward sloping during times when demand for short-term funds is running much higher than the demand for longer-term loans or when the Federal Reserve Board has increased short-term rates to combat an economy that is growing too quickly and threatening long-term price stability. With an inverted yield curve, interest rates on short-term loans far exceed the interest rates on longer-term loans. An inverted yield curve tends to normalize quickly and is often a precursor to a recession. The yield curve may also flatten out when the interest rates for both short-term and long-term loans are approximately equal to one another.

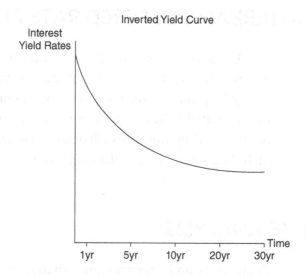

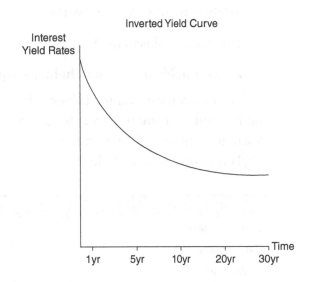

FUNDAMENTAL ANALYSIS

Fundamental analysis examines the company's financial statements and financial ratios to ascertain the company's overall financial performance. The following are used to determine a value for the company's stock:

- Balance sheet

- Income statement

- Footnotes to financial statements

- Financial ratios

- Liquidity ratios

- Valuation ratios

BALANCE SHEET

The balance sheet shows an investor everything that the corporation owns (assets) and everything that the corporation owes (liabilities) at the time the balance sheet was prepared. A balance sheet is a snapshot of the company's financial health on the day it was taken. The difference between the company's assets and its liabilities is the corporation's net worth—and the corporation's net worth is the shareholders' equity. Remember that the shareholders own the corporation. The basic balance sheet equation is:

assets − liabilities = net worth

The balance sheet equation also may be presented as follows:

assets = liabilities + shareholder's equity

The two columns on the balance sheet contain the company's assets on the left and its liabilities and shareholder's equity on the right. The total dollar amount of both sides must be equal or must balance. The entries on a balance sheet look as follows:

Assets	Liabilities
Current assets	Current liabilities
Fixed assets	Long-term liabilities
Other assets	Equity/net worth
	Preferred stock par value
	Common stock par value
	Additional paid in surplus
	Treasury stock
	Retained earnings

The assets are listed in order of liquidity. Current assets include cash and assets that can be converted into cash within 12 months. Current assets include:

- Money market instruments
- Marketable securities
- Accounts receivable net of any delinquent accounts
- Inventory including work in progress
- Prepaid expenses

Fixed assets are assets that have a long useful life and are used by the company in the operation of its business. Fixed assets include:

- Plant and equipment
- Property and real estate

Other assets are intangible/nonphysical assets that belong to the company.

Other assets include:

- Goodwill

- Trademarks

- Patents

- Contract rights

Intangible assets generally have significant value to the corporation, but are difficult to place a hard value on by outside companies.

The liabilities of the corporation are listed in the order in which they become due. Current liabilities are obligations that must be paid within 12 months. Current liabilities include:

- Wages payable, including salaries and commissions owed to employees

- Accounts payable to vendors and suppliers

- Current portion of long-term debt; that is, any portion of the company's long-term debt due within 12 months

- Taxes due within 12 months

- Short-term notes due within 12 months

Long-term liabilities are debts that will become due after 12 months. Long-term liabilities include:

- Bonds

- Mortgages

- Notes

 TAKENOTE!

The corporation's debt, which comes due in 5 years or more, is known as funded debt.

Stockholders' equity is the net worth of the company. Stockholders' equity is broken up into the following categories:

- Capital stock at par: the aggregate par for both common and preferred stock.

- Additional paid in surplus (sometimes known as capital in excess of par): any sum paid over par by investors when the shares were issued by the company.

- Retained earnings: profits that have been kept by the corporation, sometimes known as earned surplus.

CAPITALIZATION

The term capitalization refers to the sources and makeup of the company's financial picture. The following are used to determine the company's capitalization:

- Long-term debt

- Equity accounts, including par value of common and preferred stock and paid in and earned surplus

A company that borrows a large portion of its capital though the issuance of bonds is said to be highly leveraged. Raising money through the sale of common stock is considered to be a more conservative method for a corporation to raise money because it does not require the corporation to pay the money back. When a company borrows funds, it is trying to use that borrowed capital to increase its return on equity.

THE INCOME STATEMENT

The income statement details a corporation's revenue and expenses for the period for which it was produced. Income statements are usually prepared on a quarterly and annual basis. Fundamental analysis uses the income statement to determine a corporation's profitability. The three levels of earnings listed on the income statement are:

1. Operating income

2. Net income after taxes

3. Earnings available to common

Operating income: the business profit or loss from operations; also known as earnings before interest and taxes (EBIT).

Net income after taxes: corporation earnings after all federal and state taxes have been paid. Dividends to shareholders will be paid from net income after taxes.

Earnings available to common: what is left from the corporation's net income after taxes, after the corporation has paid preferred dividends. If the corporation wants to pay a dividend to common shareholders, then the preferred dividends must have already been paid.

Income Statement ABC Mills, Inc. January 1–December 31		
Net sales		$ 100,000,000
Cost of goods sold	$ 45,000,000	
General operating expenses (including $5,000,000 depreciation)	$ 32,000,000	
		$ 77,000,000
Operating income		$ 23,000,000
Interest expense		$ 2,800,000
Pretax income		$ 20,200,000
Taxes at 36%		$ 7,272,000
Net income after taxes		$ 12,928,000
Preferred dividends		$ 1,750,000
Earnings available to common		$ 11,178,000

By combining the information contained in the balance sheet and the income statement, an analyst can determine:

- Earnings per share primary.

- Earnings per share fully diluted.

- Price earnings ratio.

- Dividend payout ratio.

- Debt service ratio.

Earnings per share primary: how much of the company's earnings are credited to each common share.

Earnings per share fully diluted: how much of the company's earnings are credited to each common share, after all convertible securities and all rights and warrants have been exchanged for common stock.

Price earnings ratio: the relationship between the earnings per share and the common stock price.

Dividend payout ratio: how much of the earnings per share were paid out to shareholders as dividends.

Debt service ratio: the ability of the company to meet its debt service obligations.

Measure	Formula	Purpose
Earnings per share primary	Earnings available to common/no. of common shares	To determine the amount of the company's earnings for each share outstanding
Earnings per share fully diluted	Earnings available to common/no. of common shares	To determine the amount of the company's earnings for each share outstanding after all conversions
Price earnings ratio	Stock price/EPS	To determine a relationship between the stock price and the earnings per share
Dividend payout ratio	Annual dividends per common share/EPS	To determine how much of the company's EPS are paid out in dividends
Debt service ratio	EBIT/annual interest and principal payments	To determine the company's ability to meet its debt service needs

TAKENOTE!

Most balance sheets and income statements include footnotes which give additional details regarding the items contained in the reports. These footnotes detail the impact potential events may have on the financial information contained in the statements as well as any assumptions or calculations used to arrive at the information.

INDUSTRY FUNDAMENTALS

There are fundamental economic factors that affect different industries. Analysis determines how susceptible the company's earnings are to a change in the economy. There are three industry categories. They are:

1. Growth industries

2. Cyclical industries

3. Defensive industries

Growth industries: The earnings of companies in a growth industry will grow faster than the overall growth of the economy as whole. Growth industries include computers and technology.

Cyclical industries: The earnings of a company in a cyclical industry are highly susceptible to the condition of the overall economy. As the economy improves, the company does well. If the economy does poorly, the company performs poorly. Cyclical industries include manufacturing, raw materials, and automobiles.

Defensive industries: The earnings of a company in a defensive industry will be the least susceptible to the changes in the overall economy. Defensive industries include food and pharmaceuticals. These are things that people buy no matter how the economy is performing. It is important to note that a manufacturer of military equipment is not considered to be in a defensive industry.

Pretest

AN INTRODUCTION TO ECONOMICS AND CORPORATE FUNDAMENTALS

la.finra.intro.econ.corp.001_1811

1. Economic theories believe all of the following to be true, except:

   a. As supply rises, prices tend to fall.

   b. As supply rises, prices tend to rise.

   c. A moderately increasing money supply promotes price stability.

   d. As demand rises, prices tend to rise.

la.finra.intro.econ.corp.002_1811

2. Which one of the following interest rates is controlled by the Federal Reserve Board?

   a. Prime rate.

   b. Federal funds rate.

   c. Broker call loan rate.

   d. Discount rate.

la.finra.intro.econ.corp.003_1811

3. All of the following indicate a downturn in the business cycle, except:

   a. Rising inventories.

   b. High consumer debt.

   c. Falling inventories.

   d. Falling stock prices.

la.finra.intro.econ.corp.004_1811

4. The government has two tools it can use to try to influence the direction of the economy. They are:

    a. Monetary policy and fiscal policy.

    b. Prime rate policy and fiscal policy.

    c. Monetary policy and prime rate policy.

    d. Fiscal policy and money market policy.

la.finra.intro.econ.corp.005_1811

5. Fiscal policy is controlled by:

    I. President.

    II. FOMC.

    III. Congress.

    IV. FRB.

    a. I and IV.

    b. I and II.

    c. II and IV.

    d. I and III.

la.finra.intro.econ.corp.006_1811

6. The Federal Reserve Board sets all of the following except:

    a. Monetary policy.

    b. Reserve requirement.

    c. Governmental spending.

    d. Discount rate.

la.finra.intro.econ.corp.007_1811

7. A decline in the GDP must last at least how long to be considered a recession?

    a. Two quarters.

    b. One quarter.

    c. Six quarters.

    d. Four quarters.

sa.finra.intro.econ.corp.001_1811
8. During an inflationary period, the price of which one of the following will fall the most?

   a. Preferred stock.

   b. Treasury bills.

   c. Treasury bonds.

   d. Common stock.

sa.finra.intro.econ.corp.002_1811
9. All of the following are bullish for the stock market, except:

   a. Falling taxes.

   b. Increasing government spending.

   c. Increasing money supply.

   d. Increasing interest rates.

Issuing and Offering Corporate Securities

INTRODUCTION

Learning Objective Statements

Detail information contained in a statutory, preliminary, and free writing prospectus.

Demonstrate the various types of corporate underwritings.

List who may purchase new issues and private placements.

Illustrate the characteristics of the registration process.

The Securities Act of 1933 was the first major piece of securities industry regulation, brought about largely as a result of the stock market crash of 1929. Other major laws were also enacted to help prevent another meltdown of the nation's financial system, such as the Securities Exchange Act of 1934, but we start our review with the Securities Act of 1933 because it regulates the issuance of corporate securities.

The Securities Act of 1933 was the first major piece of securities industry legislation, and it regulates the primary market. The primary market consists exclusively of transactions between issuers of securities and investors. In a primary market transaction, the issuer of the securities receives the proceeds from the sale of the securities. The Securities Act of 1933 requires nonexempt issuers (typically corporate issuers) to file a registration statement with the Securities and Exchange Commission (SEC). The registration statement, formerly known as an S-1, is the issuer's full-disclosure document for the government. The registration statement must contain detailed information relating to the issuer's operations and financial condition and must include:

- A balance sheet dated within 90 days of the filing of the registration statement

- Profit and loss statements for the last 3 years

- The company's capitalization

- The use of proceeds

- Shareholders owning more than 10% of the company's securities

- Biographical information on the officers and directors

The registration statement will be under review by the SEC for a minimum of 20 days. During this time, known as the cooling-off period, no sales of securities may take place. If the SEC requires additional information regarding the offering, the SEC may issue a deficiency letter or a stop order that will extend the cooling-off period beyond the original 20 days. If the SEC has issued a stop order, the 20-day cooling-off period begins again once the resubmission of the registration statement has been completed. A registered representative may only begin to discuss the potential offering with customers after the filing date.

THE PROSPECTUS

While the SEC is reviewing the securities' registration statement, registered representatives are very limited as to what they may do with regard to the new issue. During the cooling-off period, the only thing that a registered representative may do is obtain indications of interest from clients by providing them with a preliminary prospectus, also known as a red herring. The term *red herring* originated from the fact that a preliminary prospectus must have a statement printed in red ink on the front cover stating: "These securities have not yet become registered with the SEC and therefore may not be sold." An indication of interest is an investor's or broker dealer's statement that they might be interested in purchasing the securities being offered. The preliminary prospectus contains most of the same information that will be contained in the final prospectus, except for the offering price, the effective date, and the proceeds to the issuer. The preliminary prospectus usually contains a price range for the security to be offered. All information contained in a preliminary prospectus is subject to change or revision. The preliminary prospectus must be given in hard copy to expected purchasers at least 48 hours before the sale is confirmed, if the company has not been a reporting company under the Securities Exchange Act of 1934. This is done to ensure that the final prospectus is not the first piece of information forwarded to the purchaser.

THE FINAL PROSPECTUS

All purchasers of new issues must be given a final prospectus before any sales are allowed. The final prospectus serves as the issuer's full-disclosure document for the purchaser of the securities. If the issuer has filed a prospectus with the SEC and the final prospectus can be viewed on the SEC's website, a prospectus will be deemed to have been provided to the investor through the access equals delivery rule. The access equals delivery rule only applies to the final prospectus during the offering and during any aftermarket delivery requirements. A preliminary prospectus must be physically sent to potential purchasers. Once the issuer's registration statement becomes effective, the final prospectus must include:

- Type and description of the securities
- Price of the security
- Use of the proceeds
- Underwriter's discount
- Date of the offering
- Type and description of underwriting
- Business history of issuer
- Biographical data for company officers and directors
- Information regarding large stockholders
- Company financial data
- Risks to purchaser
- Legal matters concerning the company
- SEC disclaimer

FREE WRITING PROSPECTUS

A free writing prospectus (FWP) is any form of written communication published or broadcast by an issuer which contains information about the securities offered for sale that does not meet the definition of a statutory prospectus. Common examples of a free writing prospectus include:

- Marketing materials
- Graphs
- Term sheets
- E-mails
- Press releases

The free writing prospectus should include a legend recommending that the individual read the statutory prospectus to obtain more information relating to the securities being offered. A hyperlink is used in many cases to direct the reader to the statutory prospectus. An issuer who meets the definition of a well-known seasoned issuer may use an FWP at any time before or after the filing of a registration statement. A seasoned issuer may only use an FWP after the filing of the registration statement with the SEC. An unseasoned or nonreporting issuer may use a free writing prospectus only after a registration statement is filed with the SEC and must either send a statutory prospectus with FWP or must include a hyperlink to a statutory prospectus. Issuers who use free writing prospectuses will file them with the SEC over the SEC's website.

PROVIDING THE PROSPECTUS TO AFTERMARKET PURCHASERS

Certain investors who purchase securities in the secondary market just after a distribution must also be provided with the final prospectus. The term for which a prospectus must be provided depends largely on the type of offering and where the issue will be traded in the aftermarket. If the security has an aftermarket delivery requirement, a prospectus must be provided by all firms that execute a purchase order for the security during the term. The after market prospectus delivery requirements may be met electronically and are as follows:

- For IPOs: 90 days after being issued for securities quoted on the OTCBB or in the Pink OTC Market (formerly pink sheets). Twenty-five days for listed or Nasdaq securities.

- Additional offerings: 40 days for securities quoted on the OTCBB or in the Pink OTC Market (formerly pink sheets). No aftermarket requirement for listed or Nasdaq securities.

SEC DISCLAIMER

The SEC reviews the issuer's registration statement and the prospectus but does not guarantee the accuracy or adequacy of the information. The SEC disclaimer must appear on the cover of all prospectuses and states: "These securities have not been approved or disapproved by the SEC nor have any representations been made about the accuracy or the adequacy of the information."

MISREPRESENTATIONS

Financial relief for misrepresentations made under the Securities Act of 1933 is available for purchasers of any security that is sold under a prospectus that is found to contain false or misleading statements. Purchasers of the security may be entitled to seek financial relief from any or all of the following:

- The issuer
- The underwriters
- Officers and directors
- All parties who signed the registration statement
- Accountants and attorneys who helped prepare the registration statement

A due diligence meeting will be held during the cooling-off period to ensure that the information contained in the prospectus is accurate.

TOMBSTONE ADS

SEC Rule 134 allows certain types of advertisements to be run relating to a new issue. Tombstone ads are the only form of advertising that is allowed during the cooling-off period. A tombstone ad is an announcement and description of the securities to be offered. A tombstone ad lists the names of the underwriters, where a prospectus may be obtained, and a statement that the tombstone ad does not constitute an offer to sell the securities and that the offer may only be made by a prospectus. Tombstone ads are traditionally run to announce the new issue, but they are not required and do not need to be filed with the SEC. Tombstone ads may also include:

- The amount of the security to be offered
- The date of sale

- A general description of the issuer's business
- The price of the security

FREE RIDING AND WITHHOLDING/FINRA RULE 5130

A broker dealer underwriting a new issue must make a complete and bona fide offering of all securities being issued to the public and may not withhold any of the securities for:

- The underwriters.
- Another broker dealer.
- A firm employee or a person who is financially dependent on the employee.
- An employee of another FINRA member.

 TAKENOTE!

An exception to FINRA Rule 5130 applies to employees of limited broker dealers who engage solely in the purchase and sale of investment company products or direct participation programs (DPPs). Employees of limited broker dealers may purchase new issues. This exemption applies only to the employees of the limited broker dealer, not to the firm itself.

These rules are in effect for initial public offerings, but they are especially prevalent when dealing with a hot issue. A hot issue is one that trades at an immediate premium to its offering price in the secondary market. A broker dealer may not free ride by withholding securities for its own account or for the accounts of those listed above. FINRA Rule 5130 covers initial offerings of common stock only. Exempt from the rule are offerings of additional issues, bonds, and preferred shares. These offerings may be purchased by registered persons. FINRA Rule 5130 requires that a broker dealer obtain an eligibility statement from all account owners who purchase a new issue of stock within 12 months prior to the purchase. Some people may purchase hot issues so long as the amount is not substantial and they have a history of purchasing new issues. These conditionally approved people are:

- Officers and employees of financial institutions
- Nonsupported family members
- Accountants, attorneys, and finders associated with the underwriting
- Accounts where the restricted persons' interest is limited to 10% or less or where a maximum of 10% of the allocation of new issue is for the benefit of such persons. This is known as the carve out procedure.

The agreement among the underwriters must clearly state how the syndicate will handle the repurchase of shares trading at a premium. If a client "flips" the hot issue in the secondary market and the shares are repurchased by the book running lead underwriter, those shares must be used to cover any syndicate short position. If no syndicate short position exists, the shares may be used to cover unfilled qualified customer orders at the offering price. Any account to receive these shares must receive the shares through a random allocation process. In the extremely unlikely event that no unfilled orders exist, the syndicate may sell the shares in the market and anonymously donate the profits to an unaffiliated charity. If a purchaser sells the stock (flips) within 30 days of the offering, the syndicate may not seek to reclaim any sales credit earned by the agent or member unless the stock is sold back to the syndicate's penalty bid. Issuers who are going public are allowed to direct stock to the officers, directors, and employees of the company. The number of shares directed to the employees of the issuer are part of and are not in addition to the number of shares being underwritten.

 TAKENOTE!

Syndicate members may not allocate shares of hot issue to the accounts of individuals who are in a position to direct business to the firm. This includes portfolio managers who may direct execution business to the member as well as officers and directors of companies who have been investment banking clients in the last 12 months or when the company is an anticipated investment banking client. Doing so is a violation known as spinning.

UNDERWRITING CORPORATE SECURITIES

Once a business has decided that it needs to raise capital to meet its organizational objectives, it must determine how to raise the needed capital. Most corporations at this point will hire an investment banker, also known as an underwriter, to advise them. The underwriter works for the issuer, and it is an underwriter's job to advise the client about what type of securities to offer. The issuer and the underwriter together determine whether stocks or bonds should be issued and what the terms will be. The underwriter is responsible for trying to obtain the financing at the best possible terms for the issuer. The underwriter will:

- Market the issue to investors.

- Assist in the determination of the terms of the offering.

- Purchase the securities directly from the issuer to resell to investors.

The issuer is responsible for:

- Filing a registration statement with the SEC.

- Registering the securities in the states in which they will be sold, also known as blue-skying the issue.

- Negotiating the underwriter's compensation and obligations to the issuer.

TYPES OF UNDERWRITING COMMITMENTS

The agreement between the issuer and the underwriter spells out the underwriter's responsibilities to the issuer. The agreement may take a variety of forms and may include:

- Firm commitment

- Best efforts

- Mini-maxi

- All or none

- Standby

FIRM COMMITMENT

In a firm commitment underwriting, the underwriter guarantees to purchase all of the securities being offered for sale by the issuer regardless of whether it can sell them to investors. A firm commitment underwriting agreement is the most desirable for the issuer because it guarantees the issuer all of the money right away. The more in demand the offering is, the more likely it is that it will be done on a firm commitment basis. If the issue is in extremely high demand and is oversubscribed, the underwriter may exercise its greenshoe provision to cover overallotments. This will allow the underwriter to purchase an additional 15% of the issue from the issuer. In a firm commitment, the underwriter puts its own money at risk if unable to sell the securities to investors.

MARKET-OUT CLAUSE

An underwriter offering securities for an issuer on a firm commitment basis is assuming a substantial amount of risk. As a result, the underwriter will insist on having a market-out clause in the underwriting agreement. A market-out clause frees the underwriter from the obligation to purchase all of the securities in the event of a development that impairs the quality of the securities or that adversely affects the issuer. If a syndicate is underwriting a new issue for a biotech company with a drug in clinical trials and the FDA rejects the drug for use, the underwriters could invoke the market-out clause. Poor market conditions are not a reason to invoke the market-out clause.

BEST EFFORTS

In a best efforts underwriting, the underwriter attempts to sell all of the securities that are being offered by the issuer but in no way is the underwriter obligated to purchase the securities for its own account. The lower the demand for an issue, the greater likelihood that it will be done on a best efforts basis. Any shares or bonds in a best efforts underwriting that have not been sold will be returned to the issuer.

MINI-MAXI

A mini-maxi is a type of best efforts underwriting that does not become effective until a minimum amount of the securities have been sold. Once the minimum has been met, the underwriter may then sell the securities up to the maximum amount specified under the terms of the offering. All funds collected from investors will be held in escrow until the underwriting is completed. If the minimum amount of securities specified by the offering cannot be reached, the offering will be canceled and the investors' funds collected will be returned to them.

ALL OR NONE (AON)

With an all-or-none underwriting, it has been determined that the issuer must receive the proceeds from the sale of all of the securities. Investors' funds are held in escrow until all of the securities are sold. If all of the securities are sold, the proceeds will be released to the issuer. If all of the securities are not sold, the issue is canceled and the investors' funds will be returned to them. All contingent offerings must have a qualified financial institute (QFI) to act as an escrow agent for the offering. A general securities broker dealer, bank, or trust company may act as an escrow agent.

STANDBY

A standby underwriting agreement is used in conjunction with a preemptive rights offering. All standby underwritings are done on a firm commitment basis. The standby underwriter agrees to purchase any shares that current shareholders do not purchase. The standby underwriter then resells the securities to the public.

TYPES OF OFFERINGS

Securities that are being sold under a prospectus may include securities that are part of different types of offerings. The different types of offerings include initial public offerings, subsequent primary offerings, and registered secondary offerings.

INITIAL PUBLIC OFFERING (IPO)/NEW ISSUE

An initial public offering is the first time that a company sells its stock to the public. The issuing company receives the proceeds from the sale minus the underwriter's compensation.

SUBSEQUENT PRIMARY/ADDITIONAL ISSUES

In a subsequent primary offering, the corporation is already publicly owned and the company is selling additional shares to raise new financing.

The shares being sold under a subsequent primary distribution may be offered at a stated price or the shares may be sold at the market once the issue is effective. If the issue is an at-the-market offering, the shares may be sold at different prices in the marketplace.

PRIMARY OFFERING VS. SECONDARY OFFERING

In a primary offering, the issuing company receives the proceeds from the sale minus the underwriter's compensation. In a secondary offering, a group of selling shareholders receives the proceeds from the sale minus the underwriter's compensation. A combined offering has elements of both the primary offering and the secondary offering, or split. Part of the proceeds go to the company and part of the proceeds go to a group of selling shareholders.

AWARDING THE ISSUE

There are two ways in which the corporation may select an underwriter. A corporation may elect to have multiple underwriters submit bids and then choose the underwriter with the best bid. This is known as competitive bid underwriting. Or, a company may elect to select one firm to sell the issue and negotiate the terms of the offering with it. This is known as a negotiated underwriting. Most corporate offerings are awarded on a negotiated basis, whereas municipal bond offerings are usually awarded through competitive bidding.

Pretest

ISSUING AND OFFERING CORPORATE SECURITIES

la.finra.iss.off.corp.001_1811

1. A syndicate has published a tombstone ad prior to the issue becoming effective. Which of the following must appear in the tombstone?

   I. A statement that the registration has not yet become effective.

   II. A statement that the ad is not an offer to sell the securities.

   III. Contact information.

   IV. No commitment statement.

   a. III and IV.

   b. II and III.

   c. I and II.

   d. I, II, III, and IV.

la.finra.iss.off.corp.002_1811

2. During a new issue registration, false information is included in the prospectus to buyers. Which of the following may be held liable to investors?

   I. Officers of the issuer.

   II. Accountants.

   III. Syndicate members.

   IV. People who signed the registration statement.

   a. I and III.

   b. I, III, and IV.

   c. I, II, and III.

   d. I, II, III, and IV.

la.finra.iss.off.corp.003_1811

3. Corporations may do all of the following, except:

    a. Issue preferred stock only.

    b. Issue nonvoting common stock.

    c. Sell stock out of the treasury.

    d. Repurchase its own shares.

la.finra.iss.off.corp.005_1811

4. The SEC has been reviewing a company's registration statement and would like clarification on a few items. The SEC would most likely:

    a. Call the company.

    b. Issue a stop order.

    c. Issue a deficiency letter.

    d. Call the lead underwriter.

la.finra.iss.off.corp.006_1811

5. Which of the following is NOT a type of underwriting commitment?

    a. Primary commitment.

    b. Standby commitment.

    c. Best efforts commitment.

    d. Firm commitment.

la.finra.iss.off.corp.007_1811

6. XYZ has just gone public and is quoted on the Nasdaq Capital Market securities market. Any investor who buys XYZ must get a prospectus for how long?

    a. 30 days.

    b. 25 days.

    c. 60 days.

    d. 45 days.

sa.finra.iss.off.corp.001_1811

7. A company doing a preemptive rights offering would most likely use what type of underwriting agreement?

   a. Best efforts.

   b. Firm commitment.

   c. All or none.

   d. Standby.

sa.finra.iss.off.corp.002_1811

8. A red herring given to a client during the cooling-off period will contain all of the following, except:

   a. Proceeds to the company.

   b. Use of proceeds.

   c. Biographies of officers and directors.

   d. A notice that all the information is subject to change.

The Underwriting Syndicate and Exempt Transactions

INTRODUCTION

Learning Objective Statements

Detail the roles of syndicate members, the selling group, and their respective compensation.

Compare exempt transactions.

Detail the conditions regarding Rule 144.

Identify various conditions under which securities can be sold without a full registration.

Because most corporate offerings involve a large number of shares and a very large dollar amount, they are offered through several underwriters known as the underwriting syndicate. The syndicate is a group of investment banks that have agreed to share the responsibility of marketing the issue. The managing underwriter, also known as the lead underwriter or book running manager, leads the syndicate. If the syndicate plans to stabilize the issue in the aftermarket to allow for an orderly distribution of the shares, only one bid may be placed, and the stabilizing bid must be entered at or below the offering price. Most underwriting agreements have an overallotment or green shoe provision that allows the syndicate to purchase additional shares from the issuer at the original price The green shoe provision allows the syndicate to purchase additional shares equal to 15% of the offering.

SELLING GROUP

The syndicate may form a selling group in an effort to help market the issue. Members of the selling group have no underwriting responsibility and may only sell the shares to investors for a fee known as the selling concession.

Occasionally the employees of the issuer may assist in selling the securities of the issuer. This is allowed with the permission of the managing underwriter as long as payment of the employees is not based on sales and the employees are not disqualified from or registered as agents of any broker dealer.

UNDERWRITER'S COMPENSATION

The group of broker dealers that make up the underwriting syndicate will be compensated based upon their role as a syndicate member. The only syndicate member that may earn the entire spread is the lead or managing underwriter.

MANAGEMENT FEE

The lead or managing underwriter will receive a fee known as a management fee for every share that is sold. In most cases, the managing underwriter is the firm that negotiated the terms of the offering with the issuer and formed the syndicate.

UNDERWRITER'S FEE

The underwriter's fee is the cost of bringing the issue to market and is a fee assessed for each share that is sold by the syndicate. If there is any money remaining after all expenses are paid, the syndicate members split it, based upon their commitment level in the underwriting.

SELLING CONCESSION

The selling concession is paid to any syndicate member or selling group member who sells the shares to the investors. The selling concession is the only fee that the selling group members may earn.

 **TAKE**NOTE!

With the approval of the syndicate manager, a member of the syndicate or selling group may sell the shares to a FINRA member firm that is not participating in the offering. The FINRA member will receive part of the selling concession known as the reallowance.

UNDERWRITING SPREAD

The total amount of the management fee, the underwriting fee, and the selling concession make up the total underwriting spread. This is the difference between the gross proceeds of the offering and the net proceeds to the issuer.

PUBLIC OFFERING PRICE: $12

SELLING CONCESSION $1.50
UNDERWRITING FEE $.75
MANAGEMENT FEE $.25

PROCEEDS TO ISSUER: $9.50 PER SHARE

In this example the underwriting spread is $2.50 per share.

FACTORS THAT DETERMINE THE SIZE OF THE UNDERWRITING SPREAD

Many factors determine the amount of the underwriter's compensation for offering the securities on behalf of the issuer. Some of these factors are:

- The type of securities to be offered
- The size of the issue
- The quality of the securities to be issued

- The perceived demand for the securities
- The type of underwriting agreement
- The quality of the issuer's business

REVIEW OF UNDERWRITING AGREEMENTS BY FINRA

With certain exceptions, underwriting agreements must be submitted to FINRA's Corporate Finance Department for review no later than 1 day after the filing of any registration with the SEC or with any state regulator. If filing of the offering is not required at either the federal or state level, as is the case with private placements, the agreement must be filed with FINRA at least 15 business days prior to the anticipated offering date. In most cases, the agreement is submitted by the managing underwriter. FINRA reviews the maximum total compensation to the underwriters to ensure that the underwriter's compensation is fair and reasonable in light of the size and complexity of the offering. The submission must include:

- The maximum offering price
- The maximum underwriter's discount
- The maximum estimated reimbursement for the underwriter's expenses

EXEMPT SECURITIES

Certain securities are exempt from the registration provisions of the Securities Act of 1933 because of the issuer or the nature of the security. Although the securities may be exempt from the registration and prospectus requirements of the act, none are exempt from the antifraud provisions of the act. Examples of exempt securities are:

- Debt securities with maturities of less than 270 days and sold in denominations of $50,000 or more
- Employee benefit plans
- Option contracts, both puts and calls on stocks and indexes

Examples of exempt issuers are:

- U.S. government

- State and municipal governments

- Foreign national governments

- Canadian federal and municipal governments

- Insurance companies

- Banks and trusts

- Credit unions and savings and loans

- Religious and charitable organizations

 TAKENOTE!

Insurance and bank holding companies are not exempt issuers.

EXEMPT TRANSACTIONS

Sometimes a security that would otherwise have to register is exempt from the registration requirements of the Securities Act of 1933 because of the type of transaction that is involved. The following are all exempt transactions:

- Private placements/Regulation D offerings

- Rule 144

- Regulation S offerings

- Regulation A offerings

- Rule 145

- Rule 147 intrastate offerings

PRIVATE PLACEMENTS/REGULATION D OFFERINGS

A private placement is a sale of securities that is made to a group of accredited investors where the securities are not offered to the general public. Accredited investors include institutional investors and individuals who:

- Earn at least $200,000 per year if single,

  or

- Earn at least $300,000 jointly with a spouse,

  or

- Have a net worth of at least $1,000,000 without the primary residence.

Sales to nonaccredited investors for private placements exceeding $1 million are limited to 35 in any 12-month period. No commission may be paid to representatives who sell a private placement to a nonaccredited investor. All investors in private placements must hold the securities fully paid for at least 6 months and sign a letter stating that they are purchasing the securities for investment purposes. Stock purchased though a private placement is known as lettered stock, legend stock, or restricted stock, because there is a legend on the stock certificate that limits the ability of the owner to transfer or sell the securities. There is no limit as to how many accredited investors may purchase the securities. The limits on the amount of money that may be raised under the various regulation D offerings are as follows:

- Regulation 504 D allows issuers to raise up to $5 million
- Regulation 506 D allows issuers to raise an unlimited amount of capital

PURCHASER'S REPRESENTATIVE

A purchaser's representative is an individual designated in writing by the prospective purchaser to represent the purchaser when evaluating the suitability of a private placement. A purchaser's representative may not:

- Receive a blanket appointment to represent the investor for all private placements.
- Own more than 10% of the issuer's stock.
- Be an officer, director, employee, or affiliate of the issuer, unless he or she is a close relative of the prospective purchaser.

For private placements exceeding $5 million, the offering will be limited to institutional, accredited, and nonaccredited investors who together with their purchaser's representative have the financial and business knowledge to evaluate the offering. The issuer in a private placement may not advertise the issue or hold a seminar open to the general public. The JOBS Act now allows investors to view private placement documents online as long as the website requires an investor to submit a questionnaire documenting assets, income, and investment experience. This questionnaire must be reviewed and, if qualified for participation, the issuer or broker dealer may assign the investor a username and password granting him or her access to view the details of the offerings.

RULE 144

Rule 144 regulates how control or restricted securities may be sold. Rule 144 designates:

- The holding period for the security.
- The amount of the security that may be sold.
- Filing procedures.
- Method of sale.

Control securities are owned by officers, directors, and owners of 10% or more of the company's outstanding stock. Control stock may be obtained by insiders through open-market purchases or through the exercise of company stock options. There is no holding period for control securities. However, insiders are not allowed to earn a short swing profit through the purchase and sale of control stock in the open market. If the securities were held less than 6 months, the insider must return any profit to the company.

Restricted securities may be purchased by both insiders and investors though a private placement or may be obtained through an offering other than a public sale. Securities obtained through a private placement or other nonpublic means need to be sold under Rule 144 in order to allow the transfer of ownership. Restricted stock must be held fully paid for, for 6 months. After 6 months the securities may be sold freely by noninsiders so long as the seller has not been affiliated with the issuer in the last 3 months. Rule 144 sets the following volume limits for both restricted and control stock during any 90-day period. The seller must file Form 144 at the time the order is entered and is limited to the greater of:

- The average weekly trading volume for the preceding four weeks,

  or

- 1% of the issuer's total outstanding stock.

Securities may be sold under Rule 144 four times per year. Restricted securities sold under Rule 144 become part of the public float and the seller, not the issuer, receives the proceeds of the sale. For orders for 5,000 shares or less and that do not exceed $50,000, Form 144 does not need to be filed. If the owner of restricted stock dies, his or her estate may sell the shares freely without regard to the holding period or volume limitations of Rule 144.

 TAKENOTE!

There is a 6-month holding period for control stock acquired through a private placement, and control stock is always subject to the volume limitations.

BROKER TRANSACTIONS UNDER RULE 144

A firm handling a customer's sale under Rule 144, except for in very limited circumstances, must execute the orders on an agency basis for the customer. The broker dealer may execute the order with a market maker or may inquire with customers who have expressed an unsolicited interest in the securities in the last 10 days or with a broker dealer who has expressed interest in the securities in the last 60 days. Firms that are classified as bona fide block positioners are allowed to purchase the stock on a principal basis.

RULE 144A

Rule 144A permits the resale of restricted stock to qualified institutional buyers (QIBs). A QIB is defined as a company that owns investments worth at least $100 million and includes:

- Corporations
- Partnerships
- Insurance companies
- Investment companies

- Banks

- Trust funds

- Pension plans

- Registered investment advisers

- Small business development companies

The broker dealer must verify that the customer meets the definition of a QIB. When determining the eligibility for a buyer to participate in a 144a transaction, the broker dealer may use any of the following:

- The purchaser's most recent, publicly available financial statements

- The purchaser's most recent publicly available information appearing in documents filed in an SRO

- The purchaser's most recent publicly available information appearing in a recognized securities manual or filed with a foreign regulator

- A certification by the purchaser's chief financial officer or other executive

The broker dealer may not rely on the information on the customer's account card.

 TAKENOTE!

A broker dealer will be considered a QIB if it owns $10 million worth of securities or if it engages in riskless principal transactions for other QIBs.

To qualify for the exemption provided under Rule 144A, the QIB must be purchasing the securities for its own account or for the account of other QIBs. Not all securities will be eligible for an exemption under Rule 144A. Ineligible securities include:

- Securities of registered investment companies

- Securities of the same class as those listed on an exchange or Nasdaq

- Certain warrants and convertible securities

All purchasers of securities under Rule 144A must be informed that the seller is relying on the exemption provided under Rule 144A, and the issuer of the securities must be willing to provide financial information to owners and prospective purchasers. The PORTAL Market has been developed to help ensure compliance with Rule 144A and to help facilitate Rule 144A transactions. Transactions that qualify under Rule 144A may be executed without regard to any holding period otherwise imposed as long as the buyer is a QIB.

PRIVATE INVESTMENT IN A PUBLIC EQUITY (PIPE)

Public companies that wish to obtain additional financing without selling securities to the general public may sell securities to a group of accredited investors through a private placement. The accredited investors in most cases will be institutional investors who wish to invest a large amount of capital. Common stock, convertible or nonconvertible debt, rights, and warrants all may be sold to investors through a PIPE transaction. Obtaining capital through a PIPE transaction benefits the public company in a number of ways:

- Reduced transaction cost
- Term disclosure only upon completion of the transaction
- Increased institutional ownership
- Quick closing

Securities sold through a PIPE transaction are subject to Rule 144. If the issuer files a registration statement after the closing of the offering, sales may begin immediately upon the effective date.

REVERSE MERGER

A reverse merger, sometimes called an alternative public offering or APO, can be used by a private company as a cost-effective alternative to a traditional public offering. In an APO transaction, a private company acquires or merges with a company that is already public, as a means of taking itself public. Once completed, the private company will be publicly traded at a significantly lower cost and with less dilution than in a traditional offering. The details of the transaction will be reported upon completion on Form 8K.

REGULATION S OFFERINGS

Domestic issuers who make a distribution of securities exclusively to offshore investors do not have to file a registration statement for the securities under the Securities Act of 1933. In order to qualify for the exemption offered under Regulation S, the issuer may make no offerings of the securities within the United States and may not announce or distribute literature relating to the securities within the United States. Securities distributed under Regulation S are subject to a distribution compliance period, during which the securities may not be resold to domestic investors. The distribution compliance period is 6 months for equities if the issuer is a reporting company and files 10-Qs, 10-Ks, and 8-Ks, and 1 year for nonreporting companies. The distribution compliance period is 40 days for debt. Sales of the securities may take place in offshore markets anytime after the initial sale. Issuers must report the sale of securities under Regulation S by filing form 8K.

REGULATION A OFFERINGS

The JOBS Act of 2012 increased the amount that may be raised under a Regulation A offering to $50 million. This exemption from full registration allows smaller companies access to the capital markets without having to go through the expense of filing a full registration statement with the SEC. The issuer will instead file an abbreviated notice of sale or offering circular known as a 1-A with the SEC, and purchasers of the issue will be given a copy of the offering circular rather than a final prospectus. Purchasers of the issue must have the preliminary or final offering circular mailed to them 48 hours before mailing the confirmation. The same 20-day cooling-off period also applies to Regulation A offerings. The JOBS Act further refined Regulation A into two tiers, with Regulation A now sometimes being referred to as Regulation A plus. Tier 1 allows issuers to raise up to $20 million. Of this $20 million, no more than $6 million may be offered by the selling shareholders. Tier 2 allows issuers to raise up to $50 million, of which no more than $15 million may be offered by the selling shareholders.

RULE 145

Rule 145 requires that shareholders approve any merger or reorganization of the company's ownership. Any merger or acquisition is reported to the

SEC on firm S-4. Stockholders must be given full disclosure of the proposed transaction or reclassification and must be sent proxies to vote on the proposal. Rule 145 covers:

- Mergers involving a stock swap or offer of another company's securities in exchange for a company's current stock.

- Reclassification involving the exchange of one class of the company's securities for another.

- Asset transfers involving the dissolution of the company or the distribution or sale of a major portion of the company's assets. In the case of a spin-off, the shareholder will retain the securities of the issuer and will receive shares of the newly independent company that was the subject of the spin off.

Rule 145 does not cover:

- Stock splits.
- Reverse splits.
- Changes in par value.

RULE 147 INTRASTATE OFFERING

Rule 147 pertains to offerings of securities that are limited to one state. Because the offering is being made only in one state, it is exempt from registration with the SEC and is subject to the jurisdiction of the state securities administrator. In order to qualify for an exemption from SEC registration, the issue must have its principal place of business in the state and meet at least one of the doing business criteria

- 80% of the offering's proceeds must be used in that state.
- 80% of the issuer's assets must be located in that state.
- A majority of the issuer's employees are based in-state.

100 percent of the purchasers must be located in the state and purchasers must agree not to resell the securities to an out-of-state resident for 9 months. If the issuer is using an underwriter, the broker dealer must have an office in that state.

RULE 415 SHELF REGISTRATION

Rule 415 allows an issuer to register securities that may be sold for its own benefit, for the benefit of a subsidiary, or in connection with business plans in an amount that may be reasonably sold by the issuer within a 2-year period. The 2-year window starts from the registration date and allows the issuer and the underwriters flexibility in the timing of the offering. Issuers who qualify as well-known seasoned issuers (WKSI) and who qualify for automatic registration may sell securities for up to 3 years. Rule 415 also allows the issuer to register to sell securities on a continuous basis in connection with an employee benefit plan or upon the conversion of other securities.

 TAKENOTE!

Any post-effective amendment to any registration will be declared effective immediately.

SECURITIES OFFERING REFORM RULES

The SEC has adopted the securities offering reform rules, which are designed to modify and streamline the filing and communication requirements of issuers under the Securities Act of 1933. The rules focus on the following areas:

- The communications related to registered securities offerings
- Registration and other procedures in the offering and capital-formation processes
- The delivery of information to investors, including the timeliness of that delivery

The rules adopted have placed an increased importance on the value of electronic communications and filing and have helped eliminate cumbersome and outdated filing requirements.

SEC RULE 405

SEC Rule 405 defines certain classes of issuers who may be entitled to use a streamlined registration process depending on how the issuer is classified. Well-known seasoned issuers and seasoned issuers may take advantage of automatically effective shelf registration of securities by filing Form S-3 or F-3. The registration of the securities covered under the filing of Form S-3 or F-3 is effective immediately upon filing.

WELL-KNOWN SEASONED ISSUER

A well-known seasoned issuer (WKSI) is an issuer that within 60 days of its eligibility determination has at least $700 million worth of voting and nonvoting common equity held by nonaffiliates or that has issued within the last 3 years at least $1 billion in nonconvertible securities for cash (excluding common equity). A WKSI also includes a company that is a majority-owned subsidiary of a WKSI. If during the course of an offering the WKSI sees the value of its securities fall below the required levels to be considered a WKSI, the issuer may continue to sell the securities until it files its next 10-K.

SEASONED ISSUER (PRIMARY S-3 ELIGIBLE)

A seasoned issuer is an issuer that has a public float of $75 million and meets the requirements of Form S-3 to register a primary offering of securities.

UNSEASONED REPORTING ISSUER (NOT PRIMARY S-3 ELIGIBLE)

An unseasoned reporting issuer is an issuer that is required to report under the Exchange Act but does not qualify with the requirements of Form S-3 or F-3 to file a primary offering of securities.

INELIGIBLE ISSUER

An ineligible issuer is a reporting issuer that is not current with the filing of reports required under the Securities Exchange Act. Ineligible issuers also include:

- Companies who have filed for bankruptcy within the last 3 years
- Blank check companies

- Shell companies

- Issuers of penny stock

- Issuers that are limited partnerships that don't have a firm commitment underwriting agreement to sell securities

- Issuers that have been subject to a stop order or have been convicted of a felony or misdemeanor under the Exchange Act directly or indirectly through a subsidiary within the last 3 years

ADDITIONAL COMMUNICATION RULES

An issuer who is a reporting company may continue to release regular business communications with forward-looking statements prior to the effective date of an additional offering of securities. A forward-looking statement is one that contains information about what may possibly happen in the future, such as projected sales or new products. If the securities being offered are the subject of an IPO for a nonreporting issuer, only standard factual business communications may be released by the company. Standard factual information contains information relating to products or services and is not intended to be used by potential investors to make an investment decision. These two safe harbors allow the companies to continue to communicate without violating the gun jumping provisions of the communications rules. The gun jumping rules are designed to limit communications during the time an issue is in registration and to prevent companies from trying to create more favorable market conditions for the securities than otherwise would exist. If the company is a reporting company under the Securities Exchange Act of 1934, the issuer may use forward-looking statements in both their prospectus and annual reports, provided that the statements are clearly identified as forward looking. Key words such as expect, predict, potential, and anticipate are all used to inform the reader that the statements are not facts but projections based on management's beliefs. If the company uses a third party to review the projections it must disclose the nature of any relationship, the qualifications of the reviewer, and the extent of the review. The company is under no obligation to have the projections reviewed.

Road shows are designed to help the company communicate the details of the offering to broker dealers and representatives. Road shows have been traditionally held at large hotels in financial centers across the country. More and more these road shows are being conducted over the Internet via webinars and are known as electronic road shows. These road shows may be broadcast live and recorded for playback and may be available on demand. If the recorded road show is for an IPO of equity securities, the recorded road show must be filed with the SEC unless at least one version is made available to the public in addition to the financial community. Recorded road shows for additional issues do not have to be filed with the SEC.

Pretest

THE UNDERWRITING SYNDICATE AND EXEMPT TRANSACTIONS

la.finra.iss.off.corp.004_1811

1. Which of the following is NOT a type of offering?

   a. Rule 149 offering.

   b. Subsequent primary offering.

   c. Secondary offering.

   d. Combined offering.

la.finra.under.synd.tran.001_1811

2. A corporation in your state wants to sell 1,000,000 shares of stock at $5 per share to investors. Which of the following is NOT true under Rule 147?

   a. 80% of corporate assets must be located in the state.

   b. 80% of proceeds must be used in the state.

   c. 80% of the income must be derived from activity within the state.

   d. 80% of the purchasers must be in the state.

la.finra.under.synd.tran.002_1811

3. During an underwriting of a hot issue, the syndicate exercises its greenshoe provision. This will allow the syndicate to buy what additional percentage of the offering?

   a. 20%.

   b. 25%.

   c. 15%.

   d. 10%.

la.finra.under.synd.tran.003_1811

4. Once a company decides to raise long-term capital to meet its needs, it will do which of the following?

   a. Approach the money market to determine how much capital can be raised.

   b. Hire an underwriter to advise the issuer about the type of securities to issue.

   c. Hire a dealer to issue stock for public purchase.

   d. Hire a broker to issue stock for public purchase.

la.finra.under.synd.tran.004_1811

5. A firm participating in the offering of a private placement may sell the private placement to no more than _____ nonaccredited investors in any 12-month period?

   a. 12.

   b. 6.

   c. 35.

   d. 15.

la.finra.under.synd.tran.005_1811

6. A Regulation A offering as amended by the Jobs Act pertains to an:

   a. Intrastate offering of securities.

   b. Offering of bonds.

   c. Offering of $50,000,000 or less.

   d. Offering of $3,000,000 or less.

la.finra.under.synd.tran.006_1811

7. For an insider to sell unregistered stock under an exemption from registration with the SEC, Form 144, Notice of Offering, which contains certain information, must be filed with the SEC. The insider can sell securities during the period of time in which the notice of offering is effective, which is:

   a. 60 days.

   b. 6 months.

   c. 90 days.

   d. 12 months.

sa.finra.under.synd.tran.001_1811

8. A syndicate may enter a stabilizing bid:

    a. Whenever the price begins to decline.

    b. At or below the offering price.

    c. To ensure an increase from the offering price.

    d. To cover overallotments only.

sa.finra.under.synd.tran.002_1811

9. Rule 145 covers which of the following?

    a. Stock splits.

    b. Stock swaps.

    c. Reverse splits.

    d. Changes in par value.

Issuing Municipal Securities

INTRODUCTION

Learning Objective Statements

Compare the details regarding competitive bid and negotiated underwritings.

Demonstrate an understanding of the registration exemptions and legal opinions.

Contrast Eastern and Western Syndicates.

Detail the order allocation process for new issue municipal bonds.

Prior to issuing any bonds, a municipal issuer must authorize the issuance of the bonds through a bond resolution and obtain a preliminary legal opinion. The bond resolution authorizes the sale of the bonds and describes the issuer's obligations to the bondholders. The preliminary legal opinion helps to determine how the bonds may be offered.

SELECTING AN UNDERWRITER

Municipal officials cannot effectively tend to their duties and try to find investors to purchase the municipality's debt. As a result, municipal issuers select an underwriter or a syndicate of underwriters to sell the bonds for them. There are two ways that the issuer may select an: either through a negotiation with the issuer or through a competitive bidding process. Most revenue bonds are awarded to the underwriter through negotiation. In a negotiated underwriting, the issuer selects the underwriter and negotiates the best terms directly with it. Most general obligation bonds are awarded through competitive bidding. In competitive bidding, the issuer invites underwriters to bid on the terms of the issue by publishing an official notice of sale in the *The Daily Bond Buyer*. The underwriter or syndicate submitting the bid with the lowest net interest cost, or NIC, to the issuer, is awarded the issue. The official notice of sale includes:

- Description of the issuer

- Description of the issue

- Dated date

- Maturity structure

- Date and place of sale, including the time of sale

- Denomination of bonds

- Call or put provisions

- Sealed bid or other bidding provisions

- Amount of good faith deposit required to accompany all bids

- Name of bond council

- Paying agent and trustee

- Expenses allocated to issuer or purchaser

- Terms of delivery

- Criteria for awarding the issue

- Right of rejection

Interested parties submit bids based on their ability to market the bonds on behalf of the issuer. The underwriter tries to provide the issuer with a competitive rate on its bonds while still being able to earn a profit by selling the bonds to investors.

The official notice of sale does not include:

- The yield to maturity (YTM)

- The bond's rating

- The name of the underwriter

- The amount of accrued interest

The municipal issuer prepares a bond contract for the benefit of the underwriter and issuer. The bond contract includes:

- Bond resolution

- Trust indenture (if any)

- Applicable state and federal laws

- Any other documentation regarding the issuer

These documents make up the bond contract, and the issuer is required to adhere to all of the terms and conditions laid out in the various documents.

CREATING A SYNDICATE

Most municipal issues are sold to raise a substantial amount of money. In order to assist with the marketing of the issue and to spread the risk of underwriting the securities, several investment banks will form a syndicate. The syndicate is a group of underwriters responsible for selling the issue. Firms participating in a syndicate, formed to submit a bid in a competitive underwriting, must sign the syndicate letter or syndicate agreement. The syndicate letter discloses all fees and expenses, including clearing expenses. Syndicate participants in a negotiated underwriting must sign the syndicate letter or syndicate contract. The syndicate agreement contains:

- Each member's participation in the offering (member's commitment)

- Method of allocating bonds

- Name of managing underwriter.

- Management fee and spread.

- Member expenses and amount of good faith deposit.

- Liability for unsold bonds.

- Type of syndicate account (eastern or western).

SYNDICATE ACCOUNTS

Each syndicate member is responsible for selling the bonds that have been allocated to it based on its participation. A syndicate member may also be responsible for selling additional bonds if another syndicate member is unable to sell its entire allocation of bonds. There are two types of syndicate accounts: eastern accounts, also known as undivided accounts, and western accounts, also known as divided accounts. In an eastern account, if any bonds remain unsold all of the underwriters must assist in selling the remaining bonds in accordance with their commitment level, regardless of which syndicate member was unable to sell them.

EXAMPLE

Let's assume that there are three investment banks participating in a syndicate to underwrite $10,000,000 worth of municipal bonds. The syndicate account is an eastern account and the investment banks' commitment levels are as follows:

Investment Bank	Commitment Percentage	Dollar Value of Bonds
A	40%	$4,000,000
B	30%	$3,000,000
C	30%	$3,000,000

If investment bank B was able to sell only $2,000,000 of its allocation, the remaining $1,000,000 of bonds would have to be sold by all syndicate members based upon their commitment levels.

The remaining bonds would be allocated as follows:

Investment Bank	Commitment Percentage	Dollar Value of Bonds
A	40%	$400,000
B	30%	$300,000
C	30%	$300,000

Even though investment bank B was responsible for the $1,000,000 of unsold bonds, it would only be required to sell 30% of the remaining bonds, or $300,000 worth, and the other syndicate members must sell the remaining bonds in line with their participation.

In a western account, or a divided account, any unsold bonds are the responsibility of the syndicate member that was unable to sell its allocation. If, in the above example, the syndicate account was a western account, syndicate member B would have to sell all $1,000,000 worth of bonds that it failed to sell originally.

SUBMITTING THE SYNDICATE BID

Syndicate members will engage in a series of meetings in order to determine the terms and conditions of their bid. The syndicate members must determine:

- The underwriter's spread.
- The reoffering yield.
- The prices and yields to be submitted to the issuer.

If all syndicate members cannot agree unanimously on one or more conditions, they must agree to accept the decision of the majority of the syndicate members. Only one bid may be submitted for each syndicate, and it will be submitted by the lead or managing underwriter.

DETERMINING THE REOFFERING YIELD

The syndicate must determine the reoffering yield that will be offered to the investing public. This is known as writing the scale. Most general obligation municipal bonds are issued with a serial maturity that matures over a period of years. The longer-term maturities carry higher yields than the bonds that mature earlier. When the syndicate has determined the prices and yields, it submits the bid to the issuer, along with the required good faith deposit. All competitive underwritings are done on a firm commitment basis, and the winning syndicate is required to purchase all of the bonds from the issuer, even if it can't sell them to investors.

AWARDING THE ISSUE

Once all bids have been submitted, the issuer and the bond council meet to determine which syndicate will be awarded the issue. The bid with the lowest net interest cost (NIC) usually wins the issue. The NIC takes into consideration the actual dollar amount of interest that will be paid over the life of the issue. Additionally, if the issuer received a premium for the bonds, the amount of the premium will be deducted from the net interest cost. If, however, the issuer sold the bonds at a discount, the amount of the discount will be added to the overall NIC. An alternative calculation used to award the issue would be based on the true interest cost of the issue, or the TIC. The TIC takes into consideration the time value of the money. Regardless of which method is used to award the issue, the syndicate with the best bid is awarded the issue. The issuer keeps their good faith deposit and returns the others. The manager of unsuccessful syndicates must return the good faith deposits to syndicate members within 2 business days. The syndicate that submits the second best bid is known as the cover bid and will be awarded the issue in the event the winning syndicate cannot meet its obligations to the issuer. The manager of the winning syndicate opens a syndicate account once the issue has been awarded, and the manager is responsible for its operation and must keep accurate books and records for all account activities.

UNDERWRITER'S COMPENSATION

The difference between the price the underwriters pay for the bonds and the price at which they resell the bonds to the public is known as the spread. The syndicate members divide up the spread according to their different roles and in accordance with their participation in the issue. The spread consists of:

- Management fee
- Underwriting fee
- Additional takedown
- Selling concession

THE MANAGEMENT FEE

The syndicate manager receives a per bond fee for its role as syndicate manager. It receives this fee on all bonds regardless of who sells them.

THE UNDERWRITING FEE

The underwriting fee is the part of the spread that is used to cover underwriting expenses. If any surplus remains after paying all expenses, the syndicate members split the fee based on their commitment to the underwriting.

THE TOTAL TAKEDOWN

The total takedown is what syndicate members can earn on sales of the bonds to their customers. The total takedown consists of the additional takedown and the selling concession.

THE SELLING CONCESSION

The selling concession may be earned on sales of bonds made by dealers who are not syndicate members. Selling group members may purchase bonds directly from a syndicate member and earn the selling concession on sales to their customers.

$1,000 Price to Investor

Selling Concession $9.00
Additional Takedown $5.00
Underwriting Fee $4.00
Management Fee $2.00

$980 Proceeds to Issuer

 TAKENOTE!

The total takedown in this example is $14 per bond. Syndicate members will purchase the bonds from the syndicate account at $986 and may earn $14 per bond.

ORDER PERIOD

The order period is the time set by the syndicate manager during which orders are solicited for the bonds. All orders are filled based upon the order priority agreed to in the syndicate letter and without regard to when the order was received. The order allocation priority is very important, especially when the issue is in high demand and there are more orders than bonds available to fill the orders.

ALLOCATION MUNICIPAL BOND ORDERS

The syndicate manager must establish a method for allocating bonds based upon the priority of orders received by the syndicate. The MSRB requires that this be done in writing, and it is usually detailed in the syndicate agreement, along with the details regarding the sending of confirmations. The method under which the orders are allocated is not left to the syndicate manager's discretion. However, there may be circumstances under which the syndicate manager may make exceptions, as long as these circumstances are detailed in the syndicate agreement. The syndicate manager must demonstrate its reasons for deviating from the agreed order, if it takes an exception to the agreed-upon allocation process.

The syndicate may receive several types of orders:

- Presale orders
- Syndicate or group net orders
- Designated orders
- Member orders
- Member-related orders

PRESALE ORDERS

Presale orders are entered by institutional investors, who agree to purchase the bonds prior to the bond's pricing and terms being finalized. Presale orders are given the highest priority when allocating bonds to customers. The total spread, less the management fee, is deposited into the syndicate account and is divided up among the syndicate members based on their participation. If any bonds remain after all presale orders are filled, they will be allocated to the syndicate orders.

SYNDICATE ORDERS/GROUP NET ORDERS

A syndicate order is one where the sales credit for the order is shared by members of the syndicate, based on their participation. A member may designate its orders as syndicate orders to give them a better chance of being filled. The entire sales credit, less the management fee, is deposited into the syndicate account. After all syndicate orders are filled, any remaining bonds will be distributed to designated orders.

DESIGNATED ORDERS

A designated order is usually submitted by a syndicate member for the account of a large institution. With a designated order, the large institution will designate which syndicate members and which syndicate member agents receive the sales credit. If any bonds remain, the next orders to be filled are the member orders.

MEMBER ORDERS

Member orders are orders submitted by syndicate members for their own customers. The syndicate member receives all of the sales credit. Member orders are traditionally smaller orders for individual accounts. If there are any bonds remaining, the last type of order to be filled is member-related orders.

MEMBER-RELATED ORDERS

The last type of order to get filled is a member-related order. A member-related order is entered for the benefit of an entity sponsored or controlled by the member, such as a proprietary mutual fund or an UIT.

All municipal securities dealers submitting an order to a syndicate, or to a member of a syndicate, must disclose the capacity in which it is acting in filling the order. The member must also disclose if the order is for the dealer's account or for an account that it controls or sponsors. Syndicate members are also required to state the name of the person for whom the order was entered, as well as the total par value of each maturity.

SALE DATE

Municipal bonds are exempt from the Securities Act of 1933 and are not subject to a cooling-off period. As a result, the bonds may be sold as soon as the issue is awarded. Sales of municipal new issues may begin on the earliest of the following:

- When the syndicate purchases the bonds from the issuer
- Specified date of sale
- When the syndicate receives the first order

WHEN ISSUED CONFIRMATIONS

Because municipal bonds can be sold almost immediately once they are awarded to the syndicate, they are usually sold before the securities are physically available for delivery. Investors who purchase municipal securities before they are physically available for delivery receive a "when issued," or initial, confirmation. A when issued confirmation will not include the:

- Settlement date
- Accrued interest
- Total amount due

A when issued confirmation will not include the settlement date because, until the certificates are physically available for delivery, the trade cannot settle. Interest on municipal bonds starts to accrue on the "dated date." It is quite possible that the certificates will not be available for delivery until after the dated date and, as a result, the purchaser of the bonds will owe the issuer accrued interest. Because the amount of accrued interest cannot be calculated, the total amount due cannot be determined.

FINAL CONFIRMATIONS

When the certificates become available for delivery, the syndicate manager gives the syndicate members 2 business days' notice of the settlement date, and the syndicate members must pay for the bonds in full upon delivery. The syndicate members must send a final confirmation to the purchasers of the municipal bonds on or before completion of the transaction, which is the settlement date. All monies are due from the customer at settlement. The final confirmation shows the:

- Settlement date
- Amount of accrued interest, if any
- Total amount due
- All relevant facts relating to the trade

OTHER TYPES OF MUNICIPAL UNDERWRITINGS

Almost all municipal underwritings are done on a firm commitment basis. However, a municipal securities dealer may accept payments from customers who purchase securities that are part of an all-or-none offering, if the proceeds are escrowed. A dealer may also accept payments for an at-the-market offering, if a separate market for the securities exists outside the one maintained by the syndicate.

SYNDICATE OPERATION AND SETTLEMENT

Once the syndicate manager has settled with the issuer, the syndicate manager has 2 business days to return the syndicate members' good faith deposits. The syndicate manager must also:

- Send a written summary detailing how orders were allocated among members within 2 business days of the sale date.

- Register bonds eligible for automated comparison with a registered clearing agency.

- Provide the clearing agency with the coupon rate and settlement date.

- Make final settlement of the syndicate account and distribute all profits within 60 days of the delivery of the securities.

- Provide all syndicate members with a detailed record of the syndicate account.

- Ensure that the miscellaneous expenses detailed in the record of the syndicate account are not excessive in relation to other expenses and the size of the offering.

The syndicate manager must also maintain complete books and records relating to all syndicate business. These records include:

- A description of the securities and the total par value

- Syndicate members and their commitment levels

- The terms of the syndicate

- A list of all orders received

- A list of all securities allocated and the price at which they were sold

- Settlement date with the issuer

- The amount of syndicate member's good faith deposit and when received

- The date the syndicate account was closed out

THE OFFICIAL STATEMENT

Municipal bonds are exempt from the registration and prospectus requirements of the Securities Act of 1933. An issuer of municipal bonds is not required to provide investors with any disclosure documents whatsoever. Should the issuer decide to prepare a disclosure document, the issuer provides investors with the official statement. The official statement provides investors with all of the details regarding the bonds being issued. Issuers who prepare an official statement must make it available to all purchasers, as well as to any investor or broker dealer who requests one. If the final official statement is not available at the time, a request is made for information. The broker dealer may send the interested party a preliminary official statement. Alternatively, the broker dealer may prepare and forward a summary or an abstract of the official statement. If the issuer decides not to prepare an official statement, purchasers must be informed in writing that no official statement will be prepared. An official statement includes:

- The terms of the offering

- Purpose of the issue

- Summary

- Description of bonds

- Description of the issuer

- Financial data for the issuer

- Regulatory matters

- Feasibility statement

- Legal proceedings

- Type of indenture (open/closed)

- Authorization of bonds

- Security pledged, if any

- Construction plans

- Tax status

All municipal issues offered through negotiated underwritings are required to provide an official statement. The official statement must disclose:

- The underwriting spread.

- The initial offering price for each maturity.

- Any fees received from the issuer.

Prior to the completion of the transaction, the member must disclose the dealer's participation in the offering and any control or other relationship issues between the issuer and the underwriter.

BOND COUNSEL

During an offering of municipal bonds, the issuer retains legal counsel to represent it in the transaction. The bond counsel will:

- Confirm that the issuer is legally allowed to issue the bonds.

- Confirm that the debt is a legally binding obligation of the issuer.

- Ensure that the issue has been properly announced.

- Ensure that the bond certificates have been legally printed.

- Issue a legal opinion.

THE LEGAL OPINION

The legal opinion is issued by the independent bond counsel. It states that the bonds are a legally binding obligation of the issuer and that the bonds may be legally offered for sale by the issuer. The legal opinion also attests to the tax treatment of the interest payments received by investors who purchase the municipal bonds. An unqualified legal opinion is the most desirable for investors. An unqualified legal opinion means that the bond counsel has no reservations whatsoever regarding the issue. Should the bond counsel issue a qualified legal opinion, it indicates that there are some concerns regarding one or more of the statements in the legal opinion. The legal opinion must be attached to every municipal bond certificate. The only exception to this is if the bond has been identified as being traded ex legal. A bond could be traded ex legal if a legal opinion was never issued, as is the case with most smaller issues. A municipal bond can also be identified as being ex legal if the legal opinion was lost.

POTENTIAL CONFLICTS OF INTEREST FOR MUNICIPAL BOND UNDERWRITERS

There are many potential conflicts of interest that may come into play when engaging in the underwriting of municipal securities. Some of these require only that they be disclosed. Other more potentially serious types of conflicts require that the underwriter take certain actions to ensure that purchasers of the securities are not adversely affected.

ACTING AS A FINANCIAL ADVISER TO THE ISSUER

Broker dealers often provide advice to state and local municipalities for a fee. Broker dealers that act as financial advisers to issuers of municipal securities provide guidance as to the timing and structure of potential offerings and other financial matters. Any investor who purchases a new municipal issue from a broker dealer with a financial advisory relationship with the issuer must be informed of the relationship in writing prior to the completion of the transaction. Although underwriters advise issuers on the timing and structure of issues, as well as other financial matters, this does not create a financial advisory relationship. A financial advisory relationship is contractual in nature and must be in writing. The contract includes:

- The terms under which fees will be paid

- Services to be provided by the broker dealer

- Use of broker dealer's services

- Use of services offered by a control party or by a party controlled by the broker dealer

INFORMATION OBTAINED WHILE ACTING AS A FIDUCIARY

A broker dealer acting in a fiduciary capacity may not use the information obtained in the furtherance of its duties for its own benefit. A municipal securities dealer, acting as a financial adviser to the issuer of municipal securities, may not use the information it obtains regarding current bondholders to solicit business from them. Examples of fiduciary capacities are:

- Financial adviser

- Transfer agent

- Paying agent
- Indenture trustee
- Clearing agent
- Correspondent for another dealer
- Registrar
- Safekeeping agent

ACTING AS A FINANCIAL ADVISER AND AN UNDERWRITER

When a firm acts as both the financial adviser and underwriter to an issuer, potential conflicts of interest arise. The MSRB has set strict rules regarding these situations. The MSRB requires:

- The nature of the financial advisory relationship to be disclosed.
- The amount of the compensation received by the member to be disclosed.
- That prior to entering into a negotiated underwriting, the firm must receive the issuer's consent and must inform the issuer of the potential conflicts and must terminate the advisory relationship.
- The issuer must acknowledge the receipt of the information relating to the conflicts, in writing.
- That prior to submitting a bid for a competitive underwriting the broker dealer must receive the issuer's approval.
- That in the event the broker dealer acts as an underwriter, all purchasers be informed of the financial advisory relationship.

POLITICAL CONTRIBUTIONS

FINRA enforces the rules enacted by the MSRB for its members that engage in municipal securities business. MSRB Rule G-38 puts strict limits on the amount of political contributions that may be made by a municipal finance professional (MFP). An MFP is an agent who is primarily engaged in any of the following:

- Soliciting municipal underwriting

- Acting as a financial adviser or consultant

- Trading or selling municipal securities

- Providing investment advice or issuing research reports relating to municipal securities to the public

- Directing supervisors of any agent acting in the above capacity

- Acting as an executive who oversees municipal dealers or departments

MFPs may only make political contributions to candidates in an election in which they are eligible to vote. The maximum amount of their contribution is limited to $250 per candidate per election. If an MFP donates more than $250 or makes a contribution to a candidate in an election in which he or she is not able to vote, a violation has occurred, and the employing firm will be banned from engaging in municipal securities business with the issuer for 2 years. The 2-year ban will follow the MFP should the MFP change firms. Both the new firm and the previous employer will be subject to the amount of time that remains on the 2-year ban. Should an MFP make a political contribution to an incumbent that would subject the employing firm to a ban, that ban will expire if the incumbent loses the election. This political contribution does not apply to federal elections such as for senators.

EXAMPLE

If an MFP donated $200 to a mayoral candidate in a district where the MFP does not live and, as a result, could not vote in the election, the employing firm could not underwrite that municipality's debt for 2 years.

If an MFP contributes more than $250 or contributes to a candidate that he or she is not entitled to vote for, the employing firm must notify the issuer by filing forms G37 and G38 by the last day of the month following the end of each calendar quarter. These forms will tell the issuer:

- The amount of the contribution and the contributor category.

- The name and title of the political official and his or her political party.

- A list of the municipal issuers the firm engages in business with.

If the contribution is in line with MSRB Rule 37, the employing firm is not required to file forms G37 and G38. If an executive officer gives more than $250, the donation must be reported, but the firm would not be banned from engaging in municipal securities business with the issuer.

Additionally, if the firm employs consultants to help the firm obtain municipal securities business from issuers, the firm must send forms G37 and G38 to the MSRB at the end of each calendar quarter listing:

- The name of the consultant or company.

- The role in which the consultant is acting and the amount of compensation.

- A list of municipal securities business obtained by using the consultant.

- A copy of all consulting agreements.

- Termination dates for consulting agreements.

The dealer must also disclose information relating to the use of consultants to the issuers. The dealer may disclose the information on an issue-specific basis or on an issuer-specific basis. If the dealer notifies issuers on an issuer basis, the dealer must send issuers updated information annually even if there have been no changes.

MUNICIPAL BOND TRADING

Municipal bonds trade over the counter in the secondary market much like OTC stocks. Municipal bond dealers provide quotes on the bonds that they deal in to other broker dealers. A two-sided market or quote consists of: (1) a bid, which is the price at which the dealer is willing to purchase the securities, and (2) an offer, which is the price at which the dealer is willing to sell the securities. However, unlike most stocks, many municipal bonds are not actively traded in the secondary market. It is not unusual to see a dealer posting a request for a quote on an issue such as "bids wanted" or "offers wanted" for an inactive municipal bond. Most municipal bonds are quoted and traded on a yield-to-maturity basis. This type of quote is known as a basis quote. Some municipal revenue term bonds are quoted and traded as a percentage of par and are known as dollar bonds.

Pretest

ISSUING MUNICIPAL SECURITIES

la.finra.under.synd.tran.001_1811

1. The state of Texas is seeking to raise $500 million through the sale of general obligation bonds. Which of the ollowing will support the repayment of the bond issue?

   a. Property taxes.

   b. Ad valorem taxes.

   c. User fees.

   d. Sales taxes.

la.finra.iss.muni.sec.002_1811

2. The city of Chicago is seeking to raise $100 million through the sale of general obligation bonds and is seeking an underwriter for the issue. Which of the following is correct?

   a. The issue will be awarded through a negotiation.

   b. The issue must be advertised and provide terms for bidding.

   c. The issue will be underwritten on a best efforts basis if the city's bonds are not in high demand.

   d. The city is looking to the lower true interest cost to finance the issue.

sa.finra.iss.muni.sec.001_1811

3. The city of Miami is seeking to raise $10 million through the sale of general obligation bonds to repair the high school's football field. The bonds are going to be issued ex-legal. Which of the following is correct?

   a. The bonds received an unqualified legal opinion.

   b. The bonds received a qualified legal opinion.

   c. The bonds received no legal opinion.

   d. The bonds' legal claim to the tax revenue is in doubt.

sa.finra.iss.muni.sec.002_1811

4. The state of Massachusetts is seeking to raise $300 million through the sale of revenue bonds to repair the roadways. Which of the following is correct?

   a. These bonds will be subject to a statutory debt limit.

   b. These bonds will be issued through a negotiation.

   c. The offering will be advertised in the daily bond buyer.

   d. The underwriters will be required to submit sealed bids.

Trading Securities in the Secondary Market

INTRODUCTION

Learning Objective Statements

Detail the features of the secondary market.

Choose the proper type of order to enter to execute a transaction.

Differentiate the benefits and risks associated with each type of order.

Indicate the role of the NYSE and its members.

Analyze how and why to sell stock short.

Investors who do not purchase their stocks and bonds directly from the issuer must purchase them from another investor. Investor-to-investor transactions are known as secondary market transactions. In a secondary market transaction, the selling security owner receives the proceeds from the sale. Secondary market transactions may take place on an exchange or in the over-the-counter market known as Nasdaq. Although both facilitate the trading of securities, they operate in very different manners. We begin by looking at the types of orders that an investor may enter and the reasons for entering the various types of orders.

TYPES OF ORDERS

Investors can enter various types of orders to buy or sell securities. Some orders guarantee that the investor's order will be executed immediately. Other types of orders may state a specific price or condition under which the investor wants the order to be executed. All orders are canceled day orders unless otherwise specified. All day orders are canceled at the end of the trading day if they are not executed. An investor may also specify that the order remain active until canceled. This type of order is known as good till cancel, or GTC.

MARKET ORDERS

A market order guarantees that the investor's order is executed as soon as the order is presented to the market. A market order to either buy or sell guarantees the execution but not the price at which the order will be executed. When a market order is presented for execution, the market for the security may be very different from the market that was displayed when the order was entered. As a result, the investor does not know the exact price at which the order will be executed. A market order takes priority over an immediately executable limit order.

BUY LIMIT ORDERS

A buy limit order sets the maximum price that the investor will pay for the security. The order may never be executed at a price higher than the investor's limit price. Although a buy limit order guarantees that the investor will not pay over a certain price, it does not guarantee an execution. If the stock continues to trade higher away from the investor's limit price, the investor will not purchase the stock and may miss a chance to realize a profit.

SELL LIMIT ORDERS

A sell limit order sets the minimum price that the investor will accept for the security. The order may never be executed at a price lower than the investor's limit price. Although a sell limit order guarantees that the investor will not receive less than a certain price, it does not guarantee an execution. If the stock continues to trade lower away from the investor's limit price, the investor will not sell the stock and may miss a chance to realize a profit or may realize a loss as a result.

 FOCUSPOINT

It's important to remember that even if an investor sees stock trading at the limit price it does not mean that the order was executed, because there could have been stock ahead of the investor at that limit price.

STOP ORDERS/STOP-LOSS ORDERS

A stop order or stop-loss order can be used by investors to limit or guard against a loss or to protect a profit. A stop order is placed away from the market in case the stock starts to move against the investor. A stop order is not a live order; it has to be elected. A stop order is elected and becomes a live order when the stock trades at or through the stop price. The stop price is also known as the trigger price. Once the stock has traded at or through the stop price, the order becomes a market order to either buy or sell the stock, depending on the type of order that was placed.

BUY STOP ORDERS

A buy stop order is placed above the market and is used to protect against a loss or to protect a profit on a short sale of stock. A buy stop order could also be used by a technical analyst to get long the stock after the stock breaks through resistance.

EXAMPLE

An investor has sold 100 shares of ABC short at $40 per share. ABC has declined to $30 per share. The investor is concerned that if ABC goes past $32 it may return to $40. To protect his profit he enters an order to buy 100 ABC at 32 stop. If ABC trades at or through $32, the order will become a market order to buy 100 shares, and the investor will cover the short at the next available price.

SELL STOP ORDERS

A sell stop order is placed below the market and is used to protect against a loss or to protect a profit on the purchase of a stock. A sell stop order could also be used by a technical analyst to get short the stock after the stock breaks through support.

EXAMPLE

An investor has purchased 100 shares of ABC at $30 per share. ABC has risen to $40 per share. The investor is concerned that if ABC falls past $38 it may return to $30. To protect her profit she enters an order to sell 100 ABC at 38 stop. If ABC trades at or through $38, the order will become a market order to sell 100 shares, and the investor will sell her short at the next available price.

If in the same example the order to sell 100 ABC at 38 stop was entered GTC, we could have a situation such as this:

ABC closes at 39.40. The following morning ABC announces that it lost a major contract, and ABC opens at 35.30. The opening print of 35.30 elected the order, and the stock would be sold on the opening or as close to the opening as practical.

STOP-LIMIT ORDERS

An investor would enter a stop-limit order for the same reasons as he or she would enter a stop order. The only difference is that once the order has been elected the order becomes a limit order instead of a market order. The same risks that apply to traditional limit orders apply to stop-limit orders. If the stock continues to trade away from the investor's limit, the investor could give back all of the profits or suffer large losses.

OTHER TYPES OF ORDERS

There are several other types of orders that an investor may enter. They are:

- All or none (AON)

- Immediate or cancel (IOC)

- Fill or kill (FOK)

- Not held (NH)

- Market on open (MOO)/market on close (MOC)

All-or-none orders: AON orders may be entered as day orders or GTC. All-or-none orders, as the name implies, indicate that the investor wants to buy or sell all of the securities or none of them. AON orders are not displayed in the market because of the required special handling, and the investor will not accept a partial execution.

Immediate-or-cancel orders: The investor wants to buy or sell whatever can be sold immediately; whatever is not filled is canceled.

Fill-or-kill orders: The investor wants the entire order executed immediately or the entire order canceled.

Not-held orders: The investor gives discretion to the floor broker as to the time and price of execution. All retail NH orders given to a representative are considered day orders unless the order is received in writing from the customer and entered GTC.

Market-on-open/market-on-close orders: The investor wants the order executed on the opening or closing of the market or as reasonably close to the opening or closing as practical. If the order is not executed, it is canceled. Partial executions are allowed.

TAKENOTE!

The SEC has granted permission to the NYSE to stop using FOK and IOC orders.

THE EXCHANGES

The most recognized stock exchange in the world is the New York Stock Exchange (NYSE). There are, however, many exchanges throughout the United States that all operate in a similar manner. Exchanges are dual-auction markets. They provide a central marketplace where buyers and sellers come together in one centralized location to compete with one another. Buyers compete with other buyers to be the highest price anyone is willing to pay for the security, and sellers compete with other sellers to be the lowest price at which anyone is willing to sell a security. All transactions in an exchange-listed security that are executed on the exchange have to take place in front of the specialist, or designated market maker (DMM), for that security. The DMM is an exchange member who is responsible for maintaining a fair and orderly market for the stock in which he or she specializes. The DMM stands at the trading post where all the buyers and sellers must go to conduct business in the security. This is responsible for the crowd that you see on the news and financial reports when they show the floor of the exchange. All securities that trade on an exchange are known as listed securities.

PRIORITY OF EXCHANGE ORDERS

Orders that are routed to the trading post for execution are prioritized according to price and time. If the price of more than one order is the same, orders will be filled as follows:

- **Priority:** The order that was received first gets filled first.

- **Precedence:** If the time and price are the same, the larger order gets filled.

- **Parity:** If all conditions are the same, the orders are matched in the crowd and the shares are split among the orders.

Pretest

TRADING SECURITIES IN THE SECONDARY MARKET

la.finra.trad.sec.mkt.001_1811

1. Which of the following may NOT trade on the floor of the NYSE?

    a. Two-dollar broker.

    b. Regular member.

    c. Commission house broker.

    d. Allied member.

la.finra.trad.sec.mkt.002_1811

2. Which of the following is NOT a type of order?

    I. All or none.
    II. Fill or kill.
    III. Mini/maxi.
    IV. Best efforts.

    a. I and II.

    b. II and IV.

    c. I and IV.

    d. III and IV.

la.finra.trad.sec.mkt.003_1811

3. INTC has been hitting a lot of resistance at $30. A technical analyst who wants to buy the stock would most likely place what type of order?

    a. Limit order to buy at $30.

    b. Market order.

    c. Buy stop at $31.

    d. Buy limit at $29.

la.finra.trad.sec.mkt.004_1811

4. The inside market is:Highest offer.Lowest offer.Highest bid.Lowest bid.

   a. II and III.

   b. I and II.

   c. I and IV.

   d. I and III.

la.finra.trad.sec.mkt.005_1811

5. Which of the following is true of the DMMs on the NYSE?

   a. They work for themselves.

   b. They are appointed by a vote of the company's board.

   c. They work for the exchange.

   d. They work for the company whose stock they trade.

la.finra.trad.sec.mkt.006_1811

6. ABC Technologies, a very volatile stock, closes at $180 per share. Your customer has placed an order to sell 500 ABC at 165 stop limit 160 GTC. After the close, the company announces bad earnings and the stock opens at 145. What happened to your customer's order?

   a. It has been canceled because the stock price is below the limit price.

   b. It has been elected and has become a limit order.

   c. It has been elected and executed.

   d. It has been canceled because the stock price is below the stop price.

sa.finra.trad.sec.mkt.001_1811

7. Which of the following subjects the investor to unlimited risk?

   a. Selling stock short.

   b. Converting a bond into the underlying common stock.

   c. Buying a speculative bond.

   d. Selling common stock long.

sa.finra.trad.sec.mkt.002_1811

8. A bullish investor would enter which of the following orders?

   a. A sell limit thinking that the stock price will rise.

   b. A sell stop below the market.

   c. A buy stop above the market.

   d. DNR GTC.

The Role of Broker Dealers and NASDAQ

INTRODUCTION

Learning Objective Statements

Detail the role of designated market makers.

Evaluate the role of broker dealers in executing a customer's order.

The DMM (formerly known as a specialist) is an independent exchange member who has been assigned a stock or group of stocks for which he or she is the designated market maker. Designated market makers are responsible for:

• Maintaining a fair and orderly market for the securities.

• Buying for their own account in the absence of public buy orders.

• Selling from their own account in the absence of public sell orders.

• Acting as an agent by executing public orders left with them.

A large amount of capital is required to fulfill the requirements of a DMM. As a result, most DMMs are employees of member firms. Although the specialist is not required to participate in every transaction, every transaction for that security that is executed on the exchange must take place in front of the designated market maker. The DMM may act as either an agent or as a principal if he or she plays a role in the transaction.

THE DMM ACTING AS A PRINCIPAL

In the absence of public orders the DMM is required to provide liquidity and price improvement for the stocks in which he or she is the designated market maker. DMMs are required to trade against the market and may now trade for their own account at prices that would compete with public orders.

EXAMPLE   If the public market for XYZ is quoted as follows:

	Bid	Offer
10 × 10	20.45	20.55

There is a 20.45 bid for 1000 shares and 1000 shares offered at 20.55.

If a public sell order came in to sell the stock, the DMM could purchase the stock for his own account at 20.45 because he is on parity with the public. The DMM could also purchase the stock for his own account at 20.50 and would be improving the price that the seller would be receiving. This is known as price improvement. Alternatively, if a public buy order came in, the DMM could sell the stock from his own account at 20.55, because he is now allowed to compete with the public. He could also sell the stock to the customer at 20.50 because, once again, that would be providing price improvement for the order.

THE DESIGNATED MARKET MAKER/DMM ACTING AS AN AGENT

The DMM is also required to execute orders that have been left with her. Orders that have been left with the DMM for execution are said to have been "left or dropped on the DMM's book." The DMM is required to maintain a book of public orders and to execute them when market conditions permit. The types of orders that may be left with the DMM are:

- Buy and sell limit orders

- Both day and GTC orders

- AON orders

The DMM executes the orders if and when she is able to and sends a commission bill to the member who left the order with her for execution. This is known as a specialist bill and is usually only a cent or two per share.

The DMM is also required to quote the best market for the security to any party that asks. The best or inside market is composed of the highest bid and lowest offer. This is made up from bids and offers contained in the DMM's book and in the trading crowd. The inside market is also the market that is displayed to broker dealers and agents on their quote system.

When quoting the inside market, the DMM will add all of the shares bid for at the highest price and all of the shares offered at the lowest price to determine the size of the market. There are certain types of orders that are not included when determining the inside market, they are:

- Stop orders

- AON orders

A DMM may not accept the following types of orders:

- Market orders

- Immediately executable limit orders

- NH orders

- IOC orders

- FOK orders

Market orders and immediately executable limit orders are filled as soon as they reach the crowd, so there is nothing to leave with the specialist. In the case of an NH order, once a floor broker is given discretion as to time and price, he or she may not give it to another party.

A DMM's book may look something like the following example:

Buy	XYZ	Sell
5 Goldman	20	
10 JPM		
	20.05	
	20.10	1 Prudential
		5 Fidelity
	20.15	2 Morgan

The inside market for XYZ based on the DMM's book would be:

	Bid	Ask
15 × 6	20.00	20.10

Buyers are bidding for 1,500 shares, and sellers are offering 600 shares of XYZ.

DO NOT REDUCE (DNR)

GTC orders that are placed underneath the market and left with the DMM for execution will be reduced for the distribution of dividends. Orders that will be reduced are:

- Buy limits
- Sell stops

These orders are reduced because when a stock goes ex dividend its price is adjusted down. To ensure that customer orders placed below the market are only executed as a result of market activity, the order will be adjusted down by the value of the dividend.

EXAMPLE   A customer has placed an order to buy 500 XYZ at 35 GTC. XYZ closed yesterday at 36.10. XYZ goes ex dividend for 20 cents and opens the next day at 35.90. The customer's order will now be an order to purchase 500 XYZ at 34.80 GTC.

If the customer had entered the order and specified that the order was not to be reduced for the distribution of ordinary dividends, it would have remained an order to purchase 500 shares at 35. The order in this case would have been entered as:

Buy 500 XYZ 35 GTC DNR

Orders placed above the market are not reduced for distributions.

ADJUSTMENTS FOR STOCK SPLITS

GTC orders that are left with the specialist must be adjusted for stock splits. Orders that are placed above and below the market will be adjusted so that the aggregate dollar value of the order remains the same.

EXAMPLE

A customer has placed a GTC order. Let's look at what happens to the order if the company declares a stock split:

Type of Split	Old Order	New Order
2:1	Buy 100 at 50	Buy 200 at 25
2:1	Sell 100 at 100	Sell 200 at 50
3:2	Buy 100 at 100	Buy 150 at 66.67
3:2	Sell 100 at 60	Sell 150 at 40

Notice that in all of the examples the value of the customer's order remained the same. To calculate the adjustment to an open order for a forward stock split, multiply the number of shares by the fraction and the share price by the reciprocal of the fraction. Such as:

Buy 100 at 50 after a 2:1 stock split

$$100 \times 2/1 = 200$$

$$50 \times 1/2 = 25$$

The value of the order was $5,000 both before and after the order.

COMMISSION HOUSE BROKER

A commission house broker is an employee of a member organization and executes orders for the member's customers and for the member's own account.

TWO-DOLLAR BROKER

A two-dollar broker is an independent member who executes orders for commission house brokers when they are too busy managing other orders.

REGISTERED TRADERS

A registered trader is an exchange member who trades for his or her own account and for his or her own profit and loss. Orders may not originate on the floor of the NYSE; however, registered traders are active on other exchanges, such as the AMEX (now part of NYSE). A supplemental liquidity provider/SLP is an off-the-floor market maker that directs orders to the floor of the NYSE for its own account. The SLP may compete with the DMM for order execution and must display a bid or offer at least 10% of the time. The SLP receives a rebate from the NYSE when an order is executed against the SLP's quote that added liquidity to the market.

SUPER DISPLAY BOOK (SDBK)

Most customer orders are never handled by a floor broker. Floor brokers usually only handle large complex institutional orders. Customer orders are electronically routed directly to the trading post for execution via the Super Display Book (SDBK) system. The SDBK bypasses the floor broker and sends the order right to the DMM for execution. If the order can be immediately executed, the system will send an electronic confirmation of the execution to the submitting broker dealer. All listed securities are eligible to be traded over the SDBK system. All preopening orders that can be matched up are automatically paired off by the system and executed at the opening price. Any preopening orders that cannot be paired off are routed to the trading post for inclusion on the display book.

SHORT SALES

An investor who believes that a stock price has appreciated too far and is likely to decline may profit from this belief by selling the stock short. In a short sale, the customer borrows the security in order to complete delivery to the buying party. The investor sells the stock high hoping that it can be bought back at a cheaper price. It is a perfectly legitimate investment strategy. The investor's first transaction is a sell and the investor exits the position by repurchasing the stock. The short sale of stock has unlimited risk because there is no limit as to how high the stock price may go. The investor loses money if the stock appreciates past the sales price.

REGULATION OF SHORT SALES/REGULATION SHO

The SEC continues to adopt new rules relating to the short sale of securities. Regulation SHO has been adopted to update prior short sale regulations and covers:

- Definitions and order marking.

- Suspension of uptick and plus bid requirements.

- Borrowing and delivery requirements for securities.

Under Regulation SHO, the SEC has prohibited any SRO from adopting any price criteria as a requirement of executing a short sale.

RULE 200 DEFINITIONS AND ORDER MARKING

Rule 200 updates the definition of who is determined to be long a security. As new derivatives and trading systems and strategies have been introduced, amendments to the short sale rules under the Securities Exchange Act of 1934 needed to be updated. Most of the prior rules and definitions remain unchanged. The new updates under Rule 200 are:

- A person is considered long the security if he or she holds a security future contract and has been notified that he or she will receive the underlying security.

- A broker dealer must aggregate its net positions in securities unless it qualifies to allow each independent trading unit to aggregate its positions independently.

A broker dealer may qualify to have its various trading departments determine their net long or short positions independently if:

- Traders are only assigned to one independent trading unit at any one time.

- Traders in each independent trading unit employ their own trading strategies and do not coordinate their trading with other independent trading units.

- The firm has documented each aggregation unit and the independent trading objectives of each unit.

- The firm supports the independent nature of each trading unit.

- At the time a sell order is entered each independent aggregation unit determines its net position for the security.

The order marking requirements of Rule 200 require the broker dealer to mark all orders long, short, or short exempt. The definition of long and short include the definitions in the affirmative determination rule and have been expanded to include the following:

- An order may be marked long if the investor or broker dealer has possession of the security and can reasonably be expected to deliver the security by the settlement date.

- An order must be marked short if the investor or broker dealer has possession of the security but cannot reasonably be expected to deliver the security by the settlement date.

- An order does not need to be marked short exempt if the seller is only relying on a price test exemption under the tick test or bid test rule.

OVER THE COUNTER/NASDAQ

Securities that are not listed on any of the centralized exchanges trade over the counter or on the Nasdaq. Nasdaq stands for National Association of Securities Dealers Automated Quotation System. It is the interdealer network of computers and phone lines that allows securities to be traded between broker dealers. Nasdaq is not an auction market but has been granted exchange status by the SEC. It is a negotiated market. One broker dealer negotiates a price directly with another broker dealer. None of the other interested parties for that particular security have any idea of what terms are being proposed. The broker dealers may communicate over their Nasdaq workstations or can speak directly to one another over the phone.

MARKET MAKERS

Because there are no specialists for the OTC markets, bids and offers are displayed by broker dealers known as market makers. A market maker is a firm that is required to display a two-sided market. A two-sided market consists of a simultaneous bid and offer for the security quoted through the Nasdaq workstation. The market maker must be willing to buy the security at the bid price, which it has displayed, as well as be willing to sell the security at the offering price, which it has displayed. These are known as firm quotes. There is no centralized location for the Nasdaq market; it is simply a network of computers that connects broker dealers throughout the world. Market makers purchase the security at the bid price and sell the security at the offering price. Their profit is the difference between the bid and the offer, which is known as the spread. Rule changes and new trading systems known as ECNs, or electronic communication networks, have narrowed the spreads on stocks significantly in recent years.

NASDAQ SUBSCRIPTION LEVELS

Broker dealers subscribe to the Nasdaq workstation services that meet their firm's requirements. The levels of service are:

- **Level I:** Nasdaq Level I subscription service only provides information relating to the inside market and provides quotes for registered representatives.

- **Level II:** Nasdaq Level II subscription service is for broker dealers that are order-entry firms. Level II allows the broker dealer to see the inside market, as well as the quotes of all market makers and to execute orders over the Nasdaq workstation.

- **Level III:** Nasdaq Level III is the highest level of service offered over the Nasdaq workstation. Level III contains all of the features of Level II and allows the firms to enter and update their own markets. Level III is only for approved market makers.

- **Nasdaq TotalView:** Nasdaq TotalView quotation service allows professionals and nonprofessionals to view the entire Nasdaq book for securities traded over Nasdaq. TotalView displays the price and size quoted by all market makers, exchanges, and ECNs. TotalView also displays the total size of the market for the five best-priced quotes as well as order imbalance information for all Nasdaq crossing sessions.

NASDAQ QUOTES

Most actively traded Nasdaq stocks are quoted by a large number of market makers. As market makers enter their quotes, some will be above or below the inside market. A market maker whose quote is above or below the inside market is said to be away from the market. As the market makers adjust their quotes, the market maker who is publishing the highest bid for the security has its bid displayed at the top of the list and its bid is published as the best bid to anyone with a Nasdaq Level I subscription. The market maker publishing the lowest offer will have its offer listed at the top of the list and published as the lowest offer to anyone with a Nasdaq Level I subscription. As a result, the best bid and offer from any two market makers will make up the inside market.

EXAMPLE

		XYAD
	Bid	Ask
	15.00	15.05
MM 1	14.90	15.10
MM 2	15.00	15.20
MM 3	14.85	15.05
MM 4	14.95	15.15
MM 5	14.98	15.18

Note: Notice how the inside market for XYAD consists of the bid from market maker 2 and the offer from market maker 3. All of the other market makers are away from the market.

NOMINAL NASDAQ QUOTES

All quotes published over the Nasdaq workstation are firm quotes. Dealers who fail to honor their quotes have committed a violation known as backing away. Dealers who provide quotes over the phone that are clearly indicated as being subject or nominal cannot be held to trade at those prices. Nasdaq qualifiers are:

- "It looks like"

- "It's around"

- "Subject"

- "Nominal"

- "Work it out"

- "Last I saw"

A response of "it is" would indicate a firm quote. A firm quote is always good for at least one round lot or 100 shares.

AUTOMATED CONFIRMATION SYSTEM (ACT)/TRADE REPORTING FACILITY (TRF)

The ACT/TRF systems facilitate the reporting and clearing of trades executed through Nasdaq and other OTC environments. ACT/TRF transactions include:

- Nasdaq Global and Capital market securities
- Non-Nasdaq OTC securities
- Third-market trades
- Nasdaq Convertible bonds

All ACT/TRF eligible transactions must be reported to ACT/TRF within 10 seconds of the transaction.

NASDAQ EXECUTION SYSTEMS

Most Nasdaq trades are executed over the Nasdaq workstation using one of its automated execution systems. These systems allow dealers to execute orders without having to speak with one another on the phone.

THE NASDAQ MARKET CENTER EXECUTION SYSTEM (NMCES)

The Nasdaq Market Center Execution System, also known as NMCES, accepts market orders and immediately executable limit orders for both customer and firm accounts. Orders may be entered for up to 999,999 shares per order. The orders will immediately be routed to dealers on the inside market for automatic execution. Larger orders may be split up to meet the maximum order volume. However, a broker dealer may not split orders, that would otherwise be able to be entered into the Nasdaq system, in an effort to increase fees or rebates. This would be considered order shredding, which is a violation. Orders executed through the Nasdaq execution system are automatically reported to ACT.

THE NASDAQ OPENING CROSS

The Nasdaq opening cross begins at 9:28 a.m. At this time, the Nasdaq execution system automatically executes orders. Orders placed after 9:28 a.m. may not be canceled. Orders placed after 9:28 a.m. may only be changed if the change to the order makes the order more aggressive. A change that increases the size of the order or improves the price would make the order more aggressive. For a buy order an improved price would be a higher limit price; for a sell order an improved price would be a lower limit price. All orders that are executed during the opening cross will be reported to ACT with a modifier. The opening cross creates the Nasdaq official opening price (NOOP). Like the opening cross, Nasdaq has developed the closing cross to determine the Nasdaq official closing price.

NON-NASDAQ OTCBB

The OTC Bulletin Board (OTCBB) provides two-sided electronic quotes for OTC securities that cannot meet the listing standard of an exchange or Nasdaq. Direct participation programs (DPPs) and American depositary receipts (ADRs) will often be quoted on the OTCBB. The OTCBB is operational from 7:30 a.m. to 6:30 p.m. The OTCBB displays:

- Real-time quotes

- Volume

- Last sale price

Quotes that may be entered over the OTCBB by a market maker include:

- Bid wanted

- Offer wanted

- Bid only

- Offer only

- Two-sided quotes

- Quote modifications

Quotes displayed over the OTCBB are firm quotes unless they are quoting DPP programs. Quotes entered on the OTCBB must be for the minimum size for that security. The minimum quote size for the security depends on the price of the security being quoted. Quotes for DPP are subject quotes and may only be updated twice per day, once between 8:30 and 9:30 a.m. and at 12:30 p.m.

PINK OTC MARKET

Securities that do not qualify for listing on the Nasdaq or that have been delisted from Nasdaq or one of the exchanges may be quoted on the Pink OTC market. The Pink OTC market is an electronic marketplace. The Pink OTC Market facilitates trading for securities that are quoted on the pink sheets that do not meet the listing standards of any exchange or marketplace. All two-sided quotes displayed in the Pink OTC Market are firm quotes. The Pink OTC Market also provides a list of phone numbers for market makers who display subject quotes. Stocks quoted on the Pink OTC Market trading at under $5 per share are known as penny stocks. A firm that executes a customer's order for a Pink OTC Market security is required to make a reasonable effort to obtain the best price for the customer. The firm is required to obtain quotes from at least three market makers for the security prior to executing the customer's order. If the security has less than three market makers, the firm is required to obtain a quote from all market makers.

THIRD MARKET

The third market consists of transactions in exchange-listed securities executed over the counter through the Nasdaq workstation. A broker dealer may wish to simply purchase or sell an exchange-listed security directly with another brokerage firm instead of executing the order on the floor of the exchange. These transactions are known as third-market transactions. All third-market transactions are reported through TRF to the consolidated tape for display.

FOURTH MARKET

A fourth-market transaction is a transaction between two large institutions without the use of a broker dealer. The computer network that facilitates these transactions is known as INSTINET. Large blocks of stock, both listed and unlisted, trade between large institutional investors in the fourth market.

Although many trades in the fourth market are executed through the INSTINET system, many large portfolio managers execute internal crosses, which go unreported. Proprietary trading systems are not considered part of the fourth market, because these systems are either registered as broker dealers or are operated by broker dealers. Trades executed by large institutions via proprietary networks are sometimes referred to as dark pools, because the supply or demand for a security is unseen by market participants.

READING THE CONSOLIDATED TAPE

The consolidated tape system reports trades as they occur in the various markets. Securities that are primarily listed on the NYSE will be reported to consolidated tape A regardless of the market where the trade was executed. Securities primarily listed on the NYSE may trade on regional exchanges such as the Pacific Stock Exchange or over Nasdaq in the third market. Consolidated tape B reports trade for securities primarily listed on the AMEX and regional exchanges. All transactions must be reported to the consolidated tape within 30 seconds of execution.

The consolidated tape reports trades for round lots as they occur. Remember that one round lot is always 100 shares unless otherwise indicated.

EXAMPLE   Let's look at the tape as it displays trades for various securities just after the market opens:

Open......KO44.05...10s.T24.02...99s.C.46.04...12,000s ABC.34.20...

The above tape reports the following:

- 100 shares of Coca Cola traded at 44.05.

- 1,000 shares of AT&T traded at 24.02.

- 9,900 shares of Citi Group traded at 46.04.

- 12,000 shares of ABC traded at 34.20.

Note: For trades in excess of 10,000 shares, the entire volume will be reported on the tape.

Let's look at another tape:

X 15s24 .24...MCD27 .05...XYZ prC 5s/s.24.04...

The above trade reports the following:

- 1,500 shares of USX traded at 24 followed by 100 shares of USX at 24.

- 100 shares of McDonalds traded at 27 followed by 100 shares at 27.05.

- 50 shares of XYZ preferred C traded at 24.04.

Note: The s/s indicates that a round lot for XYZ prC is 10 shares.

The tape can display other information and qualifiers relating to the trades reported, such as:

- SLD: A trade reported late or out of sequence

- Halt: A security that has been halted from trading

- OPD: The opening print for the security after a delayed opening or after a halt

- Pr: Preferred stock

- R/T: Rights

- W/S: Warrants

During active or fast market conditions the tape may enact one or more of the following conditions:

- Digits and volume deleted

- Repeat prices omitted

- Minimum prices omitted

During fast market conditions when digits and volume have been deleted, a trade for 500 shares of XYZ at 46.50 would appear as: XYZ6.50. When repeat prices have been omitted, only trades that differ in price from the last transaction will be displayed. When minimum price variations have been omitted, only trades that differ by the minimum increment will be displayed.

BROKER VS. DEALER

The term *broker dealer* actually refers to the two capacities in which a firm may act when executing a transaction. When a firm is acting as a broker, it is acting as the customer's agent and is merely executing the customer's order for a fee known as a commission. The role of the broker is simply to find someone willing to buy the investor's securities if the customer is selling or to find someone willing to sell the securities if the customer is seeking to buy. The firm acts as a dealer when it participates in the transaction by taking the opposite side of the trade. For example, the firm may fill a customer's buy order by selling the securities to the customer from the firm's own account or the dealer may fill the customer's sell order by buying the securities for its own account. A brokerage firm is always acting as a dealer or in a principal capacity when it is making markets over the counter.

Broker	Dealer
Executes customers' orders	Participates in the trade as a principal
Charges a commission	Charges a markup or markdown
Must disclose the amount of the commission	Makes a market in the security Must disclose the fact that it is a market maker, but not the amount of the markup or markdown

FINRA 5% MARKUP POLICY

FINRA has set a guideline to ensure that the prices investors pay and receive for securities are reasonably related to the market for the securities. As a general rule, FINRA considers a charge of 5% to be reasonable. The 5% policy is a guideline, not a rule. Factors that go toward what is considered reasonable are:

- The price of the security
- The value of the transaction
- The type of security
- The value of the member's services
- Execution expenses

When a customer is executing an order for a low priced or low total dollar amount, a firm's minimum commission may be greater than 5% of the transaction.

| EXAMPLE | A customer wants to purchase 1,000 shares of XYZ at $1. If the firm's minimum commission is $100, that would be 10% of the trade. But in this case it would be okay. |

Stocks generally carry a higher degree of risk than bonds and, as a result, stocks justify a higher commission or profit to the dealer. Full-service firms may be able to justify a larger commission simply based on the value of the services they provide.

MARKUPS/MARKDOWNS WHEN ACTING AS A PRINCIPAL

A firm that executes customer orders on a principal basis is entitled to a profit on those transactions. If the firm is selling the security to the customer, it will charge the customer a markup. In the case of the firm buying the securities from the customer, it will charge the customer a markdown. The amount of the markup or markdown that a firm charges the customer is based on the inside market for the security.

| EXAMPLE | Let's assume that the brokerage firm is a market maker in ABCD. In the morning, the firm purchased shares of ABCD for its own account at 9.50. The stock has been trading higher all day and is now quoted as follows: |

Bid	Ask
10.00	10.05

If a customer wants to purchase 100 shares ABCD from the dealer in the above example, the customer's markup would be based on the current offering price of 10.05. As a result, the maximum amount the firm could charge the customer for the stock would be 10.552 per share, or $1,055.20 for the entire order, which would include a 5% markup. Notice that the markup to the customer did not take into consideration the firm's actual cost.

If a customer wanted to sell 100 shares of ABCD using the above quote, the minimum proceeds to the customer would be 9.50 per share, or $950 for entire order, which would include a 5% markdown.

To determine the maximum or minimum prices for a customer, use the following:

- 105% of the offer price for customers who are purchasing the security

- 95% of the bid price for customers who are selling the security

When determining the amount of the markup or markdown, the following are excluded:

- The firm's actual cost

- The firm's quote if it is a market maker in the security

RISKLESS PRINCIPAL TRANSACTIONS

If a brokerage firm receives a customer order to buy or sell a security and the firm does not have an inventory position in the security, the firm may still elect to execute the order on a principal basis. If the firm elects to execute the order on a principal basis, this is known as a riskless principal transaction. Because the dealer is only taking a position in the security to fill the customer's order, the dealer is not taking on any risk. As a result, the markup or markdown on riskless transactions is based on the dealer's actual cost, not on the inside market. Let's look at an example:

EXAMPLE

Bid	Ask
10.00	10.05

A customer wants to purchase 100 shares of ABCD from the dealer, and the dealer executes the order on a principal basis by purchasing the shares for its own account at 10.02, only to immediately resell the stock to the customer. The markup in this case must be based on the dealer's actual cost of 10.02, and the maximum the dealer could charge the customer would be 10.521 per share, or $1,052.10 for the entire order.

PROCEEDS TRANSACTIONS

In a proceeds transaction, the customer sells a security and uses the proceeds from that sale to purchase another security on the same day. FINRA's 5% policy states that a firm may only charge the customer a combined commission or markup and markdown of 5% for both transactions, not 5% on each.

ARBITRAGE

Arbitrage is an investment strategy used to take advantage of market inefficiencies and to profit from the price discrepancies that result from those inefficiencies. There are three types of arbitrage. They are:

1. Market arbitrage
2. Security arbitrage
3. Risk arbitrage

Market arbitrage: Securities that trade in more than one market will sometimes be quoted and traded at different prices. Market arbitrage consists of the simultaneous purchase and sale of the same security in two different markets to take advantage of the price discrepancy.

Security arbitrage: Securities that give the holder the right to convert or exercise the security into the underlying stock may be purchased or sold to take advantage of price discrepancies between that security and the underlying common stock. Securities arbitrage consists of the purchase or sale of one security and the simultaneous purchase or sale of the underlying security.

Risk arbitrage: Risk arbitrage tries to take advantage of the price discrepancies that come about as a result of a takeover. A risk arbitrageur will short the stock of the acquiring company and purchase the stock of the company being acquired.

Pretest

THE ROLE OF BROKER DEALERS AND NASDAQ

la.finra.bkr.deal.nasdaq.001_1811

1. When making markets over the counter, the firm is acting in what capacity?

   a. Dealer.

   b. Both.

   c. Neither.

   d. Broker.

la.finra.bkr.deal.nasdaq.002_1811

2. Your brokerage firm acts as a market maker for several high-volume stocks that are quoted on the Nasdaq. What is the firm's consideration for being a market maker?

   a. Commission.

   b. Fees.

   c. Spread.

   d. 5%.

Options, Investment Companies, Variable Annuities, and Retirement Plans

Option Basics

INTRODUCTION

Learning Objective Statements

Differentiate the rights and obligations of puts and calls for the buyer and seller of the option.

Calculate the intrinsic value and time value of an option.

Determine the maximum gain loss and breakeven for option positions.

List the required disclosures for option account approval.

Describe the role of the Options Clearing Corporation.

Select the best option position based on market opinion.

An option is a contract between two parties that determines the time and price at which a stock may be bought or sold. The two parties to the contract are the buyer and the seller. The buyer of the option pays money, known as the option's premium, to the seller. For this premium, the buyer obtains a right to buy or sell the stock depending on what type of option is involved in the transaction. The seller, because of receiving the premium from the buyer, now has an obligation to perform under that contract. Depending on the option involved, the seller may have an obligation to buy or sell the stock.

OPTION CLASSIFICATION

Options are classified as to their type, class, and series. There are two types of options:

1. Calls
2. Puts

CALL OPTIONS

A call option gives the buyer the right to buy or to "call" the stock from the option seller at a specific price for a certain period of time. The sale of a call option obligates the seller to deliver or sell that stock to the buyer at that specific price for a certain period of time.

PUT OPTIONS

A put option gives the buyer the right to sell or to "put" the stock to the seller at a specific price for a certain period of time. The sale of a put option obligates the seller to buy the stock from the buyer at that specific price for a certain period of time.

OPTION CLASSES

An option class consists of all options of the same type for the same underlying stock.

For example, all XYZ calls would be one class of options and all XYZ puts would be another class of option.

Class 1	Class 2
XYZ June 50 calls	XYZ June 50 puts
XYZ June 55 calls	XYZ June 55 puts
XYZ July 50 calls	XYZ July 50 puts
XYZ July 55 calls	XYZ July 55 puts
XYZ August 50 calls	XYZ August 50 puts

OPTION SERIES

An option series is the most specific classification of options and consists of only options of the same class with the same exercise price and expiration month. For example, all XYZ June 50 calls would be one series of options and all XYZ June 55 calls would be another series of options.

BULLISH VS. BEARISH

Option investors will seek to establish positions based on their market attitude. Option investors are either bullish or bearish.

BULLISH

Investors who believe that a stock price will increase over time are said to be bullish. Investors who buy calls are bullish on the underlying stock. That is, they believe that the stock price will rise and have paid for the right to purchase the stock at a specific price known as the exercise price or strike price. An investor who has sold puts is also considered to be bullish on the stock. The seller of a put has an obligation to buy the stock and, therefore, believes that the stock price will rise.

BEARISH

Investors who believe that a stock price will decline are said to be bearish. The seller of a call has an obligation to sell the stock to the purchaser at a specified price and believes that the stock price will fall and is therefore bearish. The buyer of a put wants the price to drop so he or she can sell the stock at a higher price to the seller of the put contract. An investor who has bought puts is also considered to be bearish on the stock.

	Calls	Puts
	Bullish	Bearish
Buyers	Have right to buy stock; want stock price to rise	Have right to sell stock; want stock price to fall
	Bearish	Bullish
Sellers	Have obligation to sell stock; want stock price to fall	Have obligation to buy stock; want stock price to rise

Buyer vs. Seller

Buyer		Seller
Owner	**Known as**	Writer
Long	**Known as**	Short
Rights	**Has**	Obligations
Maximum speculative profit	**Objective**	Premium income
With an opening purchase	**Enters the contract**	With an opening sale
Exercise	**Wants the option to**	Expire

POSSIBLE OUTCOMES FOR AN OPTION

EXERCISED

If the option is exercised, the buyer has elected to exercise his or her rights to buy or sell the stock depending on the type of option involved. Exercising an option obligates the seller to perform under the contract.

SOLD

Most individual investors elect to sell their rights to another investor rather than exercise their rights. The investor who buys the option from them will acquire all the rights of the original purchaser.

EXPIRE

If the option expires, the buyer has elected not to exercise the right and the seller of the option is relieved of the obligation to perform.

EXERCISE PRICE

The exercise price is the price at which an option buyer may buy or sell the underlying stock depending on the type of option involved in the transaction. The exercise price is also known as the strike price.

CHARACTERISTICS OF ALL OPTIONS

All standardized option contracts are issued and their performance is guaranteed by the Options Clearing Corporation (OCC). Standardized options trade on the exchanges such as the Chicago Board Options Exchange and the American Stock Exchange.

All option contracts are for one round lot of the underlying stock or 100 shares. To determine the amount that an investor either paid or received for the contract, take the premium and multiply it by 100. If an investor paid $4 for 1 KLM August 70 call, they paid $400 for the right to buy 100 shares of KLM at $70 per share until August. If another investor paid $2 for 1 JTJ May 50 put, they paid $200 for the right to sell 100 shares of JTJ at $50 until May.

MANAGING AN OPTION POSITION

In an option trade, both the buyer and seller establish the position with an opening transaction. The buyer has an opening purchase and the seller has an opening sale. To exit the option position, an investor must close out the position. The buyer of the option may exit the position through:

- A closing sale.

- Exercising the option.

- Allowing the option to expire.

The seller of an option may exit or close out the position through:

- A closing purchase.

- Having the option exercised or assigned to them.

- Allowing the option to expire.

Most individual investors do not exercise their options and will simply buy and sell options in much the same way as they would buy or sell other securities.

BUYING CALLS

An investor who purchases a call believes that the underlying stock price will rise and that they will be able to profit from the price appreciation by purchasing calls. An investor who purchases a call can control the underlying stock and profit from its appreciation while limiting the loss to the amount of the premium paid for the calls. Buying calls allows the investor to maximize leverage and perhaps realize a more significant percentage return based on their investment. When looking to establish a position, the buyer must determine his or her:

- Maximum gain.

- Maximum loss.

- Breakeven.

MAXIMUM GAIN LONG CALLS

When an investor has a long call position, the maximum gain is always unlimited. The investor profits from a rise in the stock price. Because there is no limit to how high a stock price may rise, the maximum gain is unlimited just as if purchasing the stock.

MAXIMUM LOSS LONG CALLS

Whenever an investor is long or owns a stock, the maximum loss is always limited to the amount invested. When an investor purchases a call option, the amount paid for the option or the premium is always going to be the maximum loss.

DETERMINING THE BREAKEVEN FOR LONG CALLS

An investor who has purchased calls must determine where the stock price must be at expiration in order for the investor to break even on the transaction. An investor who has purchased calls pays the premium to the seller in the hopes that the stock price will rise. The stock must appreciate by enough to cover the cost of the investor's option premium in order for them to break even at expiration. To determine an investor's breakeven point on a long call, use the following formula:

breakeven = strike price + premium

EXAMPLE   An investor establlishes the following option position:

Long 1 XYZ May 30 call at 3

The investor's maximum gain, maximum loss, and breakeven are:

Maximum gain: unlimited
Maximum loss: $300 (amount of the premium paid)
Breakeven: $33 = 30 + 3 (strike price + premium)

If at expiration XYZ is at exactly $33 per share and the investor sells or exercises the option, he or she will break even excluding transactions costs.

SELLING CALLS

An investor who sells a call believes that the underlying stock price will fall and that he will be able to profit from a decline in the stock price by selling calls. An investor who sells a call is obligated to deliver the underlying stock if the buyer decides to exercise the option. When looking to establish a position, the seller must determine the:

- Maximum gain.
- Maximum loss.
- Breakeven.

MAXIMUM GAIN SHORT CALLS

For an investor who has sold uncovered or naked calls, maximum gain is always limited to the amount of the premium the investor received when he sold the calls.

MAXIMUM LOSS SHORT CALLS

An investor who has sold uncovered or naked calls does not own the underlying stock and, as a result, has unlimited risk and the potential for an unlimited loss. The seller of the calls is subject to a loss if the stock price increases. Because there is no limit to how high a stock price may rise, there is no limit to the amount of loss.

DETERMINING THE BREAKEVEN FOR SHORT CALLS

An investor who has sold calls must determine where the stock price must be at expiration in order for the investor to break even on the transaction. An investor who has sold calls has received the premium from the buyer in the hopes that the stock price will fall. If the stock appreciates, the investor may begin to lose money. The stock price may appreciate by the amount of the option premium received and the investor will still break even at expiration. To determine an investor's breakeven point on a short call, use the following formula:

breakeven = strike price + premium

EXAMPLE

An investor establishes the following option position:

Short 1 XYZ May 30 call at 3

The investor's maximum gain, maximum loss, and breakeven are:

Maximum gain: $300 (amount of the premium received)
Maximum loss: Unlimited
Breakeven: $33 = 30 + 3 (strike price + premium)

If at expiration XYZ is at exactly $33 per share and the investor closes out the transaction with a closing purchase or has the option exercised against her, the investor will break even excluding transactions costs.

Notice the relationship between the buyer and the seller:

	Call Buyer	Call Seller
Maximum gain	Unlimited	Premium received
Maximum loss	Premium paid	Unlimited
Breakeven	Strike price + premium	Strike price + premium
Wants option to	Exercise	Expire

Because an option is a two-party contract, the buyer's maximum gain is the seller's maximum loss and the buyer's maximum loss is the seller's maximum gain. Both the buyer and the seller will break even at the same point.

BUYING PUTS

An investor who purchases a put believes that the underlying stock price will fall and that he or she will be able to profit from a decline in the stock price by purchasing puts. An investor who purchases a put can control the underlying stock and profit from its price decline while limiting the loss to the amount of the premium paid for the puts. Buying puts allows the investor to maximize the leverage while limiting losses and the investor may realize a more significant percentage return based on investment. When looking to establish a position, the buyer must determine the:

- Maximum gain.
- Maximum loss.
- Breakeven.

MAXIMUM GAIN LONG PUTS

An investor who has purchased a put believes that the stock price will fall. There is, however, a limit to how far a stock price may decline. A stock price may never fall below zero. As a result, the investor who believes that the stock price will fall has a limited maximum gain. To determine the maximum gain for the buyer of a put, use the following formula:

maximum gain = strike price − premium

MAXIMUM LOSS LONG PUTS

Whenever an investor is long or owns a stock, the maximum loss is always limited to the amount invested. When an investor purchases a put option, the amount he or she pays for the option or premium is always going to be the maximum loss.

DETERMINING THE BREAKEVEN FOR LONG PUTS

Whenever an investor has purchased a put, he or she believes that the stock price will decline. In order for the investor to break even on the transaction, the stock price must fall by enough to offset the amount of the premium paid for the option. At expiration, the investor will break even at the following point:

breakeven = strike price − premium

EXAMPLE

An investor establishes the following option position:

Long 1 XYZ May 30 put at 4

The investor's maximum gain, maximum loss, and breakeven are:

Maximum gain: $26 or $2,600 for the whole position
(strike price − premium)
Maximum loss: $400 (amount of the premium paid)
Breakeven: $26 = 30 − 4 (strike price − premium)
If XYZ is at exactly $26 per share at expiration and the investor sells or exercises their option, they will break even excluding transactions costs.

SELLING PUTS

An investor who sells a put believes that the underlying stock price will rise and that he or she will be able to profit from a rise in the stock price by selling puts. An investor who sells a put is obligated to purchase the underlying stock if the buyer decides to exercise the option. When looking to establish a position, the seller must determine the:

- Maximum gain.
- Maximum loss.
- Breakeven.

MAXIMUM GAIN SHORT PUTS

For an investor who has sold uncovered or naked puts, maximum gain is always limited to the amount of the premium received when the puts were sold.

MAXIMUM LOSS SHORT PUTS

An investor who has sold a put believes that the stock price will rise. There is, however, a limit to how far a stock price may decline. A stock price may never fall below zero. As a result, the investor who believes that the stock price will rise has a limited maximum loss. The worst thing that can happen for an investor who is short a put is that the stock goes to zero and he is forced to purchase it at the strike price from the owner of the put. To determine the maximum loss for the seller of a put, use the following formula:

maximum loss = strike price – premium

DETERMINING THE BREAKEVEN FOR SHORT PUTS

Whenever an investor has sold a put, she believes that the stock price will rise. If the stock price begins to fall, she becomes subject to loss. In order for the investor to break even on the transaction, the stock price may fall by the amount of the premium she received for the option. At expiration, the investor will break even at the following point:

breakeven = strike price – premium

EXAMPLE   An investor establishes the following option position:

Short 1 XYZ May 30 put at 4

The investor's maximum gain, maximum loss, and breakeven are:

Maximum gain: $400 (amount of the premium received)
Maximum loss: $26 or $2,600 for the whole position
(strike price – premium)
Breakeven: $26 = 30 – 4 (strike price – premium)

If XYZ is at exactly $26 per share at expiration and the investor closes out the position with a closing purchase or has the option exercised against them, they will break even, excluding transactions costs.

Notice the relationship between the buyer and the seller:

	Put Buyer	Put Seller
Maximum gain	Strike price – premium	Premium received
Maximum loss	Premium paid	Strike price – premium
Breakeven	Strike price – premium	Strike price – premium
Wants option to	Exercise	Expire

Because an option is a two-party contract, the buyer's maximum gain is the seller's maximum loss and the buyer's maximum loss is the seller's maximum gain. Both the buyer and the seller will break even at the same point.

OPTION PREMIUMS

The price of an option is known as its premium. Factors that determine the value of an option and, as a result, its premium, are:

- Relationship of the underlying stock price to the option's strike price

- Amount of time to expiration

- Volatility of the underlying stock

- Supply and demand

- Interest rates

An option can be:

- In the money.
- At the money.
- Out of the money.

These terms describe the relationship of the underlying stock to the option's strike price. These terms do not describe how profitable the position is.

IN-THE-MONEY OPTIONS

A call is in the money when the underlying stock price is greater than the call's strike price.

EXAMPLE	An XYZ June 40 call is $2 in the money when XYZ is at $42 per share.
	A put is in the money when the underlying stock price is lower than the put's strike price.

EXAMPLE	An ABC October 70 put is $4 in the money when ABC is at $66 per share. It would only make sense to exercise an option if it was in the money.

AT-THE-MONEY OPTIONS

Both puts and calls are at the money when the underlying stock price equals the options exercise price.

EXAMPLE	If FDR is trading at $60 per share, all of the FDR 60 calls and all of the FDR 60 puts will be at the money.

OUT-OF-THE-MONEY OPTIONS

A call is out of the money when the underlying stock price is lower than the option's strike price.

EXAMPLE

An ABC November 25 call is out of the money when ABC is trading at $22 per share.

A put option is out of the money when the underlying stock price is above the option's strike price.

EXAMPLE

A KDC December 50 put is out of the money when KDC is trading at $54 per share.

It would not make sense to exercise an out-of-the-money option.

	Calls	Puts
In the money	Stock price > strike price	Stock price < strike price
At the money	Stock price = strike price	Stock price = strike price
Out of the money	Stock price < strike price	Stock price > strike price

INTRINSIC VALUE AND TIME VALUE

An option's total premium is comprised of intrinsic value and time value. An option's intrinsic value is equal to the amount the option is in the money. Time value is the amount by which an option's premium exceeds its intrinsic value. In effect, the time value is the price an investor pays for the opportunity to exercise the option. An option that is out of the money has no intrinsic value; therefore, the entire premium consists of time value.

EXAMPLE

An XYZ June 40 call is trading at $2 when XYZ is trading at $37 per share. The June 40 call is out of the money and has no intrinsic value; therefore, the entire $2 premium consists of time value. If an XYZ June 40 put is trading at $3 when XYZ is at $44 dollars per share, the entire $3 is time value.

If, in this example, the options were in the money and the premium exceeded the intrinsic value of the option, the remaining premium would be time value.

EXAMPLE

An XYZ June 40 call is trading at $5 when XYZ is trading at $42 per share. The June 40 call is in the money and has $2 in intrinsic value; therefore, the rest of the premium consists of the time value of $3. If an XYZ June 40 put is trading at $4 when XYZ is at $39, the put is in the money by $1 and the rest of the premium or $3 is time value.

Pretest

OPTION BASICS

la.finra.opt.bas.001_1811

1. Which of the following are true about an option?

   I. It is a contract between two parties that determines the time and place at which a security may be bought or sold.

   II. The two parties are known as the buyer and the seller. The money paid by the buyer of the option is known as the option's premium.

   III. The buyer has bought the right to buy or sell the security depending on the type of option.

   IV. The seller has an obligation to perform under the contract, possibly to buy or sell the stock depending on the option involved.

   a. I, III, and IV.

   b. I, II, III, and IV.

   c. I, II, and III.

   d. II, III, and IV.

la.finra.opt.bas.002_1811

2. An investor buys 10 XYZ Nov 75 calls at 4:10 on Monday, May 11. The trade will settle on:

   a. Thursday, May 14.

   b. Tuesday, May 12.

   c. Monday, May 11.

   d. Monday, May 18.

la.finra.opt.bas.003_1811

3. Which of the following issues standardized options?

   a. Exchanges.

   b. OCC.

   c. Company.

   d. Nasdaq.

sa.finra.opt.bas.001_1811

4. Which of the following are bearish?

   I. Call seller.

   II. Put seller.

   III. Call buyer.

   IV. Put buyer.

   a. II and III.

   b. II and IV.

   c. I and IV.

   d. I and II.

sa.finra.opt.bas.002_1811

5. The OCC is:

   a. Options Clearing Corporation.

   b. Options Counseling Committee.

   c. Options and Claims Corporation.

   d. Options Clearing Committee.

Using Options to Hedge a Position and Exercising Options

INTRODUCTION

Learning Objective Statements

Select the best option strategy to hedge a stock position.

Employ appropriate index option strategies.

Detail the impact of option exercise and expiration.

Describe the role of the Options Clearing Corporation.

Many investors use options to hedge a position that they have established in the underlying stock. Options can be used to guard against a loss or to protect a profit the investor has in a position. Options in this case operate like an insurance policy for the investor.

LONG STOCK LONG PUTS/MARRIED PUTS

An investor who is long stock and wishes to protect the position from downside risk receives the most protection by purchasing a protective put. By purchasing the put, the investor has locks in or sets a minimum sale price that he or she will receive in the event of the stock's decline for the life of the put. The minimum sale price in this case is equal to the strike price of the put. Long puts can be used with long stock to guard against a loss or to protect an unrealized profit. However, by purchasing the put, the investor has increased their breakeven point by the amount of the premium paid to purchase the put. When looking to establish a long stock long put position, the investor must determine their:

- Maximum gain.
- Breakeven.
- Maximum loss.

MAXIMUM GAIN LONG STOCK LONG PUTS

An investor who is long stock and long puts has a maximum gain that is unlimited because they own the stock.

BREAKEVEN LONG STOCK LONG PUTS

To determine an investor's breakeven when they have established a long stock long put position, you must add the option premium to the cost of the stock.

breakeven = stock price + premium

 TAKENOTE!

For the SIE exam it is important that you understand how options are used as a hedge for an underlying stock position. The examples are included to illustrate the concepts; most students will not be required to calculate the math.

EXAMPLE   An investor establishes the following position:

Long 100 XYZ at 55
Long 1 XYZ June 55 put at 3

The investor breaks even if the stock goes to $58. The stock price has to appreciate by enough to offset the amount of the premium that the investor paid for the option. If, at expiration, the stock is at $58 per share and the put expires, the investor will have broken even, excluding transaction costs.

MAXIMUM LOSS LONG STOCK LONG PUTS

In order to determine an investor's maximum loss when they have established a long stock long put position, you must first determine the breakeven as just outlined. Once you have determined the breakeven, use the following formula:

maximum loss = breakeven – strike price

Let's take another look at the previous example, only this time using it to determine the investor's maximum loss.

EXAMPLE

An investor establishes the following position:

Long 100 XYZ at 55
Long 1 XYZ June 55 put at 3

It has already been determined that the investor will break even if the stock goes to $58. To determine the maximum loss, subtract the put's strike price from the investor's breakeven as follows:

58 – 55 = 3

The investor's maximum loss is $3 per share or $300 for the entire position. Notice that the option's premium is the investor's maximum loss. When the purchase price of the stock and the strike price of the put are the same, the investor's maximum loss is equal to the premium paid for the option.

Here is another example where the investor's purchase price is different from the strike price of the put.

EXAMPLE

An investor establishes the following position:

Long 100 XYZ at 58
Long 1 XYZ June 55 put at 2

In order to find the investor's maximum loss, first determine the breakeven. This investor will break even if the stock goes to $60, found by adding the stock price to the premium the investor paid for the put. To find the maximum loss, subtract the put's strike price from the breakeven:

60 – 55 = 5

The investor's maximum loss on this position is $5 per share or $500 for the entire position.

An investor who is long stock and long puts has limited potential losses and received the maximum possible protection while retaining all of the appreciation potential.

LONG STOCK SHORT CALLS/COVERED CALLS

An investor who is long stock can receive some partial downside protection and generate some additional income by selling calls against the stock owned. The investor will receive downside protection or will hedge the position by the amount of the premium received from the sale of the call. Although the investor will receive partial downside protection, he or she also gives up any appreciation potential above the call's strike price. An investor who is going to establish a covered call position must determine his or her:

- Breakeven.

- Maximum gain.

- Maximum loss.

BREAKEVEN LONG STOCK SHORT CALLS

By selling the calls, the investor has lowered the breakeven on the stock by the amount of the premium received from the sale of the call. To determine the investor's breakeven in this case, the price to which the stock can fall, use the following formula:

purchase price of the stock – premium received

EXAMPLE

An investor establishes the following position:
    Long 100 ABC at 65
    Short 1 ABC June 65 call at 4
Using the formula, we get:

65 – 4 = 61

The stock price in this case can fall to $61 and the investor will still break even.

MAXIMUM GAIN LONG STOCK SHORT CALLS

Because the investor has sold call options on the stock owned, he or she has limited the amount of gain. Any appreciation of the stock beyond the call's strike price belongs to the investor who purchased the call. To determine an investor's maximum gain on a long stock short call position, use the following formula:

maximum gain = strike price – breakeven

Now use the same example to determine the investor's maximum gain.

EXAMPLE

An investor establishes the following position:

Long 100 ABC at 65
Short 1 ABC June 65 call at 4

Using this formula, we get:

65 – 61 = $4

The investor's maximum gain is $4 per share or $400 for the entire position. Notice that because the purchase price of the stock and the strike price of the call are the same, the investor's maximum gain is equal to the amount of the premium received on the sale of the call.

Here is an example in which the strike price and the purchase price for the stock are different.

EXAMPLE

An investor establishes the following position:

Long 100 ABC at 65
Short 1 ABC June 70 call at 2

The investor will break even at $63, found by subtracting the premium received from the investor's purchase price for the stock. To determine the maximum gain, subtract the breakeven from the strike price and we get:

70 – 63 = 7

The investor's maximum gain is $7 per share or $700 for the entire position.

MAXIMUM LOSS LONG STOCK SHORT CALLS

An investor who has sold covered calls has only received partial downside protection in the amount of the premium received. As a result, the investor is still subject to a significant loss in the event of an extreme downside move in the stock price. To determine an investor's maximum loss when they are long stock and short calls, use the following formula:

maximum loss = breakeven − 0

Said another way, an investor is subject to a loss equal to the breakeven price per share. Using the same example, we get:

EXAMPLE

An investor establishes the following position:

Long 100 ABC at 65
Short 1 ABC June 70 call at 2

The investor will break even at $63, found by subtracting the premium received from the investor's purchase price for the stock. To determine the maximum loss, we only need to look at the breakeven and we get a maximum loss of $63 per share or $6,300 for the entire position. The investor will realize the maximum loss if the stock goes to zero.

SHORT STOCK LONG CALLS

An investor who sells stock short believes that he or she can profit from a fall in the stock price by selling it high and repurchasing it cheaper. An investor who has sold stock short is subject to an unlimited loss if the stock price should begin to rise. Once again there is no limit to how high a stock price may rise. An investor who has sold stock short would receive the most protection by purchasing a call. A long call could be used to guard against a loss or to protect a profit on a short stock position. By purchasing the call, the investor has set the maximum price that they will have to pay to repurchase the stock for the life of the option. Before establishing a short stock long call position, the investor will have to determine the:

- Breakeven.
- Maximum gain.
- Maximum loss.

DETERMINING THE BREAKEVEN SHORT STOCK LONG CALLS

An investor who has sold stock short will profit from a fall in the stock price. When an investor has purchased a call to protect the position, the stock price must fall by enough to offset the premium the investor paid for the call. To determine the breakeven for a short stock long call position, use the following formula:

breakeven = stock price – premium

EXAMPLE

An investor establishes the following position:

> Short 100 ABC at 60
> Long 1 ABC October 60 call at 2

Using the formula, we get:

60 – 2 = 58

The stock would have to fall to $58 by expiration in order for the investor to break even.

MAXIMUM GAIN SHORT STOCK LONG CALLS

The maximum gain on the short sale of stock is always limited because a stock cannot fall below zero. When an investor has a short stock long call position, the maximum gain is found by using the following formula:

maximum gain = breakeven – 0

Said another way, the investor's maximum gain per share would be equal to their break-even price per share. Using the same example, we get:

EXAMPLE

An investor establishes the following position:

> Short 100 ABC at 60
> Long 1 ABC October 60 call at 2

Using this formula, we get:

58 – 0 = 58

If the stock falls to $0 by expiration, the investor would realize the maximum gain of $58 per share or $5,800 for the entire position.

MAXIMUM LOSS SHORT STOCK LONG CALLS

An investor who has sold stock short and has purchased a call to protect the position is only subject to a loss up to the strike price of the call. In order to determine the investor's maximum loss, use the following formula:

maximum loss = strike price – breakeven

Using the same example, we get the following:

EXAMPLE

An investor establishes the following position:

> Short 100 ABC at 60
> Long 1 ABC October 60 call at 2

60 – 58 = 2

The investor is subject to a loss of $2 per share or $200 for the entire position. Notice that the price at which the investor sold the stock short and the strike price of the call are the same. As a result, the investor has set a maximum repurchase price equal to the price at which he or she sold the stock short. The investor's maximum loss when the sale price and strike price are the same is the amount of the premium that the investor paid for the call.

Here's a position where the sale price of the stock and strike price of the option are different.

EXAMPLE

An investor establishes the following position:

> Short 100 ABC at 56
> Long 1 ABC October 60 call at 2

This investor will break even at $54 per share. To determine the maximum loss, subtract the breakeven from the strike price of the option.

60 – 54 = 6

The investor is subject to a loss of $6 per share or $600 for the entire position.

SHORT STOCK SHORT PUTS

An investor who has sold stock short can receive some protection and generate premium income by selling puts against the short stock position. Selling puts against a short stock position only partially hedges the unlimited upside risk associated with any short sale of stock. Additionally, the investor, in exchange for the premium received for the sale of the put, has further limited the maximum gain. Before entering a short stock short put position, an investor must determine the:

- Breakeven.

- Maximum gain.

- Maximum loss.

BREAKEVEN SHORT STOCK SHORT PUTS

An investor who has sold stock short and sold puts against the position is subject to a loss if the stock price begins to rise. To determine how high a stock price could rise after establishing a short stock short put position and still allow the investor to break even, use the following formula:

breakeven = stock price + premium

EXAMPLE

An investor establishes the following position:

> Short 100 ABC at 55
> Short 1 ABC November 55 put at 4

Using the formula, we get:

55 + 4 = 59

In this case, the stock could rise to $59 by expiration and still allow the investor to break even, excluding transaction costs.

MAXIMUM GAIN SHORT STOCK SHORT PUTS

An investor who has established a short stock short put position has limited the amount of the gain even further by selling puts, because the investor will be required to purchase the shares at the put's strike price if the stock declines.

To determine the investor's maximum gain, use the following formula:

maximum gain = breakeven – strike price

EXAMPLE   An investor establishes the following position:

Short 100 ABC at 55
Short 1 ABC November 55 put at 4

The investor will break even at 59 found by adding the stock price of 55 and the option premium of 4 together.

Using this formula, we get:

59 – 55 = 4

The investor's maximum gain in this case is $4 per share or $400 for the entire position. The investor received a total of $59 per share by establishing the position. If the stock falls to zero, they still would be required to repurchase the shares at 55 under the terms of the put contract. Notice that the sales price and the put's exercise price are the same and the amount of the investor's maximum gain is equal to the amount of the premium received.

Let's look at a position where the sale price of the stock and the strike price of the put are different.

EXAMPLE   An investor establishes the following position:

Short 100 XYZ at 60
Short 1 XYZ November 55 put at 4

The investor will break even at 64; $64 dollars per share are the total proceeds received by the investor for establishing the position. To determine the maximum gain using the previous formula, we get:

64 – 55 = 9

The investor's maximum gain is $9 per share or $900 for the total position.

MAXIMUM LOSS SHORT STOCK SHORT PUTS

An investor who has sold puts against the short stock position has only limited the loss by the amount of the premium received from the sale of the put. As a result, the investor's loss in a short stock short put position is still unlimited.

Underlying Position	Most Protection	Some Protection and Income
Long stock	Long puts	Short calls
Short stock	Long calls	Short puts

 **FOCUSPOINT**

It's important to note that anytime an investor wants the most protection, he is going to buy the hedge. If the investor wants some protection and income, he will sell the hedge.

INDEX OPTIONS

In an effort to gauge the market's overall performance, industry participants developed indexes. Two of the most widely followed indexes are the Dow Jones Industrial Average (DJIA) and the Standard and Poor's 500 (S&P 500). There are two types of indexes: broad-based indexes, such as the S&P 500 (SPX) or S&P 100 (OEX), that track a large number of stocks, and narrow indexes, such as the semiconductor index (SOX), that track only a particular industry.

INDEX OPTION SETTLEMENT

Investors who want to take a position in index options purchase calls and puts just like investors in stock options. However, an index is not a security, and it cannot be physically delivered if the option is exercised. An investor cannot call the index away from someone who is short a call and cannot put an index to an investor who is short a put. As a result, the exercise of index options is settled in cash. Option holders who elect to exercise the option have their account credited the in-the-money amount, in cash. The amount that will be credited to their account will be the in-the-money amount at the close of the market on the day of exercise. To determine the option's premium and the amount of money to be delivered upon the exercise index options, use 100 as a multiplier.

EXAMPLE

An investor establishes the following position:

Long 1 OEX March 550 call at $4

The investor has purchased an S&P 100 (OEX) 550 call for $4. The contract value is 55,000, and the total premium paid by the investor is $400. The investor is bullish on the overall market and believes the market will rise and the OEX will be higher than 550 by expiration. If at expiration the index is at 556.20, the investor's account will be credited the in-the-money amount, as follows:

556.20
$\underline{-550.00}$
6.20
$\underline{\times 100}$
$ 620.00

The investor's account will be credited $620. Because the investor paid $400 for the option, the investor's profit is $220.

EXERCISING AN INDEX OPTION

It is usually not wise to exercise an index option prior to its expiration because the investor loses any amount of time value contained in the option's premium. Additionally, if the investor exercises an option at 10:00 a.m., the investor will receive the in-the-money amount as of the close of the market that day. It is quite possible for an investor to exercise an in-the-money option at 10:00 a.m. and have the option be out of the money at the close of business because the market moved against the investor. In both scenarios, it is better to sell the option.

INDEX OPTION POSITIONS

An investor may establish all of the following positions using index options:

- Long calls and puts

- Short calls and puts

- Long spreads and straddles

- Short spreads and straddles

- Long and short combinations

Index options may also be used to:

- Speculate on the direction of the market.

- Protect a long portfolio by purchasing puts or selling calls.

- Protect a short portfolio by purchasing calls or selling puts.

THE OPTION CLEARING CORPORATION

The Option Clearing Corporation (OCC) was created and is owned by the exchanges that trade options. The OCC issues all standardized options and guarantees their performance. The OCC does not guarantee a customer against loss; it only guarantees the option's performance. The OCC guarantees that if an investor who is short an option is unable to perform the obligation under the contract, the investor who is exercising the contract will still be able to do so without any delay. Without this performance guarantee, the trading of standardized options would be impossible. The OCC issues option contracts the day after the trade date, and all standardized options settle on the next business day or trade date plus one. When an investor closes out its position through either a closing purchase or sale, the OCC eliminates the closing investor's obligations or rights from its books. All standardized options of the same series are interchangeable or fungible. For example, all XYZ April 50 calls are the same. In order to meet the prospectus requirements of the Securities Act of 1933, the OCC publishes a disclosure document known as the Characteristics and Risks of Standardized Options. All option investors must be given this document prior to or at the time their account is approved for options trading. Should the OCC update the options disclosure document, the updated risk disclosure document must be sent to all investors who transact business in the type of options subject to the update.

EXPIRATION AND EXERCISE

The OCC has set the following rules for stock and narrow-based index options expiration and exercise:

- Options cease trading at 4:00 p.m. EST (3:00 p.m. CST) on the third Friday of each month prior to expiration

- Option holders who wish to exercise their options must do so by 5:30 p.m. EST (4:30 p.m. CST) on the third Friday of each month

- All options expire at 11:59 p.m. EST (10:59 p.m. CST) on the third Friday of each month

- All options held by public customers will automatically be exercised if they are 1 cent in the money

- All options held by broker dealers will automatically be exercised if they are 1 cent in the money

The OCC has set the following rules for broad-based option expiration and exercise:

- Options cease trading at 4:15 p.m. EST (3:15 p.m. CST) on the third Friday of each month prior to expiration

- Option holders who wish to exercise their options must do so by 5:30 p.m. EST (4:30 p.m. CST) on the third Friday of each month

- All options expire at 11:59 p.m. EST (10:59 p.m. CST) on the third Friday of each month

The following rules have been set for foreign currency

- Foreign currency options trade on the Nasdaq/PHLX from 9:30 a.m. to 4:00 p.m. EST

- Options expire at 11:59 p.m. EST on the third Friday of each month

- Position limits are 600,000 contracts on the same side of the market

AMERICAN VS. EUROPEAN EXERCISE

There are two styles of options that trade in the United States: American and European. An American-style option may be exercised by the holder at any time during the life of the contract. A European-style option may only be exercised by the holder at expiration. If an investor who is long an option decides to exercise the option, the OCC will randomly assign the exercise notice to a broker dealer who is short that option. The broker dealer must then assign the exercise notice to a customer who is short that option. The broker dealer may use any fair method for randomly assigning exercise notices. The exercise of a call or put results in the delivery of the underlying stock in two business days. The exercise of an index option results in the cash settlement the next business day.

Pretest

USING OPTIONS TO HEDGE A POSITION AND EXERCISING OPTIONS

la.finra.hedge.pos.001_1811

1. You are long 10,000 shares of XYZ at 42 and are concerned about a market decline; you would like to take in some additional income. You should:

   a. Sell 10 XYZ Oct 45 puts.

   b. Sell 100 XYZ Oct 45 calls.

   c. Sell 100 XYZ Oct 45 puts.

   d. Sell 10 XYZ Oct 45 calls.

sa.finra.hedge.pos.002_1811

2. An investor is long 1000 shares of OnNet.com at $30 per share. To gain the maximum protection he should:

   a. Sell 10 OnNet June 30 calls.

   b. Sell 10 OnNet June 30 puts.

   c. Buy 10 OnNet June 30 calls.

   d. Buy 10 OnNet June 30 puts.

sa.finra.hedge.pos.003_1811

3. Your customer is long 100 shares of MSFT. The investor wants to protect the position without spending any additional money, what should he do?

   a. Buy a call.

   b. Sell a call.

   c. Sell a put.

   d. Buy a put.

Investment Companies and Mutual Funds

INTRODUCTION

Learning Objective Statements

Detail the features and functions of an investment company.

Compare the characteristics of open-end and closed-end funds.

List the function of each component of investment companies.

Detail how investment company shares are distributed.

In this lesson, we look at how an investment company pools investors' funds in order to purchase a diversified portfolio of securities. It is imperative that all candidates have a complete understanding of how an investment company operates. Some of the focus points:

• Types of investment companies

• Investment company structure

• Investment company registration

• Investment company taxation

• Investment strategies and recommendations

• Investor benefits

INVESTMENT COMPANY PHILOSOPHY

An investment company is organized as either a corporation or as a trust. Individual investor's money is then pooled together in a single account and used to purchase securities that will have the greatest chance of helping the investment company reach its objectives. All investors jointly own the portfolio that is created through these pooled funds and each investor has an undivided interest in the securities. No single shareholder has any right or claim that exceeds the rights or claims of any other shareholder regardless of the size of the investment. Investment companies offer individual investors the opportunity to have their money managed by professionals that may otherwise only offer their services to large institutions. Through diversification, the investor may participate in the future growth or income generated from the large number of different securities contained in the portfolio. Both diversification and professional management should contribute significantly to the attainment of the objectives set forth by the investment company. There are many other features and benefits that may be offered to investors that will be examined later in this lesson.

TYPES OF INVESTMENT COMPANIES

All investment company offerings are subject to the Securities Act of 1933 that requires the investment company to register with the Securities and Exchange Commission and to give all purchasers a prospectus. Investment companies are also all subject to the Investment Company Act of 1940 that sets forth guidelines on how investment companies operate. The Investment Company Act of 1940 breaks down investment companies into three different types:

1. Face-amount company (FAC)
2. Unit investment trust (UIT)
3. Management investment company (mutual funds)

FACE-AMOUNT COMPANY/FACE-AMOUNT CERTIFICATES

An investor may enter into a contract with an issuer of a face-amount certificate to contract to receive a stated or fixed amount of money (the face amount) at a stated date in the future. In exchange for this future sum, the investor must deposit an agreed lump sum or make scheduled installment payments. Face-amount certificates are rarely issued today as most of the tax advantages that the investment once offered have been lost through changes in the tax laws.

UNIT INVESTMENT TRUST (UIT)

A unit investment trust will invest either in a fixed portfolio of securities or in a nonfixed portfolio of securities. A fixed UIT traditionally invests in a large block of government or municipal debt. The bonds are held until maturity and the proceeds distributed to investors in the UIT. Once the proceeds have been distributed to the investors, the UIT has achieved its objective and will cease to exist. A nonfixed UIT purchases mutual fund shares in order to reach a stated objective. A nonfixed UIT is also known as a contractual plan. Both types of UITs are organized as a trust and operate as a holding company for the portfolio. UITs are not actively managed and they do not have a board of directors or investment advisers. Both types of UITs issue units or shares of beneficial interest to investors, which represent as undivided interest in the underlying portfolio of securities. UITs must maintain a secondary market in the units or shares to offer some liquidity to investors.

MANAGEMENT INVESTMENT COMPANIES (MUTUAL FUNDS)

A management investment company employs an investment adviser to manage a diversified portfolio of securities designed to obtain its stated investment objective. The management company may be organized as either an open-end company or as a closed-end company. The main difference between an open-end company and a closed-end company is how the shares are purchased and sold. An open-end company offers new shares to any investor who wants to invest. This is known as a continuous primary offering. Because the offering of new shares is continuous, the capitalization of the open-end fund is unlimited. Stated another way, an open-end mutual fund may raise as much money as investors are willing to put in. An open-end fund must repurchase its own shares from investors who want to redeem them. There is no secondary market for open-end mutual fund shares. The shares must be purchased from the fund company and redeemed to the fund company. A closed-end fund offers common shares to investors through an initial public offering (IPO) just like a stock. Its capitalization is limited to the number of authorized shares that have been approved for sale. Shares of the closed-end fund will trade in the secondary market in investor-to-investor transactions on an exchange or in the over-the-counter market (OTC), just like common shares.

OPEN END VS. CLOSED END

Although both open-end and closed-end funds are designed to achieve their stated investment objectives, the manner in which they operate is different. The following is a side-by-side comparison of the important features of both open-end and closed-end funds and shows how those features differ between the fund types.

Feature	Open End	Closed End
Capitalization	Unlimited continuous primary offering	Single fixed offering through IPO
Investor may purchase	Full and fractional shares	Full shares only
Securities offered	Common shares only	Common and preferred shares and debt securities
Shares purchased and sold	Shares purchased from the fund company and redeemed to the fund company	Shares may be purchased only from the fund company during IPO, then secondary market transactions between investors
Share pricing	Shares priced by formula NAV + SC = POP	Shares priced by supply and demand
Shareholder rights	Dividends and voting	Dividends, voting, and preemptive

DIVERSIFIED VS. NONDIVERSIFIED

Investors in a mutual fund achieve diversification through their investment in the fund. However, in order to determine if the fund itself is a diversified fund, the fund must meet certain requirements. The Investment Company Act of 1940 laid out an asset allocation model that must be followed in order for the fund to call itself a diversified mutual fund. It is known as the 75-5-10 test and the requirements are as follows:

75%: 75% of the fund's assets must be invested in securities of other issuers. Cash and cash equivalents are counted as part of the 75%. A cash equivalent may be a T-bill or a money market instrument.

5%: The investment company may not invest more than 5% of its assets in any one company.

10%: The investment company may not own more than 10% of any company's outstanding voting stock.

EXAMPLE	XYZ fund markets itself as a diversified mutual fund. It has $10,000,000,000 in net assets and the investment adviser thinks that the ABC Company would be a great company to acquire for $300,000,000. Since XYZ markets itself as a diversified mutual fund, they would not be allowed to purchase the company even though the price of $300,000,000 would be less than 5% of the fund's assets. The investment company must meet both the diversification requirements of 5% of assets and 10% of ownership in order to continue to market itself as a diversified mutual fund.

INVESTMENT COMPANY REGISTRATION

Investment companies are regulated by both the Securities Act of 1933 and by the Investment Company Act of 1940. An investment company must register with the SEC if the company operates to own, invest, reinvest, or trade in securities. A company must also register with the SEC as an investment company if the company has 40% or more of its assets invested in securities other than those issued by the U.S. government or one of the company's subsidiaries.

INVESTMENT COMPANY COMPONENTS

Investment companies have several different groups that serve specialized functions. Each of these groups plays a key role in the investment company's operation. They are the:

- Board of directors
- Investment adviser
- Custodian bank
- Transfer agent

BOARD OF DIRECTORS

Management companies have an organizational structure that is similar to that of other companies. The board of directors oversees the company's president and other officers who run the day-to-day operations of the company. The board and the corporate officers concern themselves with the business and administrative functions of the company. They do not manage the investment portfolio. The board of directors:

- Defines investment objectives.
- Hires the investment adviser, custodian bank, and transfer agent.
- Determines what type of funds to offer, that is, growth, income, and so forth.

The board of directors is elected by a vote of the shareholders. The Investment Company Act of 1940 governs the makeup of the board. The Investment Company Act of 1940 requires that a majority or at least 51% of the board be noninterested persons. A noninterested person is a person whose only affiliation with the fund is as a member of the board. Therefore, a maximum of 49% of the board may hold another position within the fund company or may otherwise be interested in the fund.

INVESTMENT ADVISER

The investment company's board of directors hires the investment adviser to manage the fund's portfolio. The investment adviser is a company, not a person, which must also determine the tax consequences of distributions to shareholders and ensure that the investment strategies are in line with the fund's stated investment objectives. The investment adviser's compensation is a percentage of the net assets of the fund, not a percentage of the profits, although performance bonuses are allowed. The investment adviser's fee is typically the largest expense of the fund and the more aggressive the objective, the higher the fee. The investment adviser may not borrow from the fund and may not have any security-related convictions.

CUSTODIAN BANK

The custodian bank or the exchange member broker dealer that has been hired by the investment company physically holds all of the fund's cash and securities. The custodian holds all of the fund's assets for safekeeping and provides other bookkeeping and clerical functions for the investment company, such as maintaining books and records for accumulation plans for investors. All fund assets must be kept segregated from other assets.

The custodian must ensure that only approved persons have access to the account and that all distributions are done in line with SEC guidelines.

TRANSFER AGENT

The transfer agent for the investment company handles the issuance, cancellation, and redemption of fund shares. The transfer agent also handles name changes and may be part of the fund's custodian or a separate company. The transfer agent receives an agreed fee for its services.

Pretest

INVESTMENT COMPANIES AND MUTUAL FUNDS

la.finra.invest.co.mut.001_1811

1. An investor with $20,000 invested in the XYZ growth fund is:

    a. A stockholder in XYZ.

    b. An owner of XYZ.

    c. An owner of an undivided interest in the XYZ growth portfolio.

    d. Both an owner of XYZ and an owner of an undivided interest in the XYZ growth portfolio.

la.finra.invest.co.mut.002_1811

2. The ex-dividend date on a closed-end mutual fund is set by the:

    a. Board of directors.

    b. SEC.

    c. Board of governors.

    d. FINRA/NYSE.

la.finra.invest.co.mut.003_1811

3. A mutual fund has been seeking to attract new customers to invest in its growth fund. They have been running an advertising campaign that markets them as a diversified mutual fund. How much of any one company may they own?

    a. 15%.

    b. 5%.

    c. 10%.

    d. 9%.

la.finra.invest.co.mut.004_1811

4. An investor wires $10,000 into his mutual fund on Tuesday, March 11, and the money is credited to his account at 3 p.m. He will be the owner of record on:

   a. Friday, March 14.

   b. Wednesday, March 12.

   c. Tuesday, March 11.

   d. Tuesday, March 18.

sa.finra.invest.co.mut.001_1811

5. A mutual fund's custodian bank does which of the following?

   a. Holds customers' securities.

   b. Cancels certificates.

   c. Maintains records for accumulation plans.

   d. Issues certificates.

sa.finra.invest.co.mut.002_1811

6. A long-term growth fund has a portfolio turnover ratio of 25%. How often does the fund replace its total holdings?

   a. Every 4 years.

   b. Once a year.

   c. Every 4 months.

   d. Every quarter.

Mutual Fund Investment Objectives Valuation and Sales Charges

INTRODUCTION

Learning Objective Statements

Select the appropriate mutual fund portfolio to reach stated investment objectives.

List factors that impact the net asset value and public offer price.

Analyze sales charges and fees.

Compare breakpoint schedules, rights of accumulation, and combination privileges.

Most mutual funds do not sell shares directly to investors. The distribution of the shares is the responsibility of the underwriter. The underwriter for a mutual fund is also known as the sponsor or distributor. The underwriter is selected by the fund's board of directors and receives a fee in the form of a sales charge for the shares it distributes. As the underwriter receives orders for the mutual fund shares, it purchases the shares directly from the fund at the net asset value (NAV). The sales charge is then added to the NAV as the underwriter's compensation. This process of adding the sales charge to the NAV is responsible for the mutual fund pricing formula, which is NAV + SC = POP.

SELLING GROUP MEMBER

Most brokerage firms maintain selling agreements with mutual fund distributors, which allow them to purchase mutual fund shares at a discount from the public offering price (POP). Selling group members may then sell the mutual fund shares to investors at the POP and earn part of the sales charge. In order to purchase mutual fund shares at a discount from the POP, the selling group member must be a member of FINRA. All non-FINRA members and suspended members must be treated as members of the general public and pay the public offering price.

DISTRIBUTION OF NO-LOAD MUTUAL FUND SHARES

No-load mutual funds do not charge a sales charge to the investors who invest in the mutual fund. Because there is no sales charge, the mutual fund may sell the shares directly to investors at the NAV.

DISTRIBUTION OF MUTUAL FUND SHARES

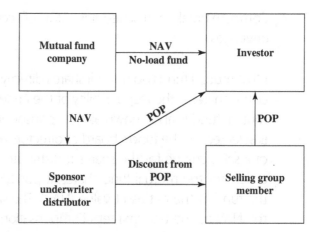

MUTUAL FUND PROSPECTUS

The prospectus is the official offering document for open-end mutual fund shares. The prospectus, or information on where to obtain a prospectus, must be presented to all purchasers of the fund either before or during the sales presentation. The prospectus is the fund's full-disclosure document and provides details regarding:

- Fund's investment objectives

- Sales charges

- Management expenses

- Fund services

- Performance data for the past 1, 5, and 10 years or for the life of the fund

The prospectus, which is given to most investors, is the summary prospectus. If investors want additional information regarding the mutual fund, they may request a statement of additional information. The statement of additional information includes details regarding the following as of the date it was published:

- Fund's securities holdings

- Balance sheet

- Income statement

- Portfolio turnover data

- Compensation paid to the board of directors and investment advisory board

A summary prospectus that contains past performance data is known as an advertising prospectus. Requirements regarding updating and using a mutual fund prospectus are as follows:

A mutual fund prospectus:

- Should be updated by the fund every 12 months.

- Must be updated by the fund every 13 months.

- May be used by a representative for up to 16 months.

- Should be discarded after 16 months from publication.

Mutual funds also are required to disclose either in the prospectus or in its annual report to shareholders:

- A performance comparison graph showing the performance of the fund.

- Names of the officers and directors who are responsible for the portfolio's day-to-day management.

- Disclosure of any factors that materially affected performance over the latest fiscal year.

Mutual funds are required to include summary information at the front of its statutory prospectus. The purpose of this summary information is to clearly convey all of the most pertinent information an investor would require to make an informed decision about the fund. The terms to be detailed in the summary information include the fund's investment objectives, past performance, costs, and the biographical information for the management of the fund. Also covered in the summary information will be the principal investment strategies, compensation, purchase and redemptions, and tax implications. Mutual funds may use this information to create a "mutual fund profile" for investors. Investors may use the profile to purchase the mutual fund shares but the investor must be given information on where to obtain a statutory prospectus and the statement of additional information for the fund.

CHARACTERISTICS OF OPEN-END MUTUAL FUND SHARES

All open-end mutual fund shares are sold through a continuous primary offering, and each new investor receives new shares from the fund company. The new shares are created for investors as their orders are received by the fund. Investors purchase shares from the fund company at the public offering price and redeem them to the fund company at the net asset value. The mutual fund has 7 calendar days to forward the proceeds to an investor after receiving a redemption request. If the investor has possession of the mutual fund certificates, the fund then has 7 calendar days from the receipt of the certificate by the custodian to forward the proceeds. Suspension of the 7-day rule may be allowed only if:

- The NYSE is closed for an extraordinary reason.

- The NYSE's trading is restricted or limited.

- The liquidation of the securities would not be practical.

- An SEC order has been issued.

ADDITIONAL CHARACTERISTICS OF OPEN-END MUTUAL FUNDS

- Diversification

- Professional management

- Low minimum investment

- Easy tax reporting, Form 1099

- Reduction of sales charges through breakpoint schedule, letter of intent, and rights accumulation

- Automatic reinvestment of dividends and capital gains distributions

- Structured withdrawal plans

MUTUAL FUND INVESTMENT OBJECTIVES

EQUITY FUNDS

The only investment that will meet a growth objective is common stock. Growth funds seeking capital appreciation invest in the common stock of a corporation whose business is growing more rapidly than other companies and more rapidly than the economy as a whole. Growth funds seek capital gains and do not produce significant dividend income.

EQUITY INCOME FUND

An equity income fund purchases both common and preferred shares that have a long track record of paying consistent dividends. Preferred shares are purchased by the fund for their stated dividend. Utility stocks also are purchased, because utilities traditionally pay out the highest percentage of their earnings to shareholders in the form of dividends. Other common shares of blue-chip companies also may be purchased.

SECTOR FUNDS

Mutual funds that concentrate 25% or more of their assets in one business area or region are known as sector funds. Technology, biotech, and gold funds would all be examples of sector funds that concentrate their investments in one business area. A Northeast growth fund would be an example of a sector fund that concentrates its assets geographically. Sector funds traditionally carry higher risk-reward ratios. If the sector does well, the investor may enjoy a higher rate of return. If, however, the sector performs poorly, the investor may suffer larger losses. The high-risk reward ratio is due to the fund's concentration in one area.

INDEX FUNDS

An index fund is designed to mirror the performance of a large market index such as the S&P 500 or the Dow Jones Industrial Average. An index fund's portfolio is comprised of stocks that are included in the index that the fund is designed to track. The fund manager does not actively seek out which stocks to buy or sell, making an index fund an example of a fund that is passively managed. If the stock is in the index, it will usually be in the portfolio. Portfolio turnover for an index fund is generally low, which helps keep the fund's expenses down.

GROWTH AND INCOME (COMBINATION FUND)

A growth and income fund, as the name suggests, invests to achieve both capital appreciation and current income. The fund invests a portion of its assets in shares of common stock that offer the greatest appreciation potential and invests a portion of its assets in preferred and common shares that pay high dividends, in order to produce income for investors.

BALANCED FUNDS

A balanced fund invests in both stocks and bonds, according to a predetermined formula. For example, the fund may invest 70% of its assets in equities and 30% of its assets in bonds.

ASSET ALLOCATION FUNDS

Asset allocation funds invest in stocks, bonds, and money market instruments, according to the expected performance for each market. For example, if the portfolio manager feels that equities will do well, he may invest more money in equities. Alternatively, if he feels that the bond market will outperform equities, they may shift more money into the debt markets.

OTHER TYPES OF FUNDS

There are other types of equity funds, such as foreign stock funds that invest outside the United States, and special situation funds that invest in takeover candidates and restructuring companies. A final type of fund is an option income fund that purchases shares of common stock and sells call options against the portfolio in order to generate premium income for investors. Because the fund has sold call options on the shares it owns, it will limit the capital appreciation of the portfolio.

BOND FUNDS

Investors who invest in bond funds are actually purchasing an equity security that represents their undivided interest in a portfolio of debt. Corporations, U.S. government, or state and local municipalities may have issued the debt in the portfolio. Bond funds invest mainly to generate current income for investors through interest payments generated by the bonds in the portfolio.

CORPORATE BOND FUNDS

Corporate bond funds invest in debt securities that have been issued by corporations. The debt in the portfolio could be investment grade, or it could be speculative, such as in a high-yield or junk-bond fund. Dividend income that is generated by the portfolio's interest payments is subject to all taxes.

GOVERNMENT BOND FUNDS

Government bond funds invest in debt securities issued by the U.S. government, such as Treasury bills, notes, and bonds. Many funds also invest in the debt of government agencies, such as those issued by the Government National Mortgage Association, also known as Ginnie Mae. Government bond funds provide current income to investors, along with a high degree of safety of principal. Dividends based upon the interest payments received from direct treasury obligations are only subject to federal taxation.

MUNICIPAL BOND FUNDS

Municipal bond funds invest in portfolios of municipal debt. Investors in municipal bond funds receive dividend income, which is free from federal taxes because the dividends are based on the interest payments received from the municipal bonds in the portfolio. Investors are still subject to taxes for any capital gains distributions or for any capital gains realized through the sale of the mutual fund shares.

MONEY MARKET FUNDS

Money market funds invest in short-term money market instruments such as banker's acceptances, commercial paper, and other debt securities with less than 1 year remaining to maturity. Money market funds are no-load funds that offer the investor the highest degree of safety of principal along with current income. The NAV for money market funds is always equal to $1, however, this is not guaranteed. Investors use money market funds as a place to hold idle funds and to earn current income. Interest is earned by investors daily and is credited to their accounts monthly. Most money market funds offer check-writing privileges, and investors must receive a prospectus prior to investing or opening an account.

ALTERNATIVE FUNDS

Alternative funds, also known as alt funds or liquid alts, invest in non-traditional assets or illiquid assets and may employ alternative investment strategies. There is no standard definition for what constitutes an alt fund, but alt funds are often marketed as a way for retail investors to gain access to hedge funds and actively managed programs that will perform well in a variety of market conditions. A hedge fund is usually offered only to large institutional investors and has significant minimum investments that are often $2 million dollars or more. Investors in hedge funds have limited access to the funds and may only withdraw money at times set by the hedge fund. These funds claim to reduce volatility, increase diversification, and produce higher returns when compared to long-only equity funds and income funds, while still providing liquidity. Recommendations for alt funds must be based on the specific strategies employed by the fund, not merely as one overall investment. Retail communication must accurately and fairly detail each fund's operations and objectives in line with the information in the prospectus. A significant concern is that investment advisers and retail investors will not understand how these funds will react in certain market conditions or how the fund manager will approach those market conditions. These funds must be reviewed during the new product review process even if the firm has a selling agreement with the fund.

VALUING MUTUAL FUND SHARES

Mutual funds must determine the net asset value of the fund's shares at least once per business day. Most mutual funds price their shares at the close of business of the NYSE (4:00 pm EST). The mutual fund prospectus provides the best answer as to when the fund calculates the price of its shares. The calculation is required to determine both the redemption price and the purchase price of the fund's shares. The price, which is received by an investor who is redeeming shares, and the price that is paid by an investor who is purchasing shares, is based upon the price, which is next calculated after the fund has received the investor's order. This is known as forward pricing. To calculate the fund's NAV, use the following formula:

assets − liabilities = net assets value

To determine the NAV per share, simply divide the total net asset value by the total number of outstanding shares.

$$\frac{\textbf{total NAV}}{\textbf{total no. of shares}}$$

 FOCUSPOINT

If XYZ mutual fund has $10,000,000 in assets and $500,000 in liabilities, what is the fund's NAV?

assets − liabilities = NAV

$10,000,000 − $500,000 = $9,500,000

If XYZ has 1,000,000 shares outstanding, its NAV per share would be:

$$\frac{\textbf{total NAV}}{\textbf{total no. of shares}} \quad \frac{\textbf{\$9,500,000}}{\textbf{1,000,000}}$$

NAV per share = $9.50

CHANGES IN THE NAV

The net asset value of a mutual fund is constantly changing as security prices fluctuate and as the mutual fund conducts its business. The following illustrates how the NAV per share will be affected given certain events.

INCREASES IN THE NAV

The net asset value of the mutual fund increases if the:

- Value of the securities in the portfolio increases.
- Portfolio receives investment income, such as interest payments from bonds.

DECREASES IN THE NAV

The net asset value decreases the:

- Value of the securities in the portfolio falls in value.
- Fund distributes dividends or capital gains.

NO EFFECT ON THE NAV

The following have no effect on the net asset value of the mutual fund share:

- Investor purchases and redemptions.
- Portfolio purchases and sales of securities.
- Sales charges.

SALES CHARGES

The maximum allowable sales charge that an open-end fund may charge is 8.5% of the POP. The sales charge that may be assessed by a particular fund is detailed in the fund's prospectus. It is important to note that the sales charge is not an expense of the fund; it is a cost of distribution, which is borne by the investor. The sales charges pay for the following:

- Underwriter's commission
- Commission to brokerage firms and registered representatives

FRONT-END LOADS

A front-end load is a sales charge that the investor pays when they purchase shares. The sales charge is added to the NAV of the fund, and the investor purchases the shares at the POP. The sales charge, in essence, is deducted from the gross amount invested, and the remaining amount is invested in the portfolio at the NAV. Shares that charge a front-end load are known as "A" shares.

EXAMPLE   XYZ mutual fund has a NAV of $9.50 and a POP of $10 and a sales charge percentage of 5%. How much in sales charges would an investor pay if they were to invest $10,000 in the fund?

$$\frac{\begin{array}{r} \$10,000 \\ \times 5\% \end{array}}{\$500 = \text{sales charge}} \qquad \frac{\begin{array}{r} \$10,000 \\ -\$500 \end{array}}{\$9,500 \ \text{invested in the portfolio at NAV}}$$

BACK-END LOADS

A back-end load is also known as a contingent differed sales charge (CDSC). An investor in a fund that charges a back-end load pays the sales charge at the time of redemption of fund shares. The sales charge is assessed on the value of the shares that have been redeemed, and the amount of the sales charge declines as the holding period for the investor increases. The following is a hypothetical back-end load schedule:

Years Money Left in Portfolio	Sales Charge
1	8.5%
2	7%
3	5%
4	3%
5	1.5%
5 years or more	0%

The mutual fund prospectus details the particular schedule for back-end load sales charges. Mutual fund shares that charge a back-end load are also known as "B" shares.

OTHER TYPES OF SALES CHARGES

There are other ways in which a mutual fund assesses a sales charge. Shares, which charge a level load based on the NAV, are known as level-load funds or "C" shares. Shares, which charge an asset-based fee and a back-end load, are known as "D" shares.

12B-1 FEES

Most mutual funds charge an asset-based distribution fee to cover expenses related to the promotion and distribution of the fund's shares. The amount of the fee is determined annually as a percentage of the NAV or as a flat fee. The 12B-1 fee is charged to the shares quarterly, reducing the investor's overall return on the fund. Because a 12B-1 fee reduces the return, it is a type of sales load. 12B-1 fees cover such things as the printing of prospectuses and certain sales commissions to agents. To start and continue a 12B-1 fee, three votes must initially approve the fee and annually reapprove it. The three votes that are required are:

1. A majority vote of the board of directors
2. A majority vote of the non-interested board of directors
3. A majority vote of the outstanding shares

To terminate a 12B-1 fee, only two votes are required. They are:

1. A majority vote of the noninterested board of directors
2. A majority vote of the outstanding shares

LIMITS OF A 12B-1 FEE

A mutual fund that distributes its own shares and markets itself as a no-load fund may charge a 12B-1 fee that is no more than .25%. If the fund charges a 12B-1 fee that is greater than .25%, it may not be called a no-load fund. Other funds that do not call themselves no-load funds are limited to .75% of assets, and the amount of the 12B-1 fee must be reasonably related to the anticipated level of expenses incurred for promotion and distribution. All 12B-1 fees are reviewed quarterly.

RECOMMENDING MUTUAL FUNDS

Mutual funds are designed to be longer-term investments and are generally not used to time the market. When determining suitability for investors, the investment advisers must first make sure that the investment objective of the mutual fund matches the investor's objective. Once several funds have been selected that meet the client's objective, the adviser must then compare costs, fees, and expenses among the funds. Priority should be given to any fund company with whom the investor maintains an investment. If the client's objective has changed, then the fund most likely offers conversions privileges that will allow the investor to move into another portfolio without paying any sales charge. If the investor is committing new capital then the fund company most likely offers combination privileges and rights of accumulation, which will help the investor reach a sale charge reduction. Switching fund companies and/or spreading out investment dollars among different fund companies are red flags for breakpoint sales violations and abusive sales practices. The amount of time the investor is seeking to hold the investment is a determining factor as to which share class is the most appropriate. Investors who have longer holding periods may be better off in B shares that assess a sales charge upon redemption based on their holding period. Investors who have shorter time horizons are better off choosing A shares over B shares as the expenses associated with B shares tend to be higher. Important to note is that making a large investment in class B shares is a red flag for a breakpoint sales violation as the large dollar amount would most likely have resulted in a reduced sales charge for the investors. Investors with relatively short holding periods or who want to actively move money between funds to try to time the market would be best off with C shares that charge a level load each year.

SALES CHARGE REDUCTIONS

The maximum allowable sales charge that may be assessed by an open-end mutual fund is 8.5% of the public offering price. If a mutual fund charges 8.5%, they must offer the following three privileges to investors:

1. Breakpoint sales charge reductions that reduce the amount of the sales charge based on the dollar amount invested

2. Rights of accumulation that reduce the sales charge on subsequent investments, based on the value of the investor's account

3. Automatic reinvestment of dividends and capital gains at the NAV

If a mutual fund does not offer all three of these benefits to investors, the maximum allowable sales charge that may be charged drops to 6.25%. Although a mutual fund that charges 8.5% must offer these features, most mutual funds that charge less than 8.5% also offer them.

BREAKPOINT SCHEDULE

As an incentive for investors to invest larger sums of money into a mutual fund, the mutual fund will reduce the sales charge based upon the dollar amount of the purchase. Breakpoint sales charge reductions are available to any person including corporations, trusts, couples, and accounts for minors. Breakpoint sales charge reductions are not available to investment clubs or to parents and their adult children investing in separate accounts. The following is an example of a breakpoint schedule that a family of funds might use:

Dollar Amount Invested	Sales Charge
$1–$24,999	8.5%
$25,000–$74,999	7%
$75,000–$149,999	5%
$150,000–$499,999	3%
$500,000 or greater	1%

A breakpoint schedule benefits all parties: the fund company, the investor, and the representative.

LETTER OF INTENT

An investor who might not be able to reach a breakpoint with a single purchase may qualify for a breakpoint sales charge reduction by signing a letter of intent. A letter of intent gives the investor up to 13 months to reach the dollar amount to which they subscribed. The letter of intent is binding only on the fund company, not on the investor. The additional shares that are purchased as a result of the lower sales charge are held by the fund company in an escrow account. If the investor fulfills the letter of intent, the shares are released to them. Should investors fail to reach the breakpoint to which they subscribed, they will be charged an adjustment to their sales charge. The investor may choose to pay the adjusted sales charge by either sending a check or by allowing some of the escrowed shares to be liquidated.

BACKDATING A LETTER OF INTENT

An investor may backdate a letter of intent up to 90 days to include a prior purchase and the 13-month window starts from the back date. For example, if an investor backdates a letter of intent by the maximum of 90 days allowed, then the investor has only 10 months to complete the letter of intent.

BREAKPOINT SALES

A breakpoint sale is a violation committed by a registered representative who is trying to earn larger commissions by recommending the purchase of mutual fund shares in a dollar amount that is just below the breakpoint that would allow the investor to qualify for a reduced sales charge. A breakpoint violation may also have been committed if a representative spreads out a large sum of money over different families of funds. A registered representative must always notify an investor of the availability of a sales charge reduction, especially when the investor is depositing a sum of money that is close to the breakpoint.

RIGHTS OF ACCUMULATION

Rights of accumulation allow the investor to qualify for reduced sales charges on subsequent investments by taking into consideration the value of the investor's account, including the growth. Unlike a letter of intent, there is no time limit and, as the investor's account grows over time, they can qualify for lower sales charges on future investments. The sales charge reduction is not retroactive and does not reduce the sales charges on prior purchases. To qualify for the breakpoint, the dollar amount of the current purchase is calculated into the total value of the investor's account.

 **FOCUS**POINT

Using the earlier breakpoint schedule, let's look at an investor's account over the last 3 years:

	Deposit	Sales Charge
Year 1	$5,000	8.5%
Year 2	$5,000	8.5%
Year 3	$5,000	8.5%

Let's assume that the investor's account has increased in value by $6,000, making the total current value of the account $21,000. The investor has another $5,000 to invest this year and, because there is a sales charge reduction available at the $25,000 level, based on the breakpoint schedule outlined earlier, the investor will pay a sales charge of 7% on the new $5,000.

AUTOMATIC REINVESTMENT OF DISTRIBUTIONS

Investors may elect to have their distributions automatically reinvested in the fund and use the distributions to purchase more shares. Most mutual funds allow the investor to purchase the shares at the NAV when they reinvest distributions. This feature has to be offered by mutual funds charging a sales charge of 8.5%. However, it is offered by most other mutual funds as well.

CLOSED-END FUNDS

Closed-end funds do not charge a sales charge to invest. An investor who wants to purchase a closed-end fund will pay the current market price plus the commission the brokerage firm charges to execute the order.

EXCHANGE-TRADED FUNDS (ETFs)

In recent years, exchange-traded funds, or ETFs, have gained a lot of popularity. ETFs are created through the purchase of a basket of securities that are designed to track the performance of an index or sector. ETFs are not actively managed. They provide investors with lower costs and the ability to buy, sell, and sell short the ETF at any point during the trading day, and they may be purchased on margin. Certain types of ETFs are designed to provide returns and performance characteristics of positions that take on the leverage. Such ETFs are often known as "ultra" or double, ETFs. These ETFs may provide returns that are double or more of the return of an index, or double or more the inverse return of an index.

ETFS THAT TRACK ALTERNATIVELY WEIGHTED INDICES

Investing in ETFs that track indices has become a popular investment strategy. As a result, new products have come to market that track the performance of alternative indices. Equally weighted, alternatively weighted, fundamentally weighted, and volatility weighted ETFs offer exposure to other investment styles and may provide enhanced performance. These ETFs present additional risk factors that both investment advisers and investors need to understand. These funds are sometimes marketed as having better performance than other indices, which could be cause for concern as the ETFs that track these indices may be complex, thinly traded, and hard to understand for both advisers and retail investors. The lack of liquidity can lead to wider spreads causing the product to be expensive to buy and sell for investors. The portfolios often have high turnover, which can lead to increased transaction costs for ETF.

Pretest

MUTUAL FUND INVESTMENT OBJECTIVES VALUATION AND SALES CHARGES

la.finra.mutual.obj.val.001_1811

1. An investor who wishes to include a prior purchase of a mutual fund in a new letter of intent, wants to backdate the letter. Which of the following is correct?

   a. He may do this within 7 business days.

   b. He may do this within 3 months.

   c. He may do this within 1 month.

   d. He may do this within 2 months.

la.finra.mutual.obj.val.002_1811

2. A no-load mutual fund may charge a 12B-1 fee that is:

   a. Up to .25 of 1% of the NAV.

   b. Less than .25 of 1% of the NAV.

   c. Up to .25 of 1% of the POP.

   d. Less than .25 of 1% of the POP.

sa.finra.mutual.obj.val.001_1811

3. A mutual fund that assesses a charge to cover promotional expenses would be charging:

   a. A 12b-1 fee.

   b. A contingent deferred sales charge.

   c. A redemption charge.

   d. A balanced load.

sa.finra.mutual.obj.val.002_1811

4. A mutual fund would be offered at a premium to its value if it's a:

   a. Back-end load fund.

   b. Front-end load fund.

   c. No load fund.

   d. A nondiversified fund.

Variable Annuities

INTRODUCTION

Learning Objective Statements

Compare the features and objectives of fixed and variable annuities.

Detail the operation of equity indexed annuities.

Detail how and why an investor purchases an annuity.

Contrast accumulation and annuity units.

Compare annuity payout options.

This lesson covers a variety of important topics relating to annuity products and retirement plans. For most people, saving for retirement has become an important investment objective for at least part of their portfolio. Many investors choose to purchase annuities to help plan for retirement. Over the years a wide range of annuity products have been developed to meet different investment objectives and risk profiles. Candidates need to fully understand how annuities and retirement plans function in order to successfully complete the exam.

ANNUITIES

An annuity is a contract between an individual and an insurance company. Once the contract is entered into, the individual becomes known as the annuitant. There are three basic types of annuities that are deigned to meet different objectives. They are:

1. Fixed annuity
2. Variable annuity
3. Combination annuity

Although all three types allow the investor's money to grow tax deferred, the type of investments made and how the money is invested varies according to the type of annuity.

FIXED ANNUITY

A fixed annuity offers investors a guaranteed rate of return regardless of whether the investment portfolio can produce the guaranteed rate. If the performance of the portfolio falls below the rate that was guaranteed, the insurance company owes investors the difference. Because the purchaser of a fixed annuity does not have any investment risk, a fixed annuity is considered to be an insurance product, not a security. Representatives who sell fixed annuity contracts must have an insurance license. Because fixed annuities offer investors a guaranteed return, the money invested by the insurance company will be used to purchase conservative investments like mortgages and real estate. These are investments whose historical performance is predictable enough that a guaranteed rate can be offered to investors. All of the money invested into fixed annuity contracts is held in the insurance company's general account. Because the rate that the insurance company guarantees is not very high, the annuitant may suffer a loss of purchasing power due to inflation risk.

VARIABLE ANNUITY

An investor seeking to achieve a higher rate of return may elect to purchase a variable annuity. Variable annuities seek to obtain a higher rate of return by investing in stocks, bonds, or mutual fund shares. These securities traditionally offer higher rates of return than more conservative investments. A variable annuity does not offer the investor a guaranteed rate of return and the investor may lose all or part of their principal. Because the annuitant bears the investment risk associated with a variable annuity, the contract is considered to be both a security and an insurance product. Representatives who sell variable annuities must have both their securities license and their insurance license. The money and securities contained in a variable annuity contract are held in the insurance company's separate account. The separate account was named this because the variable annuity's portfolio must be kept separate from the insurance company's general funds. The insurance company must have a net worth of $1,000,000, or the separate account must have a net worth of $1,000,000, in order for the separate account to begin operating. Once the separate account begins operations, it may invest in one of two ways:

1. Directly
2. Indirectly

DIRECT INVESTMENT

If the money in the separate account is invested directly into individual stocks and bonds, the separate account must have an investment adviser to actively manage the portfolio. If the money in the separate account is actively managed and invested directly, then the separate account is considered to be an open-end investment company under the Investment Company Act of 1940 and must register as such.

INDIRECT INVESTMENT

If the separate account uses the money in the portfolio to purchase mutual fund shares, it is investing in the equity and debt markets indirectly and no investment adviser is required to actively manage the portfolio. If the separate account purchases mutual fund shares, then the separate account is considered to be a unit investment trust under the Investment Company Act of 1940 and must register as such.

COMBINATION ANNUITY

For investors who feel that a fixed annuity is too conservative and that a variable annuity is too risky, a combination annuity offers the annuitant features of both a fixed and variable contract. A combination annuity has a fixed portion that offers a guaranteed rate and a variable portion that tries to achieve a higher rate of return. Most combination annuities allow the investor to move money between the fixed and variable portions of the contract. The money invested in the fixed portion of the contract is invested in the insurance company's general account and used to purchase conservative investments like mortgages and real estate. The money invested in the variable side of the contract is invested in the insurance company's separate account and used to purchase stocks, bonds, or mutual fund shares. Representatives who sell combination annuities must have both their securities license and their insurance license.

BONUS ANNUITY

An insurance company that issues annuity contracts may offer incentives to investors who purchase their variable annuities. Such incentives are often referred to as bonuses. One type of bonus is known as premium enhancement. Under a premium enhancement option, the insurance company will make an additional contribution to the annuitant's account based on the premium paid by the annuitant. For example, if the annuitant is contributing $1,000 per month, the insurance company may offer to contribute an additional 5% or $50 per month to the account. Another type of bonus offered to annuitants is the ability to withdraw the greater of the account's earnings or up to 15% of the total premiums paid without a penalty. Although the annuitant will not have to pay a penalty to the insurance company, there may be income taxes and a 10% penalty tax owed to the IRS. Bonus annuities often have higher expenses and longer surrender periods than other annuities and these additional costs and surrender periods need to be clearly disclosed to perspective purchasers. In order to offer bonus annuities the bonus received must outweigh the increased costs and fees associated with the contract. Fixed annuity contracts may not offer bonuses to purchasers.

EQUITY-INDEXED ANNUITY

Equity-indexed annuities offer investors a return that varies according to the performance of a set index such as the S&P 500. Equity-indexed annuities credit additional interest to the investor's account based on the contract's participation rate. If a contract sets the participation rate at 70% of the return for the S&P 500 index, and the index returns 5%, then the investor's account will be credited for 70% of the return or 3.5%. The participation rate may also be shown as a spread rate. If the contract has a spread rate of 3% and the index returns 10%, then the investor's contract would be credited 7%. Equity-indexed annuities may also set a floor rate and a cap rate for the contract. The floor rate is the minimum interest rate that will be credited to the investor's account. The floor rate may be zero or it may be a positive number, depending on the specific contract.

The contract's cap rate is the maximum rate that will be credited to the contract. If the return of the index exceeds the cap rate, the investor's account will only be credited up to the cap rate. If the S&P 500 index returns 11% and the cap rate set in the contract is 9%, then the investor's account will only be credited 9%.

Most equity-indexed annuities combine the guarantee features of a fixed annuity with the potential for additional returns like that of a variable annuity. Equity-indexed annuities may also be referred to as equity-indexed contracts or EICs.

The following table compares the features of fixed and variable annuities:

Feature	Fixed Annuity	Variable Annuity
Payment received	Guaranteed/fixed	May vary in amount
Return	Guaranteed minimum	No guarantee/return may vary in amount
Investment risk	Assumed by insurance company	Assumed by investor
Portfolio	Real estate, mortgages, and fixed income securities	Stocks, bonds, or mutual fund shares
Portfolio held in	General account	Separate account
Inflation	Subject to inflation risk	Resistant to inflation
Representative registration	Insurance license	Insurance and securities license

RECOMMENDING VARIABLE ANNUITIES

There are a number of factors that will determine if a variable annuity is a suitable recommendation for an investor. Variable annuities are meant to be used as supplements to other retirement accounts such as IRAs and corporate retirement plans. Variable annuities should not be recommended to investors who are trying to save for a large purchase or expense such as college tuition or a second home. Variable annuity products are more appropriate for an investor who is looking to create an income stream. A deferred annuity contract would be appropriate for someone seeking retirement income at some point in the future. An immediate annuity contract would be more appropriate for someone seeking to generate current income and who is perhaps already retired. Many annuity contracts have complex features and cost structures which may be difficult for both the representative and investor to understand. The benefits of the contract should outweigh the additional costs of the contract to ensure the contract is suitable for the investor. Illustrations regarding performance of the contract may use a maximum growth rate of 12% and all annuity applications must be approved or denied by a principal based on suitability within 7 business days of receipt. A Series 24 or Series 26 principal may approve or deny a variable annuity application presented by either a Series 6 or Series 7 registered representative. 1035 exchanges allow investors to move from one annuity contract to another without incurring tax consequences. 1035 exchanges can be a red flag and a cause for concern over abusive sales practices. Because most annuity contracts have surrender charges that may be substantial, 1035 exchanges may result in the investor being worse off and may constitute churning. FINRA is concerned about firms who employ compensation structures for representatives that may incentivize the sale of annuities over other investment products with lower costs and which may be more appropriate for investors. Firms should guard against incentivizing agents to sell annuity products over other investments. Members should ensure proper product training for investment advisers and principals for annuities and they must have adequate supervision to monitor sales practices and to test their product knowledge. The focus should be on detecting problematic and abusive sales practices. L share annuity contracts are designed with shorter surrender periods, but have higher costs to investors. The sale of L share annuity contracts can be a red flag for compliance personnel and may constitute abusive sales practices.

ANNUITY PURCHASE OPTIONS

An investor may purchase an annuity contract in one of three ways. They are:

1. Single payment deferred annuity
2. Single payment immediate annuity
3. Periodic payment deferred annuity

SINGLE PAYMENT DEFERRED ANNUITY

With a single payment deferred annuity, the investor funds the contract completely with one payment and defers receiving payments from the contract until some point in the future, usually after retirement. Money being invested in a single payment deferred annuity is used to purchase accumulation units. The number and value of the accumulation units varies as the distributions are reinvested and the value of the separate account's portfolio changes.

SINGLE PAYMENT IMMEDIATE ANNUITY

With a single payment immediate annuity, the investor funds the contract completely with one payment and begins receiving payments from the contract immediately, normally within 60 days. The money that is invested in a single payment immediate annuity is used to purchase annuity units. The number of annuity units remains fixed and the value changes as the value of the securities in the separate accounts portfolio fluctuates.

PERIODIC PAYMENT DEFERRED ANNUITY

With a periodic payment annuity, the investor purchases the annuity by making regularly scheduled payments into the contract. This is known as the accumulation stage. During the accumulation stage, the terms are flexible and, if the investor misses a payment, there is no penalty. The money invested in a periodic payment deferred annuity is used to purchase accumulation units. The number and value of the accumulation units fluctuate with the securities in the separate account's portfolio.

 TAKENOTE!

The suitability obligation for variable annuities covers the initial purchase and subaccount allocation as well as the exchange of one annuity contract for any other contract. Exempt from suitability determination are any changes made to the allocation of assets among the available sub accounts.

ACCUMULATION UNITS

An accumulation unit represents the investor's proportionate ownership in the separate account's portfolio during the accumulation or differed stage of the contract. The value of the accumulation unit will fluctuate as the value of the securities in the separate account's portfolio changes. As the investor makes contributions to the account or as distributions are reinvested, the number of accumulation units varies. An investor only owns accumulation units during the accumulation stage when money is being paid into the contract or when receipt of payments is being deferred by the investor, such as with a single payment-deferred annuity.

 TAKENOTE!

Most annuities allow the investor to designate a beneficiary who will receive the greater of the value of the account or the total premiums paid if the investor dies during the accumulation stage.

ANNUITY UNITS

When an investor changes from the pay-in or deferred stage of the contract to the payout phase, the investor is said to have annuitized the contract. At this point, the investor trades in his or her accumulation units for annuity units. The number of annuity units is fixed and represents the investor's proportional ownership of the separate account's portfolio during the payout phase. The number of annuity units that the investor receives when the contract is annuitized is based upon the payout option selected, the annuitant's age, sex, the value of the account, and the assumed interest rate.

ANNUITY PAYOUT OPTIONS

Annuity contracts are not subject to the contribution limits or the required minimum distributions of qualified plans. An investor in an annuity has the choice of taking a lump sum distribution or receiving scheduled payments from the contract. If the investor decides to annuitize the contract and receive scheduled payments, once the payout option is selected, it may not be changed. The following is a list of typical payout options in order from the largest monthly payment to the smallest. They are:

- Life only/straight life
- Life with period certain
- Joint with last survivor

LIFE ONLY/STRAIGHT LIFE

This payout option gives the annuitant the largest periodic payment from the contract and the investor receives payments from the contract for their entire life. However, when the investor dies, there are no additional benefits paid to their estate. If an investor has accumulated a large sum of money in the contract and dies unexpectedly, shortly after annuitizing the contract, the insurance company keeps the money in its account.

LIFE WITH PERIOD CERTAIN

A life with period certain payout option pays out from the contract to the investor or to their estate for the life of the annuitant or for the period certain, whichever is longer. If an investor selects a 10-year period certain when they annuitize the contract and the investor lives for 20 years, payments will cease upon the death of the annuitant. However, if the same investor dies only 2 years after annuitizing the contract, payments would go to their estate for another 8 years.

JOINT WITH LAST SURVIVOR

When an investor selects a joint with last survivor option, the annuity is jointly owned by more than one party and payments continue until the last owner of the contract dies. For example, if a husband and wife are receiving payments from an annuity under a joint with last survivor option and the husband dies, payments continue to the wife for the rest of her life. The payments received by the wife could be at the same rate as when the husband was alive or at a reduced rate, depending upon the contract. The monthly payments are based initially on the life expectancy of the youngest annuitant.

TAXATION

Contributions made to an annuity are made with after-tax dollars. The money the investor deposits becomes his or her cost base and is allowed to grow tax deferred. When the investor withdraws money from the contract, only the growth is taxed. The cost base is returned to them tax free. All money in excess of the investor's cost base is taxed as ordinary income.

TYPES OF WITHDRAWALS

An investor may begin withdrawing money from an annuity contract through any of the following options:

- Lump sum
- Random
- Annuitizing

Both lump sum and random withdrawals are done on a last in, first out (LIFO) basis. The growth portion of the contract is always considered to be the last money that was deposited and is taxed at the ordinary income rate of the annuitant. If the annuitant is under age 59.5 and takes a lump sum or random withdrawal, the withdrawal will be subject to a 10% tax penalty, as well as ordinary income taxes. An investor who needs to access the money in a variable annuity contract may be allowed to borrow from the contract. As long as interest is charged on the loan and the loan is repaid by the investor, the investor is not subject to taxes.

ANNUITIZING THE CONTRACT

When an investor annuitizes the contract and begins to receive monthly payments, part of each payment is the return of the investor's cost base and a portion of each payment is the distribution of the account's growth. To determine how much of each payment is taxable and how much is the return of principal, the investor would look at the exclusion ratio.

Contracts that are annuitized prior to age 59.5 under a life-income option are not subject to the 10% tax penalty nor are withdrawals due to disability or death.

SALES CHARGES

There is no maximum sales charge for an annuity contract. The sales charge that is assessed must be reasonable in relation to the total payments over the life of the contract. Most annuity contracts have back-end sales charges or surrender charges similar to a contingent deferred sales charge.

INVESTMENT MANAGEMENT FEES

The individuals running the separate account are professionals and are compensated for their management of the account through a fee-based agreement. A fee is deducted from the separate account to cover this management expense. The more aggressive the portfolio, the larger the management fee will be. The management fee, sales charges, and other expenses and fees all reduce the return.

VARIABLE ANNUITY VS. MUTUAL FUND

Feature	Variable Annuity	Mutual Fund
Maximum sales charge	No max	8.5%
Investment adviser	Yes	Yes
Custodian bank	Yes	Yes
Transfer agent	Yes	Yes
Voting	Yes	Yes
Management	Board of managers	Board of directors
Taxation of growth and reinvestments	Tax-deferred	Currently taxed
Lifetime income	Yes	No
Costs and fees	Higher	Lower

Pretest

VARIABLE ANNUITIES

la.finra.var.ann.ret.001_1811

1. A fixed annuity guarantees all of the following except:

   a. Income for life.

   b. Protection from inflation.

   c. Rate of return.

   d. Protection from investment risk.

Individual and Corporate Retirement Plans

INTRODUCTION

Learning Objective Statements

Compare Qualified plans versus nonqualified plans.

Detail features of Traditional and Roth IRAs.

Detail features of 529 plans and Education IRAs.

List the requirements for Corporate Sponsored retirement plans and ERISA.

For most people, saving for retirement has become an important investment objective for at least part of their portfolio. Investors may participate in retirement plans that have been established by their employers, as well as those they have established for themselves. Both corporate and individual plans may be qualified or nonqualified, and it is important for an investor to understand the difference before deciding to participate. Series 65 candidates will see a fair number of questions on the exam dealing with retirement plans.

A corporate retirement plan can be qualified or nonqualified. Nonqualified plans are reviewed first.

RETIREMENT PLANS

The following table compares the key features of qualified and nonqualified plans.

Feature	Qualified	Nonqualified
Contributions	Pretax	After-tax
Growth	Tax-deferred	Tax-deferred
Participation must be allowed	For everyone	Corporation may choose who gets to participate
IRS approval	Required	Not required
Withdrawals	100% taxed as ordinary income	Growth in excess of cost base is taxed as ordinary income

INDIVIDUAL PLANS

Individuals may set up a retirement plan for themselves that is qualified and allows contributions to the plan to be made with pretax dollars. Individuals may also purchase investment products such as annuities that allow their money to grow tax deferred. The money used to purchase an annuity has already been taxed, making an annuity a nonqualified product.

INDIVIDUAL RETIREMENT ACCOUNTS (IRAS)

All individuals with earned income may establish an IRA for themselves. Contributions to traditional IRAs may or may not be tax deductible, depending on the individual's level of adjusted gross income and whether the individual is eligible to participate in an employer-sponsored plan. Individuals who do not qualify to participate in an employer-sponsored plan may deduct their IRA contributions, regardless of their income level. The level of adjusted gross income that allows an investor to deduct his or her IRA contributions has been increasing since 1998. These tax law changes occur too frequently to make them a practical test question. Our review of IRAs focuses on the four main types, which are:

1. Traditional

2. Roth

3. SEP

4. Educational

TRADITIONAL IRA

A traditional IRA allows an individual to contribute a maximum of 100% of earned income or $6,000 per year or up to $12,000 per couple. If only one spouse works, the working spouse may contribute $6,000 to an IRA for themselves and $6,000 to a separate IRA for their spouse, under the nonworking spousal option. Investors over 50 may contribute up to $6,500 of earned income to their IRA. Regardless of whether the IRA contribution was made with pretax or after-tax dollars, the money is allowed to grow tax deferred. All withdrawals from an IRA are taxed as ordinary income regardless of how the growth was generated in the account. Withdrawals from an IRA prior to age 59.5 are subject to a 10% penalty tax as well as ordinary income taxes. The 10% penalty will be waived for first-time homebuyers or educational expenses for the taxpayer's child, grandchildren, or spouse. The 10% penalty will also be waived if the payments are part of a series of substantially equal payments. Withdrawals from an IRA must begin by April 1 of the year following the year in which the taxpayer reaches 70.5. If an individual fails to make withdrawals that are sufficient in size and frequency, the individual will be subject to a 50% penalty on the insufficient amount. An individual who makes a contribution to an IRA that exceeds 100% of earned income or $6,000, whichever is less, will be subject to a penalty of 6% per year on the excess amount for as long as the excess contribution remains in the account.

ROTH IRA

A Roth IRA is a nonqualified account. All contributions made to a Roth IRA are made with after-tax dollars. The same contribution limits apply for Roth IRAs. An individual may contribute the lesser of 100% of earned income to a maximum of $6,000 per person or $12,000 per couple. Any contribution made to a Roth IRA reduces the amount that may be deposited in a traditional IRA and vice versa. All contributions deposited in a Roth IRA are allowed to grow tax deferred and all of the growth may be taken out of the account tax free, provided that the individual has reached age 59.5 and the assets have been in the account for at least 5 years. A 10% penalty tax will be charged on any withdrawal of earnings prior to age 59.5, unless the owner is purchasing a home, has become disabled, or has died. There are no requirements for an individual to take distributions from a Roth IRA by a certain age.

> ### ◆▷ TAKE**NOTE!**
>
> Individuals and couples who are eligible to open a Roth IRA may convert their traditional IRA to a Roth IRA. The investor will have to pay income taxes on the amount converted, but will not be subject to the 10% penalty.

SIMPLIFIED EMPLOYEE PENSION (SEP) IRA

A SEP IRA is used by small corporations and self-employed individuals to plan for retirement. A SEP IRA is attractive to small employers because it allows them to set up a retirement plan for their employees rather quickly and inexpensively. The contribution limit for a SEP IRA far exceeds that of traditional IRAs. The contribution limit is the lesser of 25% of the employee's compensation or $57,000 per year. Should employees wish to make their annual IRA contribution to their SEP IRA, they may do so or they may make their standard contribution to a traditional or Roth IRA.

PARTICIPATION

All eligible employees must open an IRA to receive the employer's contribution to the SEP. If the employee does not open an IRA account, the employer must open one for them. The employee must be at least 21 years old, have worked during 3 of the last 5 years for the employer, and have earned at least $550. All eligible employees must participate as well as the employer.

EMPLOYER CONTRIBUTIONS

The employer may contribute between 0% to 25% of the employee's total compensation to a maximum of $57,000. Contributions to all SEP IRAs, including the employer's SEP IRA, must be made at the same rate. An employee who is over 70.5 must also participate and receive a contribution. All eligible employees are immediately vested in the employer's contributions to the plan.

SEP IRA TAXATION

Employer's contributions to a SEP IRA are immediately tax deductible by the employer. Contributions are not taxed at the employee's rate until the employee withdraws the funds. Employees may begin to withdraw money from the plan at age 59.5. All withdrawals are taxed as ordinary income and withdrawals prior to age 59.5 are subject to a 10% penalty tax.

IRA CONTRIBUTIONS

Contributions to IRAs must be made by April 15 of the following calendar year, regardless of whether an extension has been filed by the taxpayer. Contributions may be made between January 1 and April 15 for the previous year, the current year, or both. All IRA contributions must be made in cash.

IRA ACCOUNTS

All IRA accounts are held in the name of the custodian for the benefit of the account holder. Traditional custodians include banks, broker dealers, and mutual fund companies.

IRA INVESTMENTS

Individuals who establish IRAs have a wide variety of investments to choose from when deciding how to invest the funds. Investors should always choose investments that fit their investment objectives. The following is a comparison of allowable and nonallowable investments:

Allowable	Nonallowable
Stocks	Margin accounts
Bonds	Short sales
Mutual funds /ETFs/ETNs	Tangibles/collectibles/art
Annuities	Speculative option trading
UITs	Term life insurance
Limited partnerships	Rare coins
U.S. minted coins	Real estate

With rare exceptions an IRA may purchase real estate provided that very strict rules are followed regarding the property.

IT IS NOT WISE TO PUT A MUNICIPAL BOND IN AN IRA

Municipal bonds or municipal bond funds should never be placed in an IRA, because the advantage of those investments is that the interest income is free from federal taxes. Because their interest is free from federal taxes, the interest rate that is offered will be less than the rates offered by other alternatives. The advantage of an IRA is that money is allowed to grow tax deferred; therefore, an individual would be better off with a higher yielding taxable bond of the same quality.

ROLLOVER VS. TRANSFER

An individual may want or need to move their IRA from one custodian to another. There are two ways by which this can be accomplished. An individual may rollover their IRA or they may transfer their IRA.

ROLLOVER

With an IRA rollover, the individual may take possession of the funds for a maximum of 60 calendar days prior to depositing the funds into another qualified account. An investor may only roll over his IRA once every 12 months. The investor has 60 days from the date of the distribution to deposit 100% of the funds into another qualified account or he must pay ordinary income taxes on the distribution and a 10% penalty tax, if the investor is under 59.5.

TRANSFER

An investor may transfer her IRA directly from one custodian to another by simply signing an account transfer form. The investor never takes possession of the assets in the account and the investor may directly transfer her IRA as often as she likes.

DEATH OF AN IRA OWNER

Should the owner of an IRA die, the account becomes the property of the beneficiary named on the account by the owner. If the beneficiary is the spouse of the owner, special rules apply. The spouse may elect to rollover the IRA into her own IRA or retirement plan, such as a 401k. If this is elected there will be no tax presently due on the money. However, the spouse is still subject to the required minimum distribution rule at age 70.5. The surviving spouse may also elect to cash in the IRA. The distributions are subject to income tax but are not subject to the 10% penalty tax. If the beneficiary is not the spouse the money may not be rolled in to another IRA or retirement account. If the account owner dies prior to age 70.5, when the required distributions need to be made, the money must all be distributed prior to the end of the fifth year or the money may be distributed in equal installments based upon the beneficiary's life expectancy. If the account owner dies after the start of the required minimum distributions, the payment schedule of distributions becomes based on the life expectancy of the beneficiary.

EDUCATIONAL IRA/COVERDELL IRA

An educational IRA allows individuals to contribute up to $2,000 in after-tax dollars to an educational IRA for each student who is under the age of 18 years of age. The money is allowed to grow tax deferred and the growth may be withdrawn tax free, as long as the money is used for educational purposes. If all of the funds have not been used for educational purposes by the time the student reaches 30 years of age, the account must be rolled over to another family member who is under 30 years of age, or distributed to the original student, and is subject to a 10% penalty tax as well as ordinary income taxes.

529 PLANS

Qualified tuition plans, more frequently referred to as 529 plans, may be set up either as a prepaid tuition plan or as a college savings plan. With the prepaid tuition plan, the plan locks in a current tuition rate at a specific school.

The prepaid tuition plan can be set up as an installment plan or one where the contributor funds the plan with a lump sum deposit. Many states will guarantee the plans but may require that either the contributor or the beneficiary to be a state resident. The plan covers only tuition and mandatory fees. A room and board option is available for some plans.

A college savings account may be opened by any adult and the donor does not have to be related to the child. The assets in the college savings plan can be used to cover all costs of qualified higher education including tuition, room and board, books, computers, and mandatory fees. These plans generally have no age limit by when assets must be used. College savings accounts are not guaranteed by the state and the value of the account may decline in value depending on the investment results of the account. Collage savings accounts are not state specific and do not lock in a tuition rate. Contributions to a 529 plan are made with after-tax dollars and are allowed to grow tax deferred. The assets in the account remain under the control of the donor, even after the student reaches the age of majority. The funds may be used to meet the student's educational needs and the growth may be withdrawn federally tax-free. Most states also allow the assets to be withdrawn tax free. Any funds used for nonqualified education expenses are subject to income tax and a 10% penalty tax. If funds remain, or if the student does not attend or complete qualified higher education, then the funds may be rolled over to another family member within 60 days without incurring taxes and penalties. There are no income limits for the donors and contribution limits vary from state to state. 529 plans have an impact on a student's ability to obtain need-based financial aid. However, because the 529 plans are treated as parental assets and not as assets of the student, the plans are assessed at the expected family contribution (EFC) rate of 5.64%. This has a significantly lower impact than plans and assets that are considered to be assets of the student. Student assets are assessed at a 20% contribution rate.

LOCAL GOVERNMENT INVESTMENT POOLS (LGIPs)

Local government investment pools (LGIPs) allow states and local governments to manage their cash reserves and receive money market rates on the funds. LGIPs may also be created to invest the proceeds of a bond offering, if the proceeds of the offering are intended to be used to call in an existing bond issue. If the LGIP was created to pre-refund an existing issue, additional restrictions apply as to the type of investments that may be purchased by the pool. LGIPs that are created to manage cash reserves must only invest in securities on the state's legal or approved list. The legal list usually includes investments such as:

- Commercial paper rated in the two highest categories
- U.S. government and agency debt
- Bankers' acceptances
- Repurchase agreement
- Municipal debt issues within the state
- Investment company securities
- Certificates of deposit
- Savings accounts

Each state has an investment advisory board that works with the state treasury office to administer the pools. The main objective of these pools is safety of principal, with liquidity and interest income as secondary objectives. The pools require that the following be detailed in writing:

- Delegation of authority to make investments

- Annual investment activity reports

- Statement of safekeeping of securities

Municipal fund securities are not considered to be investment companies and are not required to register under the Investment Company Act of 1940. Additionally, prepaid tuition plans are not considered to be municipal fund securities. LGIP employees who market the plans directly to investors are exempt from MSRB (Municipal Securities Rule Making Board) rules; however, if the LGIP is marketed to investors by employees of a broker dealer, the broker dealer and all of its employees are subject to MSRB rules.

ABLE ACCOUNTS

An Achieving a Better Life Experience (ABLE) account, sometimes referred to as a 529 ABLE account, may be established as a tax-advantaged savings account to provide for the care of individuals with disabilities. ABLE account regulations were passed in order to recognize the unique financial burdens inherent in caring for a disabled person. Individuals with disabilities may only have one ABLE account at a time and the individual with the disability is deemed to be both the account owner and the designated beneficiary. ABLE accounts may be transferred or rolled over into new ABLE accounts for the same beneficiary. Contributions to the account are made with after-tax dollars and are allowed to grow tax deferred. The contributions and the growth may be used tax free by the beneficiary for qualified care and quality-of-life expenses. Tax-free withdrawals may be made by the beneficiary to cover qualified expenses incurred or in anticipation of paying expenses to be incurred. Qualified expenses would include things such as:

- Medical care

- Wellness care

- Transportation

- Housing expenses

- Assistive technology
- Education
- Job training

Withdrawals from an ABLE account for expenses that do not meet the definition of qualified expenses will be seen as part of the beneficiary's resources if retained past the month the distribution occurred. In order to qualify for an ABLE account, the individual must have been disabled by the time he or she reaches their 26th birthday. The maximum annual contribution to an ABLE account is equal to the annual tax-free gift limit of $18,000 and is subject to change each year. Anyone may make contributions to an ABLE account and the account may be rolled over to another family member if that person meets the eligibility guidelines. The assets in the ABLE account do not impact the disabled person's eligibility for many assistance programs. The first $100,000 in assets in the ABLE account is excluded when estimating the amount of resources available to the person, in calculating their eligibility for assistance. However, ABLE account balances which exceed $100,000 can cause the beneficiary of the account to be placed in a suspended status in terms of receiving supplemental security income (SSI) until all resources in the ABLE and other accounts owned by the individual fall to $100,000 or lower. Upon the death of the beneficiary of an ABLE account the remaining assets are used to repay Medicaid for any payments made to the beneficiary.

KEOGH PLANS (HR-10)

A Keogh is a qualified retirement plan set up by self-employed individuals, sole proprietors, and unincorporated businesses. If the business is set up as a corporation, a Keogh may not be used.

KEOGH CONTRIBUTIONS

Keoghs may only be funded with earned income during a period when the business shows a gross profit. If the business realizes a loss, no Keogh contributions are allowed. A self-employed person may contribute the lesser of 25% of their post-contribution income or $57,000. If the business has eligible employees, the employer must make a contribution for the employees at the same rate as their own contribution. Employee contributions are based on the employee's gross income and are limited to $57,000 per year. All money placed in a Keogh plan is allowed to grow tax deferred and is taxed as ordinary income when distributions are made to retiring employees and plan participants. From time to time, a self-employed person may make a nonqualified contribution to their Keogh plan; however, the total of the qualified and nonqualified contributions may not exceed the maximum contribution limit. Any excess contribution may be subject to a 10% penalty tax.

An eligible employee is defined as one who:

- Works full time (at least 1,000 hours per year).

- Is at least 21 years old.

- Has worked at least 1 year for the employer.

Employees who participate in a Keogh plan must be vested after 5 years. Withdrawals from a Keogh may begin when the participant reaches 59.5. Any premature withdrawals are subject to a 10% penalty tax. Keoghs, like IRAs, may be rolled over every 12 months. In the event of a participant's death, the assets will go to the individual's beneficiaries.

TAX-SHELTERED ANNUITIES (TSAs) AND TAX-DEFERRED ACCOUNTS (TDAs)

Tax-sheltered annuities and tax-deferred accounts are established as retirement plans for employees of nonprofit and public organizations such as:

- Public schools (403B)

- Nonprofit organizations (IRC 501C3)

- Religious organizations

- Nonprofit hospitals

TSAs and TDAs are qualified plans and contributions are made with pretax dollars. The money in the plan is allowed to grow tax deferred until it is withdrawn. TSAs and TDAs offer a variety of investment vehicles for participants to choose from such as:

- Stocks

- Bonds

- Mutual funds

- CDs

PUBLIC EDUCATIONAL INSTITUTIONS (403B)

In order for a school to be considered a public school and qualify to establish a TSA/TDA for their employees, the school must be supported by the state, the local government, or by a state agency. State-supported schools are:

- Elementary schools
- High schools
- State colleges and universities
- Medical schools

Any individual who works for a public school, regardless of position, may participate in the school's TSA or TDA.

NONPROFIT ORGANIZATIONS/TAX-EXEMPT ORGANIZATIONS (501C3)

Organizations which qualify under the Internal Revenue Code 501C3 as a nonprofit or tax-exempt entity may set up a TSA or TDA for their employees. Examples of nonprofit organizations are:

- Private hospitals
- Charitable organizations
- Trade schools
- Private colleges
- Parochial schools
- Museums
- Scientific foundations
- Zoos

All employees of organizations that qualify under the Internal Revenue Code 501C3 or 403B are eligible to participate as long as they are at least 21 years old and have worked full time for at least 1 year.

TSA/TDA CONTRIBUTIONS

In order to participate in a TSA or TDA, employees must enter into a contract with their employer agreeing to make elective deferrals into the plan. The salary reduction agreement states the amount and frequency of the elective deferral to be contributed to the TSA. The agreement is binding on both parties and covers only 1 year of contributions. Each year, a new salary reduction agreement must be signed to set forth the contributions for the new year. The employee's elective deferral is limited to a maximum of $19,500 per year. Employer contributions are limited to the lesser of 25% of the employee's earnings or $57,000.

TAX TREATMENT OF TSA/TDA DISTRIBUTIONS

All distributions for TSAs and TDAs are taxed as ordinary income in the year in which the distribution is made. Distributions from a TSA or TDA prior to age 59.5 are subject to a 10% penalty tax, as well as ordinary income taxes. Distributions from a TSA/TDA must begin by age 70.5 or be subject to an excess accumulation tax.

NONQUALIFIED CORPORATE RETIREMENT PLANS

Nonqualified corporate plans are funded with after-tax dollars and the money is allowed to grow tax deferred. If the corporation makes a contribution to the plan, they may not deduct the contribution from their corporate earnings until the plan participant receives the money. Distributions from a nonqualified plan, which exceed the investors cost base, are taxed as ordinary income. All nonqualified plans must be in writing and the employer may discriminate as to who may participate.

PAYROLL DEDUCTIONS

The employee may set up a payroll deduction plan by having the employer make systematic deductions from the employee's paycheck. The money, which has been deducted from the employee's check may be invested in a variety of ways. Mutual funds, annuities, and savings bonds are all usually available for the employee to choose from. Contributions to a payroll deduction plan are made with after-tax dollars.

DEFERRED COMPENSATION PLANS

A deferred compensation plan is a contract between an employee and an employer. Under the contract, the employee agrees to defer the receipt of money owed to the employee from the employer until after the employee retires. After retirement, the employee will traditionally be in a lower tax bracket and will be able to keep a larger percentage of the money for him or herself. Deferred compensation plans are traditionally unfunded and, if the corporation goes out of business, the employee becomes a creditor of the corporation and may lose all of the money due under the contract. Employees may only claim the assets if they retire, become disabled, or, in the case of death, their beneficiaries may claim the money owed. Money due under a deferred compensation plan is paid out of the corporation's working funds when the employee or their estate claims the assets. Should the employee leave the corporation and go to work for a competing company, they may lose the money owed under a noncompete clause. Money owed to the employee under a deferred compensation agreement is traditionally not invested for the benefit of the employee and, as a result, does not increase in value over time. The only product that is traditionally placed in a deferred compensation plan is a term life policy. In the case of the employee's death, the term life policy pays the employee's estate the money owed under the contract.

QUALIFIED PLANS

All qualified corporate plans must be in writing and set up as a trust. A trustee or plan administrator is appointed for the benefit of all plan holders.

TYPES OF PLANS

There are two main types of qualified corporate plans: a defined benefit plan and a defined contribution plan.

DEFINED BENEFIT PLAN

A defined benefit plan is designed to offer the participant a retirement benefit that is known or defined. Most defined benefit plans are set up to provide employees with a fixed percentage of their salary during their retirement, such as 74% of their average earnings during their 5 highest paid years. Other defined benefit plans are structured to pay participants a fixed sum of money for life. Defined benefit plans require the services of an actuary to determine the employer's contribution to the plan, based upon the participant's life expectancy and benefits promised.

DEFINED CONTRIBUTION PLAN

With a defined contribution plan, only the amount of money that is deposited into the account is known, such as 6% of the employee's salary. Both the employee and the employer may contribute a percentage of the employee's earnings into the plan. The money is allowed to grow tax deferred until the participant withdraws it at retirement. The ultimate benefit under a defined contribution plan is the result of the contributions into the plan, along with the investment results of the plan. The employee's maximum contribution to a defined contribution plan is $18,000 per year. Some types of defined contribution plans are:

- 401K

- Money purchase plan

- Profit sharing

- Thrift plans

- Stock bonus plans

All withdrawals from pension plans are taxed as ordinary income in the year in which the distribution is made.

401K AND THRIFT PLANS

401K and thrift plans allow the employee to contribute a fixed percentage of their salary to their retirement account and have the employer match some or all of their contributions. A "self-directed 401K plan" is one where the individual or plan participant selects the investments to be made in the account from a list of investment choices. The plan participant is the person who owns the account and is making contributions to the account to "plan" for their retirement. The employer, investment adviser, and plan administrator or trustee all have important roles in the creation and administration of a 401K plan.

- **The employer** is the entity that creates the plan for its employees and is known as the creator or plan sponsor.

- **The investment adviser** is the company that determines what investment choices will be offered to the participants and who executes the orders entered by the plan participants.

- **The plan administrator/trustee,** also known as a third-party administrator, is the company that has physical custody of the plan's assets and provides communication to the participants regarding the plan.

EMPLOYEE RETIREMENT INCOME SECURITY ACT OF 1974 (ERISA)

The Employee Retirement Income Security Act of 1974 (ERISA) is a federal law that establishes legal and operational guidelines for private pension and employee benefit plans. Not all decisions directly involving a plan, even when made by a fiduciary, are subject to ERISA's fiduciary rules. These decisions are business-judgment-type decisions and are commonly called "settlor" functions. This caveat is sometimes referred to as the "business decision" exception to ERISA's fiduciary rules. Under this concept, even though the employer is the plan sponsor and administrator, it will not be considered as acting in a fiduciary capacity when creating, amending, or terminating a plan. Among the decisions which would be considered settlor functions are:

- Choosing the type of plan, or options in the plan

- Amending a plan, including changing or eliminating plan options

- Requiring employee contributions or changing the level of employee contributions

- Terminating a plan, or part of a plan, including terminating or amending as part of a bankruptcy process

ERISA also regulates all of the following:

- Pension plan participation

- Funding

- Vesting

- Communication

- Beneficiaries

PLAN PARTICIPATION

All plans governed by ERISA may not discriminate among who may participate in the plan. All employees must be allowed to participate if:

- They are at least 21 years old.
- They have worked at least 1 year full time (1,000 hours).

FUNDING

Plan funding requirements set forth guidelines on how the money is deposited into the plan and how the employer and employee may contribute to the plan.

VESTING

Vesting refers to the process of how the employer's contribution becomes the property of the employee. Employers may be as generous as they like but may not be more restrictive than either one of the following vesting schedules:

- 3- to 6-year gradual vesting schedule
- 3-year cliff; the employee is not vested at all until 3 years, when they become 100% vested

COMMUNICATION

All corporate plans must be in writing at inception and the employee must be given annual updates.

BENEFICIARIES

All plan participants must be allowed to select a beneficiary who may claim the assets in case of the plan participant's death.

Pretest

INDIVIDUAL AND CORPORATE RETIREMENT PLANS

la.finra.indiv.corp.ret.001_1811

1. An investor has placed a sum equal to 50% of the annual contribution limit into his traditional IRA. The investor is seeking to maximize his contributions to his retirement savings. Which of the following is correct?

   a. The investor may contribute 100% of the annual limit to a Roth IRA.

   b. The investor may not contribute to a Roth IRA.

   c. The investor may contribute a sum equal to 50% of the annual limit to a Roth IRA.

   d. The investor may only contribute to a traditional IRA if one has been established.

la.finra.indiv.corp.ret.002_1811

2. Which of the following accounts would not subject the account owner to required minimum distributions?

   I. A Roth IRA.
   II. A variable annuity.
   III. A joint account with survivorship rights.
   IV. A traditional IRA.

   a. I and III.

   b. II and IV.

   c. I, II, and III.

   d. I only.

la.finra.indiv.corp.ret.003_1811

3. A doctor makes the maximum contribution to his Keogh plan while earning $300,000 per year. How much can he contribute to an IRA?

   a. $57,000.

   b. $17,000.

   c. $9,000.

   d. $6,000.

la.finra.indiv.corp.ret.004_1811

4. The maximum amount that a couple may contribute to their IRAs at any one time is:

   a. 100% of the annual contribution limit.

   b. 200% of the annual contribution limit.

   c. 300% of the annual contribution limit.

   d. 400% of the annual contribution limit.

la.finra.indiv.corp.ret.005_1811

5. An investor has deposited $100,000 into a qualified retirement account over a 10-year period. The value of the account has grown to $175,000 and the investor plans to retire and take a lump sum withdrawal. The investor will pay:

   a. Capital gains tax on $75,000 only.

   b. Ordinary income taxes on the $75,000 only.

   c. Ordinary income taxes on the whole $175,000.

   d. Ordinary income taxes on the $100,000 and capital gains on the $75,000.

la.finra.indiv.corp.ret.006_1811

6. A 42-year-old investor wants to put $20,000 into a plan to help meet the educational expenses of his 12-year-old son. He wants to make a lump sum deposit. Which would you recommend?

   a. 529 plan.

   b. Coverdell IRA.

   c. Roth IRA.

   d. Growth mutual fund.

la.finra.indiv.corp.ret.007_1811

7. A self-employed individual may open a SEP IRA to plan for his retirement. The maximum contribution to the plan is:

    a. $4,000.

    b. $8,000.

    c. $16,000.

    d. The lesser of 25% of the post-contribution income, up to $57,000.

sa.finra.indiv.corp.ret.001_1811

8. A school principal has deposited $15,000 in a tax-deferred annuity through a payroll deduction plan. The account has grown in value to $22,000. The principal plans to retire and take a lump sum distribution. On what amount does he pay taxes?

    a. $22,000.

    b. $15,000.

    c. $7,000.

    d. $0.

sa.finra.indiv.corp.ret.002_1811

9. A client who is 65 years old has invested $10,000 in a Roth IRA. It has now grown to $14,000. He plans to retire and take a lump sum distribution. He will pay taxes on:

    a. $0.

    b. $14,000.

    c. $4,000.

    d. $10,000.

Customer Accounts, Client Recommendations, Professional Conduct, and Industry Regulations

Customer Accounts, UGMAs, Accounts for Employees of Broker Dealers, and Customer Privacy

INTRODUCTION

Learning Objective Statements

List the information required to open a new account.

Detail the options customers have to holding securities.

Detail when confirmations statements and other communications must be sent.

Detail features of joint accounts.

Select the appropriate account choice for investors.

Assess if discretionary authority is required to execute an order.

Determine how to establish an account for a minor.

Evaluate the duties of a custodian.

Detail the procedures for employees of broker dealers opening an account at another firm.

List the requirements to establish a margin account.

List the procedures to ensure customer privacy.

Prior to executing a customer's order, the firm must open an account for the customer. NYSE rules require that representatives obtain all vital information relating to the customer. Candidates will see many types of questions dealing with customer accounts on their exam.

Prior to opening an account for any new customer, a registered representative must complete and sign a new account form. Account ownership is divided into five main types:

1. Individual
2. Joint
3. Corporate
4. Trust
5. Partnership

The registered representative should try to obtain as much information about the customer as possible. The representative should obtain the following information:

- Full name and address
- Home and work phone numbers
- Social security or tax ID number
- Employer, occupation, and employer's address
- Net worth
- Investment objectives
- Estimated annual income
- Bank/brokerage firm reference
- Whether the client is employed by a bank or broker dealer
- Any third-party trading authority
- Citizenship
- Legal age
- How account was obtained
- Whether client is an officer, a director, or a 10% stockholder of a publicly traded company

All new accounts must be accepted and signed by a principal of the firm. The principal must accept the account in writing for the firm either before or promptly after the first trade is executed. The principal accepts the account by signing the new account card. The representative who introduced the account and the name of the representative who will manage the account should be noted on the new account card as evidence that he or she introduced the account to the firm. Once the account is opened, the firm must send the customer a copy of the new account form within 30 days of the opening of the account and within 30 days of any material change in the customer's information. Firms are also required to verify the account information at least once every 36 months. The customer never has to sign anything to open a new cash account. However, some firms have the customer sign a customer agreement upon opening a new account, but this is not required. The customer agreement states the policies of the firm and usually contains a predispute arbitration clause. The predispute clause requires that any potential dispute arising out of the relationship be settled in binding arbitration. The predispute arbitration clause must be presented in a certain format and include:

- A disclosure that arbitration is final and binding.

- A disclosure that the findings of the arbitrators are not based on legal reasoning.

- A statement that the discovery process is generally more limited than the discovery process in a legal proceeding.

- A statement that the parties are waiving their right to a jury trial.

- A statement that the customer must be provided with a copy of the predispute clause and must verify its receipt with a signature.

- A disclosure that a minority of the arbitration panel will be affiliated with the securities industry.

If the predispute clause is contained in the customer agreement, there must be a highlighted disclosure just above the signature line.

If the customer requests a copy of the predispute arbitration agreement the firm must send it to the customer within 10 days. A firm may also have the customer sign a signature card. A signature card allows the firm to verify the customer's written instructions that are sent in to the firm.

Customers who do not wish to disclose financial information may still open an account if there is reason to believe that the customer can afford to maintain the account. All registered representatives should update the customer's information regularly and note any changes in the following:

- Address
- Phone number
- Employer
- Investment objectives
- Marital status

Registered representatives are also required to maintain an accurate and up-to-date listing of all of their customers' transactions and investment holdings.

Customers are not required to provide their educational background when opening an account.

HOLDING SECURITIES

Upon opening an account, the investor must decide where the securities are to be held. The following methods are available:

- Transfer and ship
- Transfer and hold in safekeeping
- Hold in street name
- Receipt versus payment (RVP)/delivery versus payment (DVP)

TRANSFER AND SHIP

Securities that are to be transferred and shipped are registered in the customer's name and sent to the customer's address of record.

TRANSFER AND HOLD IN SAFEKEEPING

Securities that are to be transferred and held in safekeeping are registered in the customer's name and held by the brokerage firm. The broker dealer may charge a fee for the safekeeping of the securities. Customers may now elect to hold securities registered in their name electronically in the book entry form through the Direct Registration System (DRS). The DRS offered through the depository trust corporation allows investors to hold their securities on the books of the issuer or the transfer agent. Investors who hold securities with the DRS receive a statement from the issuer or transfer agent.

HOLD IN STREET NAME

Securities that are held in street name are registered in the name of the brokerage firm as the nominal owner of the securities, and the customer is the beneficial owner. Most securities are held in this manner to make transfer of ownership easier.

RECEIPT VS. PAYMENT (RVP)/DELIVERY VS. PAYMENT (DVP)

These accounts are normally reserved for trusts and other institutional accounts that require that securities be delivered prior to releasing payment for the securities. These accounts are set up as cash-on-delivery (COD) accounts.

At the time the customer opens the account, the customer decides what to do with the distributions from the account. Investors may have the distributions sent directly to them or they may have them reinvested or swept into a money market account.

MAILING INSTRUCTIONS

All confirmations and statements are sent to the customer's address of record. Statements and confirmations may be sent to an individual with power of attorney if the duplicates are requested in writing. A customer's mail may be held by a brokerage firm for up to 2 months if the customer is traveling within the United States and for up to 3 months if the customer is traveling outside the United States. Customers who are on active duty with the militarily and have no fixed address should be advised to open a military P.O. Box where statements may be sent.

TYPES OF ACCOUNTS

INDIVIDUAL ACCOUNT

An individual account is an account that is owned by one person. That person makes the determination as to what securities are purchased and sold. In addition, that person receives all of the distributions from the account.

JOINT ACCOUNT

A joint account is an account that is owned by two or more adults. Each party to the account may enter orders and request distributions. The registered representative does not need to confirm instructions with both parties. Joint accounts require the owners to sign a joint account agreement prior to the opening of the account. All parties must endorse all securities and all parties must be alive. Checks drawn from the account must be made out in the names of all parties.

JOINT TENANTS WITH RIGHTS OF SURVIVORSHIP (JTWROS)

In a joint account with rights of survivorship (JTWROS), all the assets are transferred into the name of the surviving party in the event of one tenant's death. The surviving party becomes the sole owner of all of the assets in the account. Both parties on the account have an equal and undivided interest in the assets in the account.

JOINT TENANTS IN COMMON (JTIC)

In a joint account that is established as tenants in common, if one party dies all the assets of the tenant who has died become the property of the decedent's estate. They do not become the property of the surviving tenant. An account registered as JTIC allows the assets in the account to be divided unequally. One party on the account could own 60% of the account's assets.

 TAKENOTE!

Any securities registered in the names of two or more parties must be signed by all parties and all parties must be alive to be considered good delivery.

TRANSFER ON DEATH (TOD)

An account that has been registered as a transfer-on-death (TOD) account allows the account owner to stipulate to whom the account is to go to in the event of his or her death. Transfer on death accounts is sometimes referred to as pay on death or POD accounts. The party who will become the owner of the account in the event of the account holder's death is known as the beneficiary. The beneficiary may only enter orders for the account if he or she has power of attorney for the account. Unlike an account that is registered as JTWROS, the assets in the account will not be at risk should the beneficiary be the subject of a lawsuit, such as in a divorce proceeding.

DEATH OF A CUSTOMER

If an agent is notified of the death of a customer the agent must immediately cancel all open orders and mark the account deceased.

The representative must await instructions from the executor or administrator of the estate. In order to sell or transfer the assets, the agent must receive:

- Letters testamentary.

- Inheritance tax waivers.

- Certified copy of the death certificate.

The death of a customer with a discretionary account automatically terminates the discretionary authority.

CORPORATE ACCOUNTS

Corporations, like individuals, purchase and sell securities. In order to open a corporate account, the registered representative must obtain a corporate resolution that states which individuals have the power to enter orders for the corporation. If a corporation wants to purchase securities on margin, then the registered representative must obtain a corporate charter and the bylaws that state that the corporation may purchase securities on margin. Finally, a certificate of incumbency must be obtained for the officers who are authorized to transact business for the corporation, within 60 days of the account opening.

TRUST ACCOUNTS

Trusts may be revocable or irrevocable. With a revocable trust, the individual who established the trust and contributes assets to the trust, known as the grantor or settlor, may, as the name suggests, revoke the trust and take the assets back. The income generated by a revocable trust is generally taxed as income to the grantor. If the trust is irrevocable, the grantor may not revoke the trust and take the assets back. With an irrevocable trust, the trust usually pays the taxes as its own entity or the beneficiaries of the trust are taxed on the income they receive. If the trust is established as a simple trust all income generated by the trust must be distributed to the beneficiaries in the year the income is earned. If the trust is established as a complex trust, the trust may retain some or all of the income earned and the trust will pay taxes on the income that is not distributed to the beneficiaries. The grantor of an irrevocable trust is generally not taxed on the income generated by the trust unless the assets in the trust are held for the benefit of the grantor, the grantor's spouse, or if the grantor has an interest in the income of the trust greater than 5%.

A trust may also be established to hold or to distribute assets after a person's death under the terms of their will. Trusts that are established under the terms of a will are known as testamentary trusts. All assets placed into a testamentary trust are subject to both estate taxes and probate. A representative who opens a trust account must obtain documentation of the trustees investment powers over the trust's assets.

PARTNERSHIP ACCOUNTS

When a professional organization, such as a law partnership, opens an account, the registered representative must obtain a copy of the partnership agreement. The partnership agreement states who may enter orders for the account of the partnership. If the partnership wishes to purchase securities on margin, it must not be prohibited by the partnership agreement. A family limited partnership is often used for estate planning. Parents may place significant assets into a family limited partnership as a way to transfer their ownership. Usually, the parents act as the general partners and transfer limited partnership interests to their children. As the interests are transferred to the children, the parents may become subject to gift taxes. However, the gift taxes lower than they would have suffered without the partnership.

TRADING AUTHORIZATION

From time to time, people other than the beneficial owner of the account may be authorized to enter orders for the account. All discretionary authority must be evidenced in writing for the following accounts:

- Discretionary account
- Custodial account
- Fiduciary account

OPERATING A DISCRETIONARY ACCOUNT

A discretionary account allows the registered representative to determine the following, without consulting the client first:

- The asset to be purchased or sold.
- The amount of the securities to be purchased or sold.
- The action to be taken in the account, whether to buy or sell.

The principal of the firm must accept the account and review it more frequently to ensure against abuses. The customer is required to sign a limited power of attorney that awards discretion to the registered representative. The limited power of attorney is good for up to 3 years; the customer is bound by the decisions of the representative, but may still enter orders. Once discretion is given to the representative, the representative may not, in turn, give discretion to another party. If the representative leaves the firm or stops managing the customer's account, the discretionary authority is automatically terminated. A standard power of attorney also terminate upon the death or incapacitation of the account owner. A durable power of attorney continues in full effect in the case of incapacitation and terminates only upon the account owner's death. A full power of attorney allows an individual to deposit and withdraw cash and securities from the account. A full power of attorney is usually not given to a registered representative. A full power of attorney is more appropriate for fiduciaries such as a trustee, custodian, or a guardian. If a FINRA or MSRB broker dealer has a control relationship with an issuer of securities, the customer must be informed of the relationship and must give specific authorization for the purchase of the securities.

MANAGING DISCRETIONARY ACCOUNTS

All discretionary accounts must have the proper paperwork kept in the account file and must have:

- Every order entered marked discretionary, if discretion was exercised by the representative.
- Every order approved promptly by a principal.
- A designated principal to review the account.
- A record of all transactions.

Discretion may not be exercised by a representative until the discretionary papers have been received by the firm and approved by the principal.

THIRD-PARTY AND FIDUCIARY ACCOUNTS

A fiduciary account is one that is managed by a third party for the benefit of the account holder. The party managing the account has responsibility for making all of the investments and other decisions relating to the account. The individual with this responsibility must do as a prudent person would do for him or herself and may not speculate. This is known as the prudent man rule. Many states have an approved list of securities, known as the legal list, that may be purchased by fiduciaries. The authority to transact business for the account must be evidenced in writing by a power of attorney. The fiduciary may have full power of attorney, also known as full discretion, under which the fiduciary may purchase and sell securities, as well as withdraw cash and securities from the account. Under a limited power of attorney or limited discretion, the fiduciary may only buy and sell securities; assets may not be withdrawn. The fiduciary has been legally appointed to represent the account holder and may not use the assets in the account for his or her own benefit. The fiduciary may, however, be reimbursed for expenses incurred in connection with the management of the account. Examples of fiduciaries include:

- Administrators
- Custodians
- Receivers
- Trustees
- Conservators
- Executors
- Guardians
- Sheriffs/marshals

When opening a third party or fiduciary account, the registered representative is required to obtain documentation of the individual's appointment and authority to act on behalf of the account holder. Trust accounts require that the representative obtain a copy of the trust agreement. The trust agreement states who has been appointed as the trustee and any limitations on the trust's operation. Most trusts may only open cash accounts and may not purchase securities on margin, unless specifically authorized to do so in the agreement. When opening an account for a guardian, the representative must obtain a copy of the court order appointing the guardian. The court order must be dated within 60 days of the opening of the account. If the court order is more than 60 days old, the representative may not open the account until a new court order is obtained. Guardians are usually appointed in cases of mentally incompetent adults and orphaned children.

UNIFORM GIFT TO MINORS ACCOUNT (UGMA)

Minors are not allowed to own securities in their own name because they are not old enough to enter into legally binding contracts. The decision to purchase or sell a security creates a legally binding contract between two parties. The Uniform Gift to Minors Act (UGMA) regulates how accounts are operated for the benefit of minors. All UGMA accounts must have:

- One custodian

- One minor

- UGMA and the state in the account title

- Assets registered to the child's name after he or she reaches the age of majority

All securities in an UGMA account are registered in the custodian's name as the nominal owner for the benefit of the minor who is the beneficial owner of the account. For example, the account should be titled: Mr. Jones as custodian for Billy Jones under New Jersey Uniform Gift to Minors Act.

Only one custodian and one minor are allowed on each account. A husband and wife cannot be joint custodians for their minor child. If there is more than one child, a separate account must be opened for each one. The same person may serve as custodian on several accounts for several minors, and the minor may have more than one account established by different custodians. The donor of the security does not have to be the custodian for the account. If the parents are not the custodians of the accounts, they have no authority over the accounts.

RESPONSIBILITIES OF THE CUSTODIAN

The custodian has a fiduciary duty to manage the account prudently for the benefit of the minor child within certain guidelines, such as:

- No margin accounts.

- No high-risk securities (i.e., penny stocks).

- The custodian may not borrow from the account.

- No commodities.

- No speculative option strategies.

- The custodian may not give discretion to a third party.

- All distributions must be reinvested within a reasonable time.

- The custodian may not let rights or warrants expire; they must be exercised or sold.

- The custodian must provide support for all withdrawals from the account.

- Withdrawals may only be made to reimburse the custodian for expenses incurred in connection with the operation of the account or for the benefit of the minor.

CONTRIBUTIONS OF ANUGMA ACCOUNT

Gifts of cash and securities or other property may be given to the minor. There is no dollar limit as to the size of the gift that may be given. The limit on the size of the tax-free gift is $15,000 per year. An individual may give gifts valued at up to $15,000 to any number of people each year without incurring a tax liability. Once a gift has been given, it is irrevocable. Gifts to an UGMA account carry an indefeasible title and may not be taken back for any reason whatsoever. The custodian may, however, use the assets for the minor's welfare and educational needs.

 TAKENOTE!

A husband and wife may give up to $30,000 per year per person. The IRS considers half of the gift to be coming from each spouse. The annual gift limit is indexed for inflation since 1999.

UGMA TAXATION

The minor is responsible for the taxes on the account. However, any unearned income that exceeds $1,500 per year is taxed at the parent's marginal tax rate if the child is younger than 14 years old. For gifts that exceed $15,000 per year, the tax liability is on the donor of the gift, not on the minor.

DEATH OF A MINOR OR CUSTODIAN

If the minor dies, the account becomes part of the child's estate. It does not automatically go to the parents. If the custodian dies, a court or the donor may appoint a new custodian.

UNIFORM TRANSFER TO MINORS ACT

Some states have adopted the Uniform Transfer to Minors Act rather than the Uniform Gifts to Minors Act. The main difference is that with an

UTMA account the custodian may determine when the assets become the property of the child. The maximum age is 25 years old.

 TAKENOTE!

No evidence of custodial rights is required to open an UGMA or UTMA account.

ACCOUNTS FOR EMPLOYEES OF OTHER BROKER DEALERS

FINRA Rule 3210 requires that an employee of a broker dealer who wishes to open an account at another broker dealer must obtain the employer's written permission prior to opening the account. The employee must present written notification to the broker dealer opening the account that he /she is employed by a FINRA member firm at the time the account is opened. This rule is in effect for the employee or any of the employee's immediate family members. This rule also requires the employee to obtain the employer's written permission for accounts that were opened within 30 days of the start of employment. Excluded from this rule are accounts opened by the employee where no transactions may take place in individual securities such as accounts opened to purchase open end mutual funds, variable annuities, and UITs. (Prior to the effective date of this rule only employer notification is required).

NUMBERED ACCOUNTS

A broker dealer, at the request of the customer, may open an account that is simply identified by a number or a symbol, so long as there is a statement signed by the customer attesting to the ownership of the account.

OPTION ACCOUNTS

A customer wishing to trade options must be given a copy of the OCC's risk disclosure document and sign the firm's option agreement. The customer's account may be initially approved by a branch manager who is not a registered option and security futures principal (ROSFP), so long as the account is approved by a ROSFP within a reasonable amount of time.

A branch manager with more than three representatives conducting options business is required to qualify as a registered option and security futures principal.

MARGIN ACCOUNTS

A margin account allows the investor to purchase securities without paying for the securities in full. The investor is required to deposit a portion of the securities' purchase price and may borrow the rest from the broker dealer. The portion of the securities' purchase price that an investor must deposit is called margin. The amount of the required deposit or margin is controlled by the Federal Reserve Board under Regulation T of the Securities Exchange Act of 1934. Regulation T gave the Federal Reserve Board the authority to regulate the extension of credit for securities purchases. The Federal Reserve Board controls:

- Which securities may be purchased on margin.
- The amount of the initial required deposit.
- Payment dates.

Unlike when opening a cash account, when a customer opens a margin account he or she is required to sign certain account documents. The customer is asked to sign the following:

- Credit agreement
- Hypothecation agreement
- Loan consent

THE CREDIT AGREEMENT
The credit agreement states the terms and conditions under which credit is extended to the customer. It includes information about how interest is charged as well as information about the rates that are charged. A margin loan does not amortize, meaning that the principal is not paid down on a regular schedule. The brokerage firm simply charges interest to the account.

THE HYPOTHECATION AGREEMENT
The hypothecation agreement pledges the customer's securities that were purchased on margin as collateral for the loan. It also allows the brokerage

firm to take the same securities and repledge or rehypothecate them as collateral for a loan at a bank to obtain a loan for the customer.

LOAN CONSENT

By signing a loan consent agreement, the customer allows the brokerage firm to lend out the securities to customers who wish to sell the securities short. This is the only part of the margin agreement that the customer is not required to sign. The credit and hypothecation agreement must be signed prior to the account being approved to purchase securities on margin.

All securities purchased in a margin account are held in street name, the name of the brokerage firm, so that the broker dealer may sell the securities to protect itself if the value of the securities falls significantly. Day trading is an investment strategy defined by the entering of round-trip orders, consisting of both a buy and sell order, on the same day for the same security. Firms that promote the use of day trading strategies to individual investors must adhere to special account opening requirements. A broker dealer is considered to be promoting day trading strategies if it holds seminars, advertises, or uses another company to promote its services. If the firm promotes day trading, it must provide the customer with a risk disclosure document and approve the account for day trading. If the customer is not approved for day trading, the customer may still open an account so long as the firm obtains a written statement from the customer stating that he or she will not be engaging in day-trading strategies. A firm is considered to be promoting day trading if the registered representatives promote day trading strategies with the knowledge of the firm's principal.

RULES COVERING THE OPERATION OF MARGIN ACCOUNTS

The Federal Reserve Board sets the amount that must be deposited when customers purchase securities using borrowed funds. This is known as the initial margin requirement. The initial margin requirement has been equal to 50% of the purchase price for many years. For example, if a customer wanted to purchase $50,000 worth of stock on margin, the customer would be required to deposit $25,000 and the broker dealer could loan the customer the rest. Alternatively, if the customer wanted to sell stock short in the hope that the securities would fall in value, the customer would be required to deposit 50% of the price of the stock sold short. For example, if the customer sold a stock short with a market value of $60,000, the customer would be required to deposit, $30,000 to hold the position. Once a position has been established in a margin account, customers are required to maintain a minimum level of equity. The minimum equity requirement is set by the NYSE and FINRA in both new and established margin accounts.

Customers who want to establish a new margin account must have at least $2,500 in equity prior to the broker dealer loaning the customer any funds. Customers who have established margin accounts and who purchase securities on margin are required to maintain equity equal to 25% of the long market value. Going back to our customer who purchased $50,000 worth of stock on margin, the minimum equity requirement at the $50,000 level would be $12,500. Alternatively, customers who have sold stock short would be subject to a minimum equity requirement of 30% of the short market value. The investor who sold $60,000 worth of stock short would be subject to a minimum equity requirement of $18,000. Investors whose equity falls below the minimum level will be required to deposit additional money to restore the account to at least the minimum level. This is known as a margin call. When the equity in an account is below the initial requirement of 50% and above the minimum equity requirement, the account is said to be a restricted margin account. The term restricted only refers to the relationship of the equity to the market value. No limitations are placed on the account and the investor is free to increase his/her positions at will by depositing 50% of the price of the new securities. Special rules apply for customers who sell low-priced stocks short. A customer who sells a stock short worth $5 or less is subject to a marginal requirement of the greater of $2.50 per share or 100% of the value of the stock sold short. For example, a customer who sold 1,000 shares of stock short at $3 per share would be required to deposit $3,000.

> ▶ **TAKENOTE!**
>
> A customer can never be required to pay more than 100% of the stock price when purchasing a stock on margin. A customer who purchased 1,000 shares of stock at $2 in a new margin account would be required to deposit $2,000, as the minimum equity is $2,500 prior to any loan being made by the customer.

COMMINGLING CUSTOMER'S PLEDGED SECURITIES

A broker dealer may not commingle a customer's pledged securities with another customer's pledged securities as joint collateral to obtain a loan from a bank without both customers' written authorization. This authorization is required by SEC Rule 15c2-1 and is part of most margin agreements. A customer's securities may never be commingled with the firm's securities.

WRAP ACCOUNTS

A wrap account is an account that charges the customer a set annual fee for both advice and execution costs. The fee is based on the assets in the account. Wrap account holders must be given Schedule H, which details how fees are to be charged prior to opening the account. A firm that offers wrap accounts to its clients must be registered as investment advisers. Agents who service wrap accounts must have passed the Series 65 or Series 66 exams. Wrap accounts and other asset-based fee accounts are usually not appropriate for clients who trade infrequently and use a buy-and-hold strategy. The practice of placing these types of accounts into fee-based programs constitutes a violation known as reverse churning.

REGULATION S-P

Regulation S-P requires that the firm maintain adequate procedures to protect the financial information of its customers. Firms must guard against unauthorized access to customer financial information and must employ policies to ensure its safety. Special concerns arise over the ability for a person to "hack" into a firm's customer database by gaining unauthorized access. Firms must develop and maintain specific safeguards for its computer systems and WiFi access. Regulation S-P was derived from the privacy rules of the Gramm-Leach-Bliley Act. A firm must deliver:

- An initial privacy notice to customers, no later than when the account was opened.

- An annual privacy notice to all customers.

The annual privacy notice may be delivered electronically via the firm's website, so long as the customer has agreed to receive it in writing and it is clearly displayed. Regulation S-P also states that a firm may not disclose nonpublic personal information to nonaffiliated companies for clients who have opted out of the list.

The method by which a client may opt out may not be unreasonable. It is considered unreasonable to require a customer to write a letter to opt out. Reasonable methods are e-mails or a toll-free number. The rule also differentiates between who is a customer and who is a consumer. A customer is anyone who has an ongoing relationship with the firm (i.e., has an account). A consumer is someone who is providing information to the firm and is considering becoming a customer or who has purchased a product from the firm and has no other contact with the firm. The firm must give the privacy notice to consumers prior to sharing any nonpublic information with a nonaffiliated company.

 TAKENOTE!

A client of a brokerage firm may not opt out of the sharing of information with an affiliated company.

Regulation S-AM prohibits broker dealers from soliciting business based on information received from affiliated third parties unless the potential marketing had been clearly disclosed to the potential customer, the potential customer was provided an opportunity to opt out, but did not opt out.

IDENTITY THEFT

The fraudulent practice of identity theft may be used by criminals in an attempt to obtain access to the assets or credit of another person. The Federal Trade Commission (FTC) requires banks and broker dealers to establish and maintain written identity theft prevention programs. A broker dealer's written supervisory procedures manual must reference its identity theft program. The program must be designed to detect red flags relating to the known suspicious activity employed during an attempt at identity theft. The identity theft prevention program should be designed to allow the firm to respond quickly to any attempted identity theft to mitigate any potential damage.

Pretest

CUSTOMER ACCOUNTS, UGMAS, ACCOUNTS FOR EMPLOYEES OF BROKER DEALERS, AND CUSTOMER PRIVACY

la.finra.cus.ugma.emp.priv.001_1811

1. In which type of account does the nominal owner of the account enter all orders for the beneficial owner of the account?

    a. Custodial account.

    b. Fiduciary account.

    c. Authorized account.

    d. Discretionary account.

la.finra.cus.ugma.emp.priv.002_1811

2. Which of the following is NOT allowed as a joint account?

    a. A registered representative and a customer.

    b. A registered representative and a spouse.

    c. A registered representative and a friend.

    d. A registered representative and his 16-year-old child.

la.finra.cus.ugma.emp.priv.003_1811

3. A customer and his spouse have an account registered as joint tenants in common. If the customer dies, what would happen to the account?

    a. The decedent's assets will be distributed according to his will.

    b. The executor of the estate will determine how all of the assets are to be distributed.

    c. All of the assets in the account will be distributed according to the trustee.

    d. The spouse would get the assets in the account.

la.finra.cus.ugma.emp.priv.004_1811

4. To open a guardian account, the firm must obtain:

   a. Trust papers.

   b. Power of attorney.

   c. Declaration papers.

   d. Affidavit of domicile.

la.finra.cus.ugma.emp.priv.005_1811

5. In which type of account does a trustee enter all orders for the owners of the account?

   a. Custodial account.

   b. Fiduciary account.

   c. Authorized account.

   d. Discretionary account.

la.finra.cus.ugma.emp.priv.006_1811

6. The maximum allowable gift to a minor under UGMA is:

   a. $15,000.

   b. $1,500.

   c. $30,000.

   d. There is no limit.

la.finra.cus.ugma.emp.priv.007_1811

7. The nominal owner of an UGMA account is the:

   a. Custodian.

   b. Minor.

   c. Trustee.

   d. Parent.

la.finra.cus.ugma.emp.priv.008_1811

8. A representative may borrow money from a client:

   a. If the client is the issuer of securities.

   b. If the client is a credit union.

   c. If the client is a wealthy individual who regularly makes private loans.

   d. Under no circumstances.

la.finra.cus.ugma.emp.priv.009_1811

9. You have just opened up a new account for a customer. You are required to have all of the following, except the:

   a. Agent's name or ID number.

   b. Principal's signature.

   c. Customer's signature.

   d. Customer's social security number.

la.finra.cus.ugma.emp.priv.010_1811

10. A customer calls in asking about how to put money aside for his children. He wants to open a custodial account for his two children, Bobby and Sue. What should you recommend?

    a. Open two accounts for both children, with him and his wife as custodian.

    b. Open two accounts for the two children, with him being the custodian on one and his wife being custodian on the other, as one parent may only be custodian for one child.

    c. Open one account immediately for both children.

    d. Open two accounts, one for each child, with he or his wife as custodians for both or for either.

la.finra.cus.ugma.emp.priv.011_1811

11. Which of the following is true?

    a. Representatives and broker dealers may not disclose any information regarding a client to a third party without the client's expressed consent or a court order.

    b. A representative may not obtain outside employment because of the potential conflict of interest.

    c. A client may not have a numbered account for his investment account.

    d. Broker dealers may not give gifts to the employees of other broker dealers.

la.finra.cus.ugma.emp.priv.012_1811

12. A potential customer that you have been trying to get to open an account with you for some time has agreed to put some money in a mutual fund you have recommended. Which of the following customer information is NOT required on the new account form?

a. Address.

b. Social security number.

c. Educational information.

d. Investment objective.

la.finra.cus.ugma.emp.priv.013_1811

13. Two brothers, both married with children, have opened an account with your firm as JTWROS. One brother has passed away. All of the following will not happen with regard to the account except:

a. All assets will become the property of the surviving party.

b. The account will be retitled in the name of the surviving party.

c. The portion of the assets belonging to the deceased will go to his estate.

d. The original account will become an individual account.

la.finra.cus.ugma.emp.priv.014_1811

14. Before opening a new account for any customer, a registered representative must:

a. Fill out and submit the account for principal review.

b. Send a declaration of investor intent (DII) to the IRS.

c. Fill out a new account form and present it to the investor for his signature.

d. Fill out and sign a full financial declaration.

sa.finra.cus.ugma.emp.priv.001_1811

15. A registered representative may accept orders for a client's account from which of the following?

    I. Client.
   II. Client's spouse.
  III. Client's attorney.
   VI. Client's investment adviser.

a. I and II.

b. I, II, and III.

c. I only.

d. I, II, III, and IV.

sa.finra.cus.ugma.emp.priv.002_1811

16. Which of the following is NOT required in the account title for a custodial account?

   a. The state.

   b. The minor's social security number.

   c. The name of the custodian.

   d. UGMA.

Employee Conduct and Reportable Events

INTRODUCTION

Learning Objective Statements

Identify prohibited conduct and market manipulation.

Contrast churning, trading ahead, and front running.

Identify blanket recommendations.

Evalute interactions with customers.

All recommendations to customers must be suitable based on the customers' investment objectives, financial profile, and attitudes toward investing. Representatives usually make verbal recommendations to customers. The representative reviews the customer's investment objective and offers facts to support the basis for his or her recommendations, as well as an explanation as to how the recommendations will help the customer meet the desired objective. Any predictions about the performance of an investment should be stated strictly as an opinion or belief, not as a fact. If the firm uses reports that cite past performance of the firm's previous recommendations, the report must contain:

• The prices and dates when the recommendations were made.

• General market conditions.

• The recommendations in all similar securities for 12 months.

• A statement disclosing that the firm is a market maker (if applicable).

• A statement regarding whether the firm or its officers or directors own any of the securities being recommended or options or warrants for the same security.

• Information as to whether the firm managed or comanaged an underwriting of any of the issuer's securities in the last 3 years.

• A statement regarding the availability of supporting documentation for the recommendations.

PROFESSIONAL CONDUCT IN THE SECURITIES INDUSTRY

The securities industry is a highly regulated industry. All broker dealers are required to regulate their employees. A broker dealer must designate a principal to supervise all of the actions of the firm and its employees. The broker dealer and all of its employees are also regulated by a self-regulatory organization (SRO), such as FINRA or the NYSE. The SROs and all industry participants answer to the SEC. The SEC is the ultimate securities industry authority. Additionally, each state has adopted its own rules and regulations regarding securities transactions that occur within the state. Violations of industry regulations may lead to fines and expulsion from the industry. Violations of state and federal laws may result in fines, expulsion from the state or industry, or a jail term. Industry participants are expected to adhere to all of the industry's rules and regulations, as well as all state and federal laws.

FAIR DEALINGS WITH CUSTOMERS

All broker dealers are required to act in good faith in all of their dealings with customers and are required to uphold just and equitable trade practices. FINRA's rules of fair practice, also known as the rules of conduct, regulate how business is conducted with members of the general public. The rules of conduct prohibit all of the following:

• Churning
• Manipulative and deceptive practices
• Unauthorized trading

- Fraudulent acts
- Blanket recommendations
- Misrepresentations
- Omitting material facts
- Making guarantees
- Selling dividends
- Recommending speculative securities without knowing the customer can afford the risk
- Short-term trading in mutual funds
- Switching fund families

CHURNING

Most representatives are compensated when the customer makes a transaction based on their recommendations. Churning is a practice of making transactions that are excessive in size or frequency, with the intention to generate higher commissions for the representative. When determining if an account has been churned, regulators look at the frequency of the transactions, the size of the transactions, and the amount of commission earned by the representative. Customer profitability is not an issue when determining if an account has been churned.

In addition to churning, where the agent or firm executes too many transactions to increase revenue, a practice known as reverse churning is also a violation. Reverse churning is the practice of placing inactive accounts or accounts that do not trade frequently into fee-based programs that charge an annual fee based on the assets in the account. This fee covers all advice and execution charges. Since these inactive accounts do not trade frequently the total fees charged to the account will increase. This makes a fee-based account unsuitable for inactive accounts and for accounts that simply buy and hold securities for a long period of time. These accounts generally are charged an annual fee in the range of 1%–2% of the total value of the assets, in lieu of commissions when orders are executed.

MANIPULATIVE AND DECEPTIVE DEVICES

It is a violation for a firm or representative to engage in or employ any artifice or scheme that is designed to gain an unfair advantage over another party. Some examples of manipulative or deceptive devices are:

- Capping
- Pegging
- Front running
- Trading ahead
- Painting the tape/matched purchases/matches sales

Capping: A manipulative act designed to keep a stock price from rising or to keep the price down.

Pegging: A manipulative act designed to keep a stock price up or to keep the price from falling.

Front running: The entering of an order for the account of an agent or firm prior to entering a large customer order. The firm or agent is using the customer's order to profit on the order it entered for its own account.

Trading ahead: The entering of an order for a security based on prior knowledge from a soon to be released research report.

Painting the tape: A manipulative act by two or more parties designed to create false activity in the security without any beneficial change in ownership. The increased activity is used to attract new buyers.

UNAUTHORIZED TRADING

An unauthorized transaction is one that is made for the benefit of a customer's account at a time when the customer has no knowledge of the trade and the representative does not have discretionary power over the account.

FRAUD

Fraud is defined as any act that is employed to obtain an unfair advantage over another party. Fraudulent acts include:

- False statements
- Deliberate omissions of material facts
- Concealment of material facts
- Manipulative and deceptive practices
- Forgery
- Material omission
- Lying

BLANKET RECOMMENDATIONS

It is inappropriate for a firm or a representative to make blanket recommendations in any security, especially low-priced speculative securities. No matter what type of investment is involved, a blanket recommendation to a large group of people will always be wrong for some investors. Different investors have different objectives, and the same recommendation will not be suitable for everyone.

EXAMPLE

Mr. Jones, an agent with XYZ brokers, has a large customer base that ranges from young investors who are just starting to save to institutions and retirees. Mr. Jones has been doing a significant amount of research on WSIA industries, a mining and materials company. Mr. Jones strongly believes that WSIA is significantly undervalued, based on its assets and earning potential. Mr. Jones recommends WSIA to all his clients. In the next 6 months the share price of WSIA increases significantly as new production dramatically increases sales, just as Mr. Jones's research suggested. The clients then sell WSIA at Mr. Jones's suggestion and realize a significant profit.

ANALYSIS

Even though the clients who purchased WSIA based on Mr. Jones's recommendation made a significant profit, Mr. Jones has still committed a violation because he recommended it to all of his clients. Mr. Jones's clients have a wide variety of investment objectives, and the risk or income potential associated with an investment in WSIA would not be suitable for every client. Even if an investment is profitable for the client it does not mean it was suitable for the client. Blanket recommendations are never suitable.

SELLING DIVIDENDS

Selling dividends is a violation that occurs when a registered representative uses a pending dividend payment as the sole basis of a recommendation to purchase the stock or mutual fund. Additionally, using the pending dividend as a means to create urgency on the part of the investor to purchase the stock is a prime example of this type of violation. If the investor was to purchase the shares just prior to the ex dividend date simply to receive the dividend, the investor in many cases will end up worse off. The dividend in this case will actually be a return of the money that the investor used to purchase the stock, and then the investor will have a tax liability when the dividend is received.

MISREPRESENTATIONS

A representative or a firm may not knowingly make any misrepresentations regarding:

- A client's account status
- The representative
- The firm
- An investment
- Fees to be charged

OMITTING MATERIAL FACTS

A representative of a firm may not omit any material fact, either good or bad, when recommending a security. A material fact is one that an investor would need to know in order to make a well-informed investment decision. The representative may, however, omit an immaterial fact.

GUARANTEES

No representative, broker dealer, or investment adviser may make any guarantees of any kind. A profit may not be guaranteed, and a promise of no loss may not be made.

RECOMMENDATIONS TO AN INSTITUTIONAL CUSTOMER

FINRA recognizes an institutional customer as one that has at least $10,000,000 in assets. The agent's or member's suitability determination can be met if the customer:

- Can independently evaluate the investment risks and merits.
- Can independently make his or her own investment decisions.

If the customer meets the above criteria, the member or agent may recommend almost any investment to the customer and allow the customer to determine if it is suitable.

RECOMMENDING MUTUAL FUNDS

A representative recommending a mutual fund should ensure that the mutual fund's investment objective meets the customer's investment objective. If the mutual fund company or broker dealer distributes advertising or sales literature regarding the mutual fund, the following should be disclosed:

- The highest sales charge charged by the fund
- The fund's current yield based on dividends only
- Graph performance of the fund versus a broad-based index
- The performance of the fund for 10 years or the life of the fund, whichever is less
- Not imply that a mutual fund is safer than other investments
- Source of graphs and charts

MUTUAL FUND CURRENT YIELD

When advertising or recommending a mutual fund, any statement of claim regarding its current yield must be based solely on the annual dividends paid by the fund and may not include any capital gains distributions. Additionally, the public offering price used to calculate the current yield must contain the highest sales charge charged by the fund and may not be based on a breakpoint schedule or sales reduction charge.

EXAMPLE   ABC balanced fund has a POP of $10, has paid dividends totaling $1, and has distributed $.75 in capital gains distributions. What is the fund's current yield?

$$\text{current yield} = \text{annual income/current price}$$
$$\text{current yield} = \frac{\$1}{\$10} = 10\%$$

If the capital gains distributions were included, it would make the current yield look much higher than 10%. If the capital gains distribution of $.75 were included, the current yield would have been quoted at 17.5%.

DISCLOSURE OF CLIENT INFORMATION

Registered representatives and broker dealers may not disclose any information regarding clients to a third party without the client's expressed consent or without a court order. If the client is an issuer of securities and the broker dealer is an underwriter, transfer agent, or paying agent for the issuer, then the broker dealer is precluded from using the information it obtains regarding the issuer's security holders for its own benefit.

BORROWING AND LENDING MONEY

Borrowing and lending of money between registered persons and customers is strictly regulated. If the member firm allows borrowing and lending between representatives and customers the firm must have policies in place that will allow for the loans to be made. Loans may be made between an agent and a customer if the customer is a bank or other lending institution, where there is a personal or outside business relationship and that relationship is the basis for the loan, or between two agents registered with the same firm. The firm must provide the agent with written preapproval for the loan unless the loan is being made between the agent and an immediate family member or a bank. The approval documentation must be maintained for 3 years from the date when the loan was repaid or 3 years from the rep's termination from the firm.

GIFT RULE

Broker dealers may not pay compensation to employees of other broker dealers. If a broker dealer wants to give a gift to an employee of another broker dealer, it must:

- Be valued at less than $100 per person per year.
- Be given directly to the employing member firm for distribution to the employee.
- Have the employing member's prior approval for the gift.

The employing member must obtain a record of the gift, including the name of the giver, the name of the recipient, and the nature of the gift. These rules have been established to ensure that broker dealers do not try to influence the employees of other broker dealers. An exception to this rule would be in cases where an employee of one broker dealer performs services for another broker dealer under an employment contract. Occasional meals, tickets to sporting events, and lucite plaques and prospectuses are all acceptable.

OUTSIDE EMPLOYMENT

If a registered representative wants to obtain employment outside of his or her position with a member firm, the registered representative must first notify the employing member prior to engaging in the activity. Prior approval is not required but the employer has the right to refuse or limit the outside business activity. Exceptions to this rule are if the registered representative is a passive investor in a business or if the representative owns rental property. All other outside business activities must be disclosed to the member firm.

PRIVATE SECURITIES TRANSACTIONS

A registered representative may not engage in any private securities transactions without first obtaining the broker dealer's prior approval. The registered representative must provide the employing firm with all documentation regarding the investment and the proposed transaction. An example of a private securities transaction would be if a representative helped a startup business raise money through a private placement. If the representative is going to receive compensation, the employing member firm must supervise the transaction as if the firm itself executed the transaction. If a representative sells investment products that the employing member does not conduct business in without the member's knowledge, then the representative has committed a violation known as selling away.

CUSTOMER COMPLAINTS

All written complaints received from a customer or from an individual acting on behalf of the customer must be reported promptly to the principal of the firm. The firm is required to:

- Maintain a copy of the complaint in a supervising office of supervisory jurisdiction for 4 years.
- Electronically report all complaints to FINRA within 15 days of the end of each calendar quarter.
- Report complaints within 10 days to FINRA if the complaint alleges misappropriation of funds or securities or forgery.

Pretest

EMPLOYEE CONDUCT AND REPORTABLE EVENTS

la.finra.emp.con.ev.001_1811

1. Creating false activity in a security to attract new purchases is a fraudulent practice known as:

   a. Trading ahead.

   b. Painting the tape.

   c. Active concealment.

   d. Front running.

la.finra.emp.con.ev.002_1811

2. Which of the following is not a violation of the rules of conduct?

   a. Recommending a security because of its future price appreciation.

   b. Recommending a mutual fund based on a pending dividend to an investor seeking income.

   c. Implying that FINRA has approved the firm.

   d. Showing a client the past performance of a mutual fund for the last 3 years since its inception.

sa.finra.emp.con.ev.001_1811

3. A customer has a large position in GJH, a thinly traded stock whose share price has remained flat for some time. The customer contacts the agent and wants to sell his entire position. The customer is most subject to which of the following?

   a. Liquidity risk.

   b. Credit risk.

   c. Conversion risk.

   d. Execution risk.

sa.finra.emp.con.ev.002_1811

4. An investor gets advance notice of a research report being issued and enters an order to purchase the security that is the subject of the research report. This is known as:

   a. Front running.

   b. Trading ahead.

   c. Insider trading.

   d. Advance trading.

Customer Recommendations, Professional Conduct, and Taxation

INTRODUCTION

Learning Objective Statements

Select the appropriate investment given a stated objective

Analyze the various types of risk associated with investments in securities.

Calculate the impact of taxes on investment returns.

All broker dealers that carry customer accounts must send their customers information detailing FINRA's BrokerCheck public disclosure program at least once per calendar year. The BrokerCheck program, accessible via the FINRA website, provides detailed registration and disciplinary history for firms and agents maintained at the central registration depository (CRD). The information must contain the program's 800 number, FINRA's website address, and a statement that an investor brochure includes the same information and is available.

NYSE/FINRA KNOW YOUR CUSTOMER

The NYSE and FINRA both require that any recommendation to a customer be suitable for the customer. The representative has an affirmative obligation to determine the suitability of the recommendations made to customers. The suitability obligation is triggered at the time the investment is discussed with the client, not based on if the customer makes the investment. The rules require that the agent obtain enough information about the customer to ensure that all recommendations are suitable based on a review of the client's:

- Investment objectives.
- Financial status.
- Income.
- Investment holdings.
- Retirement needs.
- College and other major expenses.
- Tax bracket.
- Attitude toward investing.

The more you know about a customer's financial position, the better you will be able to help the customer meet his or her objectives. You should always ask questions like:

- How long have you been making these types of investments?
- Do you have any major expenses coming up?
- How long do you usually hold investments?
- How much risk do you normally take?
- What tax bracket are you in?
- How much money do you have invested in the market?
- Have you done any retirement planning?

Of course there are other questions that you should ask, but these are examples of the type of questions all representatives should ask.

Other questions a representative should ask the customer include:

- How old are you?
- Are you married?
- Do you have any children?
- How long have you been employed at your current job?

Registered representatives must make sure that their recommendations meet their customers' objectives. Should a client have a primary and a secondary objective, a representative must make sure that the recommendation meets the investor's primary objective first and the secondary objective second.

INVESTMENT OBJECTIVES

All investors want to make or preserve money. However, these objectives can be met in different ways. Some of the different investment objectives are:

- Income
- Growth
- Preservation of capital
- Tax benefits
- Liquidity
- Speculation

INCOME

Many investors are looking to have their investments generate additional income to help meet their monthly expenses. Some investments that will help to meet this objective are:

- Corporate bonds
- Municipal bonds
- Government bonds
- Preferred stocks
- Money market funds
- Bond funds

GROWTH

Investors who seek capital appreciation over time want their money to grow in value and are not seeking any current income. The only investments that can achieve this goal are:

- Common stocks
- Common stock funds

PRESERVATION OF CAPITAL

Investors who have preservation of capital as an investment objective are very conservative and are more concerned with keeping the money they have saved. For these investors, high-quality debt is an appropriate recommendation. The following are good investments for preserving capital:

- Money market funds
- Government bonds
- Municipal bonds
- High-grade corporate bonds

TAX BENEFITS

For investors seeking tax advantages, the only two possible recommendations are:

- Municipal bonds
- Municipal bond funds

LIQUIDITY

Investors who need immediate access to their money need to own liquid investments that will not fluctuate wildly in value in case they need to use the money. The following investments are listed from most liquid to least liquid:

- Money market funds
- Stocks/bonds/mutual funds
- Annuities
- Collateralized mortgage obligations (CMOs)
- Direct participation programs
- Real estate

SPECULATION

A customer investing in a speculative manner is willing to take a high degree of risk in order to earn a high rate of return. Some of the more speculative investments are:

- Penny stocks
- Small cap stocks
- Some growth stocks
- Junk bonds

RISK VS. REWARD

Risk is the reciprocal of reward. An investor must be offered a higher rate of return for each unit of additional risk the investor is willing to assume. There are many types of risk involved with investing money. They are as follows:

- Capital risk
- Market risk
- Nonsystematic risk
- Legislative risk
- Timing risk
- Credit risk
- Reinvestment risk
- Call risk
- Liquidity risk

CAPITAL RISK

Capital risk is the risk that an investor may lose all or part of the capital that has been invested.

MARKET RISK

Market risk is also known as a systematic risk, and it is the risk that is inherent in any investment in the markets. For example, you could own stock in the greatest company in the world and you could still lose money because the value of your stock goes down, simply because the market as a whole goes down.

NONSYSTEMATIC RISK

Nonsystematic risk is the risk that pertains to one company or industry. For example, the problems that the tobacco industry faced a few years ago would not have affected a computer company.

LEGISLATIVE RISK

Legislative risk is the risk that the government will do something that adversely affects an investment. For example, beer manufacturers probably did not fare too well when the government enacted prohibition.

TIMING RISK

Timing risk is simply the risk that an investor will buy and sell at the wrong time and lose money as a result.

CREDIT RISK

Credit risk is the risk of default inherent in debt securities. An investor may lose all or part of an investment because the issuer has defaulted and cannot pay the interest or principal payments owed to the investor.

REINVESTMENT RISK

When interest rates decline and higher yielding bonds have been called or have matured, investors will not be able to receive the same return given the same amount of risk. This is reinvestment risk, and the investor is forced to either accept the lower rate or must take more risk to obtain the same rate.

CALL RISK

Call risk is the risk that, as interest rates decline, higher yielding bonds and preferred stocks will be called and investors will be forced to reinvest the proceeds at a lower rate of return or at a higher rate of risk to achieve the same return. Call risk only applies to preferred stocks and bonds with a call feature.

LIQUIDITY RISK

Liquidity risk is the risk that an investor will not be able to liquidate an investment when needed or will not be able to liquidate the investment without adversely affecting the price.

PRODUCTS MADE AVAILABLE THROUGH MEMBER FIRMS

All products offered through member firms must meet a reasonable basis suitability requirement. The reasonable basis suitability requirement has two parts. The member must understand the risks and performance characteristics of the investment and the agents offering the products for sale must understand the risks and performance characteristics of the investment. The member is required to educate agents about the risks and rewards of the products it allows agents to recommend to clients. If a member maintains a new product committee to review potential investments offered to clients the committee must believe that the products are suitable for at least some of the firm's clients. FINRA member firms should train representatives about the characteristics relating to specific products including product features, risks, and pricing. Members should also provide representatives with suitability guidance in recommending products and product-related risk assessments and reviews. It is the responsibility of the representative to meet the client-specific suitability requirement. The representative's principal will review the transaction promptly to ensure client specific suitability.

 TAKENOTE!

If the firm's product committee understands the risks and allows agents to offer the securities to clients, but the representative does not, neither the firm nor the representative has met their obligations under suitability standards.

Members must track ongoing changes that impact suitability such as changes in interest rates, and oil prices that can impact the suitability of an investment. Specifically, members should discuss and disclose how changing interest rates may impact a portfolio of fixed income securities such as high yield bonds, CMOs, and other mortgaged-backed products.

RECOMMENDATIONS THROUGH SOCIAL MEDIA

The use of social media such as Linkedin, Facebook, and Twitter all need to be closely supervised by the member firm, specifically in cases where the communication posted by the firm or its agents could be deemed to be a recommendation. Being able to determine when communication reaches the level of a recommendation is a key element on the exam and for supervisors in general. When communication is deemed to be a recommendation it becomes subject to the suitability requirements of

FINRA Rule 2111. Certain types of communications that are deemed to be recommendations are as follows:

- Targeted e-mail distributions and tweets that advise the reader to buy or sell a security or securities within a sector
- Targeted pop-up, redirect, and mouse-over messages displayed to website visitors that advise the visitor to buy or sell a security or securities within a sector.

If the firm maintains a website that allows access to a library of research containing pervious buy and sell recommendations the ability to access the library will not constitute a recommendation.

Due to the complex compliance issues social media present, member firms are within their rights to limit or restrict employees' use of social media. Should a member firm allow its representatives to communicate over social media, the level of supervision required will depend on the type of social media used and the content of the communication. Member firms must properly train its employees on the use of social media and maintain written policies and procedures regarding its use and supervision. Static content that may be accessed by a visitor at any time requires prior approval from a principal before the static post is made. Static content includes Facebook walls, LinkedIn profiles, blogs, and Twitter posts. Aggressively tweeting positive or negative messages about an investment is a cause for concern and may result in sanctions being imposed on both the agent and the firm. Only agents who have the approval of their firm to tweet about investments should do so. Interactive blogs and chatroom conversations are deemed to be public appearances. These public appearances do not require prior principal approval but are subject to FINRA rules. Statements made must be factual and not exaggerated and no statements should be made about a security during a quiet period. It is important to note that most blogs are static and require prior approval for posts. Merely updating a blog on a regular basis does not constitute an interactive blog. FINRA members must carefully supervise the use of social media by its agents and must have systems in place designed to detect potential violations. These systems should be designed to detect red flag words such as "guarantee" and "can't lose." Agents who have a history of questionable sales practices or who have been sanctioned should be prohibited from using social media for business purposes. A post on social media from a client of the firm or from an unrelated third party will not be deemed to have been made by the firm and is not subject to supervision unless the firm assisted in preparing such post or approved the content.

> ◀▶ **TAKE**NOTE!
>
> One way for a firm to keep close supervision for representatives who make recommendations using social media is to have a preapproved catalog of research available for the representatives to use.

TAX STRUCTURE

There are two types of taxes: progressive and regressive. A progressive tax levies a larger tax on higher income earners. Examples of progressive taxes are:

- Income taxes
- Estate taxes

Regressive taxes level the same tax rate on everyone, regardless of their income. As a result, a larger portion of the lower income earner's earnings go toward the tax. Examples of regressive taxes are:

- Sales taxes
- Property taxes
- Gasoline taxes
- Excise taxes

INVESTMENT TAXATION

Investors must be aware of the impact that federal and state taxes have on their investment results. A taxable event will occur in most cases when an investor:

- Sells a security at a profit.
- Sells a security at a loss.
- Receives interest or dividend income.

CALCULATING GAINS AND LOSSES

When investors sell their shares, in most cases they will have a capital gain or loss. In order to determine if there is a gain or loss, the investor must first calculate the cost basis, or cost base. An investor's cost base, in most cases, is equal to the price the investor paid for the shares plus any commissions or fees. Once an investor knows the cost base, calculating any gain or loss becomes easy. A capital gain is realized when the investor sells the shares at a price that is greater than the cost base. Any gain on an asset held more than 1 year is considered a long-term capital gain and is taxed at a maximum rate of 15%. Any gain on an asset held for less than 1 year is considered a short-term capital gain and is taxed at the investor's ordinary income tax rate. The investor's holding period begins the day after the purchase and ends on the sale date.

EXAMPLE

An investor who purchased a stock at $10 per share 3 years ago and receives $14 per share when he sells the shares has a $4 capital gain. This is found by subtracting the cost base from the sales proceeds: $14 − $10 = $4. If the investor had 1,000 shares, he would have a capital gain of $4,000.

An investor's cost base is always returned to the investor tax-free. A capital loss is realized when investors sell shares at a price that is less than their cost base. If the investor in the previous example were to have sold the shares at $8 instead of $14, the investor would have a $2 capital loss, or a total capital loss of $2,000 for the entire position.

Again this is found by subtracting the cost base from the sales proceeds: $8 − $10 = −$2. Capital gains, like dividends, are taxed at a 15% rate for ordinary income earners and at a 20% rate for high income earners.

COST BASE OF MULTIPLE PURCHASES

Investors who have been accumulating shares through multiple purchases must determine their cost base at the time of sale through one of the following methods:

- FIFO (first in, first out)
- Share identification
- Average cost

FIFO (FIRST IN, FIRST OUT)

If the investor does not identify which shares are being sold at the time of sale, the IRS will assume that the first shares that were purchased are the first shares that are sold under the FIFO method. In many cases, this results in the largest capital gain, and, as a result, the investor has the largest tax liability.

SHARE IDENTIFICATION

An investor may at the time of the sale specify which shares are being sold. By keeping a record of the purchase prices and the dates that the shares were purchased, the investor may elect to sell the shares that create the most favorable tax consequences.

AVERAGE COST

An investor may decide to sell shares based on their average cost. An investor must determine the shares' average cost by using the following formula:

$$\text{average cost} = \frac{\textbf{total dollars invested}}{\textbf{total \# of shares purchases}}$$

Once an investor has elected to use the average cost method to calculate gains and losses, another method may not be used without IRS approval.

DEDUCTING CAPITAL LOSSES

An investor may use capital losses to offset capital gains dollar for dollar in the year in which they are realized. A net capital loss may be used to reduce the investor's taxable ordinary income by up to $3,000 in the year in which it is realized. Any net capital losses that exceed $3,000 may be carried forward into future years and may be deducted at a rate of $3,000 from ordinary income every year until the loss is used up. If the investor has a capital gain in subsequent years, the investor may use the entire amount of the net capital loss remaining to offset the gain, up to the amount of the gain.

TAXATION OF INTEREST INCOME

Interest earned by investors may or may not be subject to taxes. The following table illustrates the tax consequences of various interest payments received by investors:

Resident	Investment	Taxation
New Jersey	Corporate bond	All taxes
New Jersey	CMO	All taxes
New Jersey	GNMA	All taxes
New Jersey	T-bond	Federal taxes only
New Jersey	New York muni bond	New Jersey taxes only
New Jersey	New Jersey muni bond	No taxes
New Jersey	Puerto Rico/Guam muni bond	No taxes

 TAKENOTE!

Investors may deduct margin interest only to the extent of their investment income. Investors may not deduct margin expenses from municipal bonds.

GIFT TAXES

When gifts are made to family members or other individuals, the donor does not receive any tax deduction. The donor's cost base transfers to the recipient for tax purposes. Individuals may give gifts of up to $15,000 per person per year without incurring any tax liability. If a gift in excess of $15,000 is given to an individual, the donor owes the gift tax.

 TAKENOTE!

A husband and wife may give up to $30,000 per year per person. The IRS considers half of the gift to be coming from each spouse. The annual tax-free gift limit is updated periodically to adjust for inflation.

WITHHOLDING TAX

All broker dealers are required to withhold 31% of all sales proceeds if the investor has not provided a social security number or a tax identification number. In addition, 31% of all distributions from a mutual fund will also be withheld without a social security number or a tax identification number.

ALTERNATIVE MINIMUM TAX (AMT)

Certain items that receive beneficial tax treatment must be added back into the taxable income for some high-income earners. These items include:

- Interest on some industrial revenue bonds.
- Some stock options
- Accelerated depreciation
- Personal property tax on investments that do not generate income
- Certain tax deductions passed through from DPPs

Pretest

CUSTOMER RECOMMENDATIONS, PROFESSIONAL CONDUCT, AND TAXATION

la.finra.rec.prof.tax.001_1811

1. Which of the following could be subject to an investor's AMT?

    a. A limited partnership.

    b. An open-end mutual fund.

    c. A convertible preferred stock owned by a wealthy investor.

    d. An industrial revenue bond.

la.finra.rec.prof.tax.002_1811

2. An investor has a conservative attitude towards investing and is seeking to invest $50,000 into an interest-bearing instrument that will provide current income and safety. You would most likely recommend which of the following?

    a. Treasury bill.

    b. Ginnie Mae pass-through certificate.

    c. Treasury STRIP.

    d. Bankers' acceptance.

la.finra.rec.prof.tax.003_1811

3. An investor who is concerned with changes in interest rates would be least likely to purchase which of the following?

    a. Long-term warrants.

    b. Long-term corporate bonds.

    c. Long-term equity.

    d. Call options.

la.finra.rec.prof.tax.004_1811

4. An investor is looking for a risk-free investment. An agent should recommend which of the following to this investor?

   a. Preferred stock.

   b. 90-day T-bill.

   c. Convertible preferred stock.

   d. Bankers' acceptances.

la.finra.rec.prof.tax.005_1811

5. Which of the following is true?

   a. If an investor buys shares just prior to the ex date, he will have his investment money returned.

   b. After an investor's money is returned, the investor is still liable for taxes on the dividend amount.

   c. A registered representative may not use the pending dividend payment as the sole basis for recommending a stock purchase.

   d. All of the above.

la.finra.rec.prof.tax.006_1811

6. A new investor is in the 15% tax bracket and is seeking some additional current income. Which of the following would you recommend?

   a. Growth fund.

   b. Government bond fund.

   c. Municipal bond fund.

   d. Corporate bond fund.

la.finra.rec.prof.tax.007_1811

7. An investor has a conservative attitude toward investing and is seeking to invest $100,000 into an instrument that will provide current income and the most protection from interest rate risk. You would most likely recommend which of the following?

   a. Ginnie Mae pass-through certificate.

   b. Bankers' acceptance.

   c. Treasury STRIP.

   d. A portfolio of T-bills.

la.finra.rec.prof.tax.008_1811

8. Mr. and Mrs. Jones, a couple in their early forties, enjoy watching their son play baseball on the weekends. He is planning to go to college 11 years from September and they are looking to start saving for college expenses. Which of the following would you recommend?

    a. Educational IRA.

    b. Growth fund.

    c. Treasury STRIPS.

    d. Custodial account.

la.finra.rec.prof.tax.009_1811

9. A couple in their early thirties are seeking an investment for the $40,000 they have saved. They are planning on purchasing a new home in the next 2 years. You should most likely recommend which of the following?

    a. Preferred stock.

    b. Common stock and common stock funds.

    c. Money market funds.

    d. Municipal bonds.

sa.finra.rec.prof.tax.001_1811

10. An investor who may lose part or all of his investment is subject to which of the following?

    a. Capital risk.

    b. Market risk.

    c. Reinvestment risk.

    d. Credit risk.

sa.finra.rec.prof.tax.002_1811

11. A client has phoned in concerned about what will happen to his investment in a waste management company if the new EPA laws are enacted, requiring disposal companies to reduce pollution. What type of risk is he concerned with?

    a. Call risk.

    b. Environmental risk.

    c. Investment risk.

    d. Legislative risk.

Securities Industry Rules and Regulations

INTRODUCTION

Learning Objective Statements

Explain the Securities Exchange Act of 1934 and the role of the SEC.

Detail FINRA bylaws and apply them to a given situation.

Federal and state securities laws, as well as industry regulations, have been enacted to ensure that all industry participants adhere to a high standard of just and equitable trade practices. In this lesson, we will review the rules and regulations, as well as the registration requirements, for firms, agents, and securities.

THE SECURITIES EXCHANGE ACT OF 1934

The Securities Exchange Act of 1934 was the second major piece of legislation that resulted from the market crash of 1929. The Securities Exchange Act of 1934 regulates the secondary market that consists of investor-to-investor transactions. All transactions between two investors that are executed on any of the exchanges or in the over-the-counter (OTC) market are secondary market transactions. In a secondary market transaction, the selling security holder, not the issuing corporation, receives the money. The Securities Exchange Act of 1934 also regulates all individuals and firms that conduct business in the securities industry. The Securities Exchange Act of 1934:

- Created the Securities and Exchange Commission (SEC).
- Requires registration of broker dealers and agents.

- Regulates the exchanges and the NASD (now part of FINRA).
- Requires net capital for broker dealers.
- Regulates short sales.
- Regulates insider transactions.
- Requires public companies to solicit proxies.
- Requires segregation of customer and firm assets.
- Authorized the Federal Reserve Board to regulate the extension of credit for securities purchases under Regulation T.
- Regulates the handling of client accounts.

The Securities Exchange Act of 1934 also regulates the issuers of publicly owned securities and requires issuers of these securities to file annual reports (10-Ks) and quarterly reports (10-Qs). Issuers are also required to report material information to the public by filing form 8-K with the SEC. Issuers who file 10-K and 10-Qs are known as reporting issuers. All publicly traded corporations must solicit proxies from investors to vote on major issues relating to the corporation.

THE SECURITIES AND EXCHANGE COMMISSION (SEC)

One of the biggest components of the Securities Exchange Act of 1934 was the creation of the SEC. The SEC is the ultimate securities industry authority and is a direct government body. Five commissioners are appointed to 5-year terms by the president of the United States, and each must be approved by the Senate. The SEC is not a self-regulatory organization (SRO) or a designated examining authority (DEA). An SRO is an entity that regulates its own members, such as the NYSE or the NASD (now part of FINRA). A DEA is an entity that inspects a broker dealer's books and records, and it can also be the NYSE or FINRA. All broker dealers, exchanges, agents, and securities must register with the SEC. All exchanges are required to file a registration statement with the SEC that includes the articles of incorporation, bylaws, and constitution. All new rules and regulations adopted by the exchanges must be disclosed to the SEC as soon as they are enacted. Issuers of securities with more than 500 shareholders and with assets exceeding $5,000,000 must register with the SEC, file quarterly and annual reports, and solicit proxies from stockholders. A broker dealer that conducts business with the public must register with the SEC and maintain a certain level of financial solvency known as net capital. All broker dealers are required to forward a financial statement to all customers of the firm. Additionally, all employees of the broker dealer who are involved in securities sales, have access to cash and securities, or who supervise employees must be fingerprinted.

EXTENSION OF CREDIT

The Securities Act of 1934 gave the authority to the Federal Reserve Board (FRB) to regulate the extension of credit by broker dealers for the purchase of securities by their customers. The following is a list of the regulations of the different lenders and the regulation that gave the FRB the authority to govern their activities:

- Regulation T: Broker dealers
- Regulation U: Banks
- Regulation G: All other financial institutions

THE NATIONAL ASSOCIATION OF SECURITIES DEALERS (NASD)

The Maloney Act of 1938 was an amendment to the Securities Exchange Act of 1934 that allowed for the creation of the NASD. The NASD was the SRO for OTC market, and its purpose was to regulate the broker dealers who conduct business in the OTC market. The NASD is now part of FINRA and has four major bylaws. They are:

1. The rules of fair practice
2. The uniform practice code
3. The code of procedure
4. The code of arbitration

THE RULES OF FAIR PRACTICE/RULES OF CONDUCT

The rules of fair practice are designed to ensure just and equitable trade practices among members in their dealings with the public. In short, the rules of fair practice require members to deal fairly with the public.

The rules of fair practice may also be called the conduct rules or the rules of conduct. Among other things, they govern:

- Commissions and markups
- Retail and institutional communication
- Customer recommendations
- Claims made by representatives

THE UNIFORM PRACTICE CODE

The uniform practice code sets forth guidelines for how FINRA members transact business with other members. The uniform practice code sets standards of business practices among its members and regulates:

- Settlement dates.
- Ex dividend dates.
- Rules of good delivery.
- Confirmations.
- Don't know (DK) procedures.

THE CODE OF PROCEDURE

The code of procedure regulates how FINRA investigates complaints and violations. The code of procedure regulates the discovery phase of alleged violations of rules of fair practice. The code of procedure is not concerned with money; it is only concerned with rule violations.

THE CODE OF ARBITRATION

The code of arbitration provides a forum to resolve disputes. Arbitration provides a final and binding resolution to disputes involving a member and:

- Another member.
- A registered agent.
- A bank.
- A customer.

FINRA is divided into districts based on geography. Each district elects a committee to administer the association's rules. The committee is composed of up to 12 members who serve up to a 3-year term. The committee appoints the Department of Enforcement to handle all trade practice complaints within the district and has the power to assess penalties against members who have violated one or more of the association's rules. FINRA's executive committee, which consists of the Board of Governors, oversees the national business of FINRA.

BECOMING A MEMBER OF FINRA

FINRA sets forth strict qualification standards that all prospective members must meet, prior to being granted membership with FINRA. Any firm that engages in interstate securities transactions with public customers is required to become a FINRA member. Additionally, any broker dealer that wishes to participate as a selling group member in the distribution of mutual fund shares must also be a FINRA member.

In order to become a FINRA member, a firm must:

- Meet net capital requirements (solvency).
- Have at least two principals to supervise the firm.
- Have an acceptable business plan detailing its proposed business activities.
- Attend a premembership interview.

  Members must also agree to:

- Abide by all of the association's rules.
- Abide by all federal and state laws.
- Pay dues, fees, and membership assessments as required by the association.

  FINRA members must pay the following fees:

- Basic membership fee
- Fee for each representative and principal
- Fee based on the gross income of the firm
- Fee for all branch offices

Pretest

SECURITIES INDUSTRY RULES AND REGULATIONS

la.finra.reg.con.edu.001_1811

1. You are the owner of a restaurant and you would like to have a guitarist play in the lounge on Saturday evenings. You have known your representative for 15 years and know her to be a great jazz guitarist. You think she would like to play and ask her if she is available to do so. She would have to notify which of the following before accepting your offer?

   a. Her firm.

   b. No one, because it is not securities related and she is on her own time.

   c. FINRA.

   d. NYSE.

la.finra.sec.ind.reg.002_1811

2. A FINRA member has failed to receive a stock certificate in good form from the selling FINRA firm. Which FINRA bylaw defines good delivery?

   a. Rules of Fair Practice.

   b. Code of Procedure.

   c. Code of Arbitration.

   d. Uniform Practice Code.

la.finra.sec.ind.reg.003_1811

3. Which act gave the NASD (now part of FINRA) the authority to regulate the OTC market?

   a. The NASD Act of 1929.

   b. The Securities Act of 1933.

   c. The Securities Act of 1934.

   d. The Maloney Act of 1938.

la.finra.sec.ind.reg.004_1811

4. As it relates to a member firm conducting business with the public, all of the following are violations, except:

   a. Charging a customer a larger than normal commission for executing a specific order.

   b. Failing to execute a customer's order for a speculative security.

   c. Stating that a new issue has been approved for sale by the SEC.

   d. Printing "FINRA" in large type on business cards.

sa.finra.sec.ind.reg.001_1811

5. In the securities industry, which of the following is the ultimate industry authority regulating conduct?

   a. NYSE.

   b. SRO.

   c. SEC.

   d. FINRA.

Registration of Agents and Continuing Education

INTRODUCTION

Learning Objective Statements

List the information required to be disclosed on Form U4 and U5.

Evaluate reasons for terminating a representative.

Explain the need to qualify or re-qualify by exam.

Detail the registration requirements for broker dealers, investment advisers, and agents.

Contrast the continuing education requirements for Firm Element and Regulatory Element Training.

Once an agent passes both the SIE and appropriate top off exam, the agent qualifies for registration with a broker dealer. In this lesson we cover the specific registration, disclosure and ongoing continuing education requirements you must be familiar with to pass your exam.

HIRING NEW EMPLOYEES

A registered principal of a firm is the individual who interviews and screens potential new employees. The principal is required to make a thorough investigation into the candidate's professional and personal backgrounds. With few exceptions, other than clerical personnel, all new employees are required to become registered as an associated person with the firm. The new employee begins the registration process by filling out and submitting a Uniform Application for Securities Industry Registration, also known as Form U4. Form U4 is used to collect the applicant's personal and professional history, including:

- 10 year employment history
- 5 year resident history
- Legal name and any aliases used
- Any legal or regulatory actions

The principal of the firm is required to verify the employment information for the last 3 years and must attest to the character of the applicant by signing Form U4 prior to its submission to FINRA. All U4 forms are sent to the Central Registration Depository (CRD), along with a fingerprint card for processing and recording. Any applicant who has answered yes to any of the questions on the form regarding his or her background must give a detailed explanation in the DRP pages attached to the form. The applicant is not required to provide information regarding:

- Marital status.
- Educational background.
- Income or net worth.

Information regarding the employee's finances is disclosed on Form U4 if the associated person has ever declared bankruptcy and if the employee has any unsatisfied judgments or liens. Any development that would cause an answer on the associated person's U4 to change requires that the member update the U4 within 30 days of when the member becomes informed of the event. In the case of an event that could cause the individual to become statutorily disqualified, such as a felony conviction or misdemeanor involving cash or securities, the member must update the associated person's U4 within 10 business days of learning of the event.

> ▶ **TAKENOTE!**
>
> Broker dealers are required to perform background checks on its employees every 5 years to ensure that no judgements, liens, or disclosable events have gone unreported by the registered person. Registered persons who fail to disclose unsatisfied judgements or liens are subject to significant regulatory action that could result in the person being barred from the industry, in extreme cases.

DISCIPLINARY ACTIONS AGAINST A REGISTERED REPRESENTATIVE

If another industry regulator takes disciplinary action against a representative, the employing member firm must notify FINRA. Actions by any of the following should be immediately disclosed to the association:

- The SEC
- An exchange or association
- A state regulator
- A clearing firm
- A commodity regulatory body

Also immediately reportable to FINRA are any of the following:

- A customer complaint alleging theft, forgery, or misappropriation of customer assets
- Indictment, conviction, or plea of guilty or no contest to a criminal matter
- If the agent becomes a respondent or defendant in a matter in excess of $15,000 or if the firm becomes a respondent or defendant in a matter in excess of $25,000
- An agent is disciplined by the employing member firm or commissions are withheld from an agent or the agent is fined in either case in amounts in excess of $2,500

FINRA defines immediate notification for the previously listed matters as being within 10 days. All disclosures must include the type of action brought as well as the name of the party bringing the actions and the name of the representative involved. The firm makes the disclosure on Form U4. FINRA submits disciplinary actions that are taken by FINRA on Form U6 and they are recorded on the employee's record. All disciplinary actions, along with a record of the agent's registrations and employment history, are available through FINRA's BrokerCheck program. Arbitration awards and settlements reported by the agent on his or her U4 as well as those reported by FINRA appear in the BrokerCheck online report. FINRA members are required to regulate the activities of its associated people and must disclose to the association any action that the member takes against a registered representative. Should a registered representative feel that the information disclosed through the BrokerCheck program is inaccurate, the representative may request an amendment to the disclosure by filling out and submitting a BrokerCheck comment form. Generally information filed as part of an agent's termination from an employer is not disclosed through the BrokerCheck Program. Any information regarding regulatory action or customer actions that are required to be disclosed are reported through the agent's U4. The information reported on the U4 will become part of the BrokerCheck report.

RESIGNATION OF A REGISTERED REPRESENTATIVE

If a registered representative voluntarily terminates his or her association with a member firm, the member must fill out and submit a uniform termination notice known as a U5 to FINRA within 30 days. An associated person's registration is nontransferable. A representative may not simply move the registration from one firm to another. The employing firm that the representative is leaving must fill out and submit a U5 to FINRA, which terminates the representative's registration. The new employing firm must fill out and submit a new U4 to begin a new registration for the associated person with the new employer. A representative who leaves the industry for more than 24 months is required to requalify by exam.

During a period of absence from the industry of 2 years or less, FINRA retains jurisdiction over the representative in cases involving customer complaints and violations. Agents who volunteer or who are called to active duty with the military have their registrations and continuing education requirements "tolled" and their registrations are placed in "special inactive" status. During their time of active military duty, the 24-month requirement is not in effect and the agent may continue to receive compensation from transactions but may not contact customers. Once active duty ends the agent has 90 days to reenter the business. If the person is not associated with a member at that time the 24-month window will begin.

CONTINUING EDUCATION

Most registered agents and principals are required to participate in industry-mandated continuing education programs. The continuing education program consists of a firm element, which is administered by the broker dealer, and a regulatory element, which is administered by the regulators.

FIRM ELEMENT

Every FINRA member firm at least annually must identify the training needs of its covered employees and develop a written training plan based on their employees' needs. A covered employee is a registered person who engages in sales of securities to customers, trading and investment banking, and their immediate supervisors. The firm, at a minimum, should institute a plan that increases the covered employees' securities knowledge and focus on the products offered by the firm. The plan should also highlight the risks and suitability requirements associated with the firm's investment products and strategies. The firm is not required to file its continuing education plan with FINRA unless it is specifically requested to do so. However, firms that fail to adequately document their continuing education program, including their covered agents' compliance with the program, may be subject to disciplinary action.

REGULATORY ELEMENT

All registered agents who were not registered on or before July 1, 1988, must participate in the regulatory element of the continuing education requirement. Agents subject to the requirement must complete the computer-based training at an approved facility on the second anniversary of their initial registration and every 3 years thereafter. The content of the exam is developed by The Securities Industry Regulatory Council on Continuing Education and is not the responsibility of the broker dealer. FINRA will notify the agent 30 days prior to their anniversary date. This notification provides the agent with a 120-day window to complete the regulatory continuing education requirement. An agent who fails to complete the requirement within that period will have their registration become inactive. Agents whose registrations have become inactive may not engage in any securities business that requires a license and may not receive commissions until their registration is reactivated. Registered representatives are subject to Series 101 of the regulatory element, while registered principals are subject to Series 201 of the requirement. Agents who were exempt from the regulatory element as a result of having been registered for 10 years or more with a clean disciplinary history on July 1,

1998, who become the subject of a significant disciplinary action, are now required to participate in the regulatory element of the continuing education requirement. Additionally, if an agent who was exempt from the regulatory element subsequently becomes registered as a principal, they will become subject to the Series 201 requirement. The one-time exemption is only for the regulatory element; there is no exemption from the firm element of the continuing education program. An agent who leaves the industry for more than 24 months will have to requalify by exam and will have a regulatory education requirement based on the date of reassociation (the date they passed the exam for the second time). An agent who temporarily leaves the industry (less than 24 months), who is not required to requalify by exam, will have a regulatory continuing education requirement based on the original sate of association.

TERMINATION FOR CAUSE

A member may terminate a registered representative for cause if the representative has:

- Violated firm policy.
- Violated the rules of the NYSE, FINRA, SEC, or any other industry regulator.
- Violated state or federal securities laws.

A firm may not terminate a representative who is the subject of investigation by any securities industry regulator until the investigation is complete.

RETIRING REPRESENTATIVES/CONTINUING COMMISSIONS

Retiring representatives may continue to receive commissions from the business that they have built over their career provided that a contract is in place prior to the representative's retirement. A retiring representative may continue to receive commissions on old business only. The retiring representation may not receive commissions on any new business and may not receive finder's fees. If the retired representative dies, the representative's beneficiary may continue to receive the commissions that were due the representative.

STATE REGISTRATION

In addition to registering with FINRA, all broker dealers and agents must register in their home state as well as in any state in which they transact business. An agent who lives in one state and who commutes to an office in a nearby state must be registered in both of those states.

REGISTRATION EXEMPTIONS

The following individuals are exempt from registration:

- Clerical
- Nonsupervising officers and managers not dealing with customers
- Non-U.S. citizens working abroad
- Floor personnel

PERSONS INELIGIBLE TO REGISTER

Individuals applying for registration must meet the association's requirements in the following areas:

- Training
- Competence
- Experience
- Character

Anyone who fails to meet the association's requirements in any of the above listed areas may not become registered. An individual may also be disqualified by statute or through rules for any of the following:

- The individual incurred expulsion, suspension, or disciplinary actions by the SEC or any foreign or domestic SRO.
- The individual caused the expulsion or suspension of a broker dealer or principal.

- The individual made false or misleading statements on the application for registration on form U4 or form BD.

- The individual has had a felony conviction or misdemeanor involving securities within the last 10 years.

- There is a court injunction or order barring the individual.

Anyone who is not registered as an agent or who has lost his or her registration as a result of a disqualifying event or action by a regulator may not act in the capacity of an agent and may not be paid commissions for securities transactions. If a firm pays commissions to an unregistered person or otherwise allows an unregistered person to act in the capacity of a registered agent, both the firm and the unregistered person or agent are subject to severe penalties.

Pretest

REGISTRATION OF AGENTS AND CONTINUING EDUCATION

la.finra.reg.con.edu.001_1811

1. You are the owner of a restaurant and you would like to have a guitarist play in the lounge on Saturday evenings. You have known your representative for 15 years and know her to be a great jazz guitarist. You think she would like to play and ask her if she is available to do so. She would have to notify which of the following before accepting your offer?

   a. Her firm.

   b. No one, because it is not securities related and she is on her own time.

   c. FINRA.

   d. NYSE.

la.finra.reg.con.edu.002_1811

2. At a member firm, which of the following must be registered?

   a. A corporate officer whose sole function is to act as liaison between the board of directors and management.

   b. A part-time sales assistant who occasionally takes verbal orders from customers.

   c. A back-office margin clerk who assists the head of the margin department.

   d. A receptionist who takes messages from customers inquiring about their accounts.

sa.finra.reg.con.edu.001_1811

3. An individual applying for registration with a FINRA member firm would be required to include which of the following on Form U4?

    a. 5-year employment history.

    b. Educational background.

    c. 5-year residence history.

    d. A divorce.

sa.finra.reg.con.edu.002_1811

4. Which of the following is an associated person of a member firm?

    I. Registered representative.
    II. Trader.
    III. Director.
    IV. Manager.

    a. I and III.

    b. I and II.

    c. I, II, and IV.

    d. I, II, III, and IV.

Communications with the Public, Dispute Resolution, Insider Trading, SIPC, and AML

INTRODUCTION

Learning Objective Statements

Contrast Retail and Institutional Communications.

Understand how to use the do not call list and other customer contact.

Explain and apply SIPC coverage for customers of broker dealers.

Compare the features of mediation and arbitration.

Detail the dispute resolution process with FINRA.

Identify the stages and acts of money laundering.

In order to be successful on your exam you must have a full and complete understanding of the rules regarding the customer agent relationship. A detailed mastery regarding customer contact, dispute resolution and customer identification procedures will go a long way to making sure that you pass your exam.

COMMUNICATIONS WITH THE PUBLIC

Member firms seek to increase their business and exposure through the use of both retail and institutional communications. There are strict regulations in place in order to ensure all communications with the public adhere to industry guidelines. Some communications with the public are available to a general audience and include:

- Television/radio
- Publicly accessible websites
- Motion pictures
- Newspapers/magazines
- Telephone directory listings
- Signs/billboards
- Computer/Internet postings
- Video tape displays
- Other public media
- Recorded telemarketing messages

Other types of communications are offered to a targeted audience. These communications include:

- Market reports
- Password-protected websites
- Telemarketing scripts
- Form letters or e-mails (sent to more than 25 people)
- Circulars
- Research reports
- Printed materials for seminars
- Option worksheets
- Performance reports
- Prepared scripts for TV or radio
- Reprints of ads

REGULATION BEST INTEREST

Regulation Best Interest (Reg BI) was adopted by the SEC in June of 2019 as an amendment to The Securities Exchange Act of 1934. All broker dealers, investment advisers and agents are subject to standards of conduct that require the firm and its agents to act in the best interest of retail customers. Reg BI covers all recommendations to effect securities transactions as well as all recommendations regarding account establishment. That is to say that when recommending that a client open a joint, transfer on death, trust or fee-based account, the type of account established must be in the client's best interest. In June of 2020, as part of Reg BI, all broker dealers and investment advisers will be required to provide retail clients with a client relationship summary (CRS) and will be required to post the CRS on their publicly available website. The CRS may be provided in hardcopy or electronically. If the CRS is provided in hardcopy, the CRS may not be more than two pages long and the CRS must be the first page among any documents sent in the same package. The following rules are in place relating to the CRS:

- The CRS must be written in plain English using everyday terms.

- The CRS should be written using "active voice" with a strong, direct and clear meaning.

- The CRS must follow the standard format and order as detailed by the SEC.

- The CRS should be written as if speaking to the retail investor directly.

- The CRS must be factual and avoid boilerplate, vague or exaggerated language.

- The CRS may not include disclosures other than those required under Reg BI.

- Electronic CRSs should use graphs and charts, specifically dual-column charts to compare services.

- Electronic CRSs may use videos and popups and must provide access to any referenced information via hyperlink or other means.

- Electronic CRSs may be delivered via e-mail provided that the e-mail contains a direct link to the CRS.

Some of the required disclosures are referred to as "conversation starters." These conversation starters should be in bold or in other text to ensure that they are more noticeable than other disclosures. These conversation starters include questions such as:

1. Who is my primary contact and does he or she represent a broker dealer or an investment adviser?

2. Who can I speak to about how the person is treating me?

3. Given my financial situation should I choose a brokerage service, why or why not?

4. Given my financial situation should I choose an investment advisory service, why or why not?

5. How will you choose investments to recommend to me?

6. What is your relevant experience including licenses, education and qualifications? What do these qualifications mean?

7. What fees will I pay?

8. How will these fees affect my investments? If I give you $10,000 how much will go towards fees and expenses and how much will be invested for me?

9. What are your legal obligations to me when providing recommendations (broker dealer)?

10. What are your legal obligations to me when acting as my investment adviser?

11. How else does your firm make money?

12. How do your financial professionals make money?

13. What conflicts of interest do you have?

14. Does the firm or its financial professionals have legal or disciplinary history?

Both broker dealers and investment advisers are required to adhere to the standards of conduct under Reg BI. As such both must disclose that they must put the interests of the client ahead of theirs when making a recommendation and that the way the firm makes money for providing the services causes a conflict of interest. These conflicts include recommending proprietary products, receiving payments from third parties, principal trading or revenue sharing.

Online broker dealers who only provide access to trading as well as investment advisers who only offer automated services and who do not offer access to specific registered individuals, must disclose this fact in the CRS and must provide a section on their website that answers questions relating to the conversation starters. If a broker dealer or investment adviser provides both online services and access to registered personnel, a registered person must be made available to discuss the conversation starters.

Broker dealers are required to provide the CRS to customers before or upon the earlier of recommending the type of account to establish, an investment strategy or upon opening an account or placing an order. Investment advisers must provide the CRS to clients prior to or at the time the contract is entered into even if the contract is oral. The CRS is now known as ADV Part 3. For entities who are registered as both a broker dealer and as an investment adviser, the CRS must be delivered upon the earliest requirement for either registration. Any changes required to be made to the CRS must be completed within 30 days and an updated CRS clearly reflecting the changes must be sent to existing customers within 60 days. All broker dealers and investment advisers are required to file the CRS along with any changes with the SEC. Broker dealers will file through the Central Registration Depository (CRD) system and investment advisers will file through the Investment Adviser Registration Database (IARD). The relationship summary must be provided to a client upon request within 30 days.

FINRA RULE 2210 COMMUNICATIONS WITH THE PUBLIC

FINRA Rule 2210 replaces the advertising and sales literature rules previously used to regulate member communications with the public. FINRA Rule 2210 streamlines member communication rules and reduces the number of communication categories from six to three. The three categories of member communication are:

1. Retail communication

2. Institutional communication

3. Correspondence

RETAIL COMMUNICATION

Retail communication is defined as any written communication distributed or made available to 25 or more retail investors in a 30-day period. The communication may be distributed in hard copy or in electronic formats. This includes texts, e-mails, instant messages, and form letters where the body of the information is the same. The definition of a retail investor is any investor who does not meet the definition of an institutional investor. Retail communications now contain all components of advertising and sales literature. All retail communications must be approved by a registered principal prior to first use. The publication of a post in a chat room or other online forum will not require the prior approval of a principal so long as such post does not promote the business of the member firm and does not provide investment advice. Additionally, generic advertising is also exempt from the prior approval requirements. All retail communications must be maintained by the member for 3 years. If the member firm is a new member firm, which has been in existence for less than 12 months based on the firm's approval date in the central registration depository or CRD, the member must file all retail communications with FINRA 10 days prior to its first use unless the communication has been previously filed and contains no material changes or has been filed by another member such as an investment company or ETF sponsor. Member firms who have been established for more than 12 months may file retail communications with FINRA 10 days after the communication is first used. Investment companies, ETF sponsors, and retail communications regarding variable annuities must be filed 10 days prior to first use if the communication contains nonstandardized performance rankings. Should FINRA determine that a member firm is making false or misleading statements in its retail communications with the public, FINRA may require the member to file all of its retail communications with the public with the association 10 days prior to its first use.

 **TAKENOTE!**

Research reports concerning only securities listed on a national securities exchange are excluded from Rule 2210's filing requirements. Additionally, a free writing prospectus is exempt from filing with the SEC and not subject to Rule 2210's filing or content standards.

INSTITUTIONAL COMMUNICATIONS

Institutional communication is defined as any written communication distributed or made available exclusively to institutional investors. The communication may be distributed in hard copy or in electronic formats. Institutional communications do not have to be approved by a principal prior to first use so long as the member has established policies and procedures regarding the use of institutional communications and has trained its employees on the proper use. Institutional communications are also exempt from FINRA's filing requirement, but like retail communications, must be maintained by a member for 3 years. If the member believes that the institutional communication or any part thereof may be seen by even a single retail investor, the communication must be handled as all other retail communications and is subject to the approval and filing requirements as if it was retail communication. An institutional investor is a person or firm that trades securities for his or her own account or for the account of others. Institutional investors are generally limited to large financial companies. Because of their size and sophistication, fewer protective laws cover institutional investors. It is important to note that there is no minimum size for an institutional account. Institutional investors include:

- Broker dealers
- Investment advisers
- Investment companies
- Insurance companies
- Banks
- Trusts
- Savings and loans
- Government agencies
- Employment benefit plans with more than 100 participants
- Any nonnatural person with more than $50,000,000 in assets

CORRESPONDENCE

Correspondence consists of electronic and written communications between the member and up to 25 retail investors in a 30-calendar-day period. With the increase in acceptance of e-mail as business communication, it would be impractical for a member to review all correspondence between the member and a customer. The member instead may set up procedures to review a sample of all correspondence, both electronic and hard copy. If the member reviews only a sample of the correspondence, the member must train his or her associated people on their firm's procedures relating to correspondence and must document the training and ensure that procedures are followed. Even though the member is not required to review all correspondence, the member must still retain all correspondence. The member should, where practical, review all incoming hard copy correspondence. Letters received by the firm could contain cash, checks, securities, or complaints.

BROKER DEALER WEBSITES

A broker dealer will not be deemed to have a place of business in a state where it does not maintain an office simply by virtue of the fact that the publicly available website established by the firm or one of its agents is accessible from that state so long as the following conditions are met:

- The website clearly states that the firm may only conduct business in states where it is properly registered to do so.

- The website only provides general information about the firm and does not provide specific investment advice.

- The firm or its agent may not respond to Internet inquiries with the intent to solicit business without first meeting the registration requirements in the state of the prospective customer.

The content of any website must be reviewed and approved by a principal prior to its first use and must be filed with FINRA within 10 days of use. If the firm or its agent updates the website and the update materially changes the information contained on the website, the updates must be reapproved by a principal and refiled with FINRA. The website may use the FINRA logo so long as the use is only to demonstrate that the firm is a FINRA member and a hyperlink to the FINRA website is included in close proximity to the logo. Member firms are not required to display the FINRA logo.

BLIND RECRUITING ADS

A blind recruiting ad is an ad placed by the member firm for the specific purpose of finding job applicants. Blind recruiting ads are the only form of advertising that does not require the member's name to appear in the ad. The ads may not distort the opportunities or salaries of the advertised position. All other ads are required to disclose the name of the member firm, as well as the relationship of the member to any other entities that appear in the ad.

GENERIC ADVERTISING

Generic advertising is generally designed to promote firm awareness and to advertise the products and services generally offered through the firm. Generic ads will generally include:

- Securities products offered (i.e., stocks, bonds, mutual funds)
- Contact name, number, and address
- Types of accounts offered (i.e., individual, IRA, 401K)

TOMBSTONE ADS

A tombstone ad is an announcement of a new security offering coming to market. Tombstone ads may be run while the securities are still in registration with the SEC and may only include:

- Description of securities
- Description of business
- Description of transaction
- Required disclaimers
- Time and place of any stockholders meetings regarding the sale of the securities

    All tombstone ads must include the following:

- A statement that the securities registration has not yet become effective
- A statement that responding to the ad does not obligate the prospect
- A statement as to where a prospectus may be obtained
- A statement that the ad does not constitute an offer to sell the securities and that an offer may only be made by the prospectus

All retail communication is required to be approved by a principal of the firm prior to its first use. A general security principal (Series 24) may approve most retail communication. Any retail communication relating to options, must be approved by a registered option principal or the compliance registered options principal. Research reports must be approved by a supervisory analyst.

TESTIMONIALS

From time to time, firms will use testimonials made by people of national or local recognition in an effort to generate new business for the firm. If the individual giving the testimonial is quoting past performance relating to the firm's recommendations, it must be accompanied by a disclaimer that past performance is not indicative of future performance. If the individual giving the testimony was compensated in any way, the fact that the person received compensation must also be disclosed. Should the individual's testimony imply that the person making the testimony is an expert, a statement regarding the person's qualifications as an expert must also be contained in the ad or sales literature. Research prepared by outside parties must disclose the name of the preparer.

FREE SERVICES

If a member firm advertises free services to customers or to people who respond to an ad, the services must actually be free to everyone with no strings attached.

MISLEADING COMMUNICATION WITH THE PUBLIC

The following are some examples of misleading statements, which are not allowed to appear in communication with the public:

- Excessive hedge clauses
- Implying an endorsement by FINRA, the NYSE, or the SEC
- Printing the FINRA logo in type that is larger than the type of the member's name
- Implying that the member has larger research facilities than it actually has
- Implying that an individual has higher qualifications than he or she actually has

SECURITIES INVESTOR PROTECTION CORPORATION ACT OF 1970

The Securities Investor Protection Corporation (SIPC) is a government-sponsored corporation that provides protection to customers in the event of a broker dealer's failure. All broker dealers that are registered with the SEC are required to be SIPC members. All broker dealers are required to pay annual dues to SIPC's insurance fund to cover losses due to broker dealer failure. If a broker dealer fails to pay its SIPC assessment, it may not transact business until the assessment is paid.

NET CAPITAL REQUIREMENT

All broker dealers are required to maintain a certain level of net capital in order to ensure that they are financially solvent. A broker dealer's capital requirement is contingent upon the type of business that it conducts. The larger and more complex the firm's business is, the greater the net capital requirement. Should a firm fall below its net capital requirement, it is deemed to be insolvent, and SIPC will petition in court to have a trustee appointed to liquidate the firm and protect the customers. The trustee must be a disinterested party and, once the trustee is appointed, the firm may not conduct business or try to conceal any assets.

CUSTOMER COVERAGE

SIPC protects customers of a brokerage firm in much the same way that the FDIC protects customers of banks. SIPC covers customer losses that result from broker dealer failure, not for market losses. SIPC covers customers for up to $500,000 per separate customer. Of the $500,000, up to $250,000 may be in cash. Most broker dealers carry additional private insurance to cover larger accounts, but SIPC is the industry-funded insurance and is required by all broker dealers. The following are examples of separate customers:

Customer	Securities Market Value	Cash	SIPC Coverage
Mr. Jones	$320,000	$75,000	All
Mr. & Mrs. Jones	$290,000	$90,000	All
Mrs. Jones	$397,000	$82,000	All

All of the accounts shown would be considered separate customers, and SIPC would cover the entire value of all of the accounts. If an account has in excess of $250,000 in cash, the individual would not be covered for any amount exceeding $250,000 and would become a general creditor for the rest. SIPC does not consider a margin account and a cash account as separate customers and the customer would be covered for the maximum of $500,000. SIPC does not offer coverage for commodities contracts, and all member firms must display the SIPC sign in the lobby of the firm. Many firms purchase excess insurance for customers that go above and beyond SIPC coverage. If the firm reduces or eliminates this excess coverage it must inform customers 30 days prior to the effective date of the change.

FIDELITY BOND

All SIPC members are required to obtain a fidelity bond to protect customers in the event of employee dishonesty. Some things that a fidelity bond will insure against are check forgery and fraudulent trading. The minimum amount of the fidelity bond is $25,000; however, large firms are often required to carry a higher amount.

THE SECURITIES ACTS AMENDMENTS OF 1975

The Securities Acts Amendments of 1975 gave the authority to the Municipal Securities Rule Making Board (MSRB) to regulate the issuance and trading of municipal bonds. The MSRB has no enforcement division. Its rules are enforced by other regulators.

POLITICAL CONTRIBUTIONS

FINRA enforces the rules enacted by the MSRB for its members that engage in municipal securities business. MSRB Rule G-38 puts strict limits on the amount of political contributions that may be made by a municipal finance professional (MFP). An MFP is an agent who is primarily engaged in any of the following:

- Soliciting municipal underwriting
- Acting as a financial adviser or consultant

- Trading or selling municipal securities

- Providing investment advice or issuing research reports relating to municipal securities to the public

- Directing supervisors of any agent acting in the above capacity

- Acting as an executive who oversees municipal dealers or departments

MFPs may only make political contributions to candidates in an election in which they are eligible to vote. The maximum amount of their contribution is limited to $250 per candidate per election. If an MFP donates more than $250 or makes a contribution to a candidate in an election in which he or she is not able to vote, a violation has occurred, and the employing firm will be banned from engaging in municipal securities business with the issuer for 2 years. The 2-year ban will follow the MFP should the MFP change firms. Both the new firm and the previous employer will be subject to the amount of time that remains on the 2-year ban. Should an MFP make a political contribution to an incumbent that would subject the employing firm to a ban, that ban will expire if the incumbent loses the election. This political contribution does not apply to federal elections such as for senators.

EXAMPLE If an MFP donated $200 to a mayoral candidate in a district where the MFP does not live and, as a result, could not vote in the election, the employing firm could not underwrite that municipality's debt for 2 years.

If an MFP contributes more than $250 or contributes to a candidate that he or she is not entitled to vote for, the employing firm must notify the issuer by filing forms G37 and G38 by the last day of the month following the end of each calendar quarter. These forms will tell the issuer:

- The amount of the contribution and the contributor category.

- The name and title of the political official and his or her political party.

- A list of the municipal issuers the firm engages in business with.

If the contribution is in line with MSRB Rule 37, the employing firm is not required to file forms G37 and G38. If an executive officer gives more than $250, the donation must be reported, but the firm would not be banned from engaging in municipal securities business with the issuer. Additionally, if the firm employs consultants to help the firm obtain municipal securities business from issuers, the firm must send forms G37 and G38 to the MSRB at the end of each calendar quarter listing:

- The name of the consultant or company.

- The role in which the consultant is acting and the amount of compensation.

- A list of municipal securities business obtained by using the consultant.

- A copy of all consulting agreements.

- Termination dates for consulting agreements.

The dealer also must disclose information relating to the use of consultants to the issuers. The dealer may disclose the information on an issue-specific basis or on an issuer-specific basis. If the dealer notifies issuers on an issuer basis, the dealer must send issuers updated information annually, even if there have been no changes.

CONDUCT OF MSRB MEMBERS

Every broker dealer who is a member of the MSRB shall provide a written notice to all clients as required by MSRB Rule G10 informing them of the following:

1. That the broker dealer is registered with both the SEC and the MSRB

2. The Web address for the MSRB

3. Information regarding the availability of the investor brochure as well as the location of the brochure posted on the MSRB website

4. Information regarding the protections available to the investor through the MSRB and how to file a complaint

This information may be provided in either hard copy or electronically. The above information must be provided to municipal advisory clients as well as to investors. A municipal advisory client is a municipal entity as well as any obligated person or entity who the advisor engages to perform municipal advisory activities. All municipal advisors including the associated persons who solicit business from municipal issuers and entities shall deal honestly and fairly with their clients and shall not misrepresent or omit facts, risks, or other material information. If the member firm is acting as an underwriter of municipal fund securities that are not interests in local government investment pools/LGIPS, the member shall be required under MSRB Rule G45 to file information relating to the offering no later than 60 days after each semiannual report required on June 30th and December 31st of each year. This report may be filed directly by the member or on behalf of the member by an electronic submission agent. Performance data for each plan shall be submitted annually within 60 days of the December 31st submission.

THE INSIDER TRADING & SECURITIES FRAUD ENFORCEMENT ACT OF 1988

The Insider Trading & Securities Fraud Enforcement Act of 1988 sets forth guidelines and controls for the use and dissemination of nonpublic material information. Nonpublic information is information that is not known by people outside the company. Material information is information regarding a situation or development that materially affects the company in the present or in the future. It is not just that insiders have this type of information, but it is required in order for them to do their jobs effectively. It is, however, unlawful for an insider to use this information to profit from a forthcoming move in the stock price. An insider is defined as any officer, director, 10% stockholder, or anyone who is in possession of nonpublic material information, as well as the spouse of any such person. Additionally, it is unlawful for the insider to divulge any of this information to any outside party. Trading on inside information has always been a violation of the Securities Exchange Act of 1934, and the Insider Trading Act prescribed penalties for violators, which include:

- A fine up to 300% of the amount of the gain or 300% of the amount of the loss avoided for the person who acts on the information

- A civil or criminal fine for the person who divulges the information

- Insider traders can be sued by the affected parties

- Criminal prosecutions and a criminal fine of up to $1,000,000 and 20 years in prison

Information becomes public information once it has been disseminated over public media. The SEC will pay a reward of up to 10% to informants who turn in individuals who trade on inside information. In addition to the insiders already listed, the following are also considered insiders:

- Accountants

- Attorneys

- Investment bankers

FIREWALL

Broker dealers who act as underwriters and investment bankers for corporate clients must have access to information regarding the company in order to advise the company properly. The broker dealer must ensure that no inside information is passed between its investment banking department and its retail trading departments. The broker dealer is required to physically separate these divisions by a firewall. The broker dealer must maintain written supervisory procedures to adequately guard against the wrongful use or dissemination of inside information.

TELEMARKETING RULES

FINRA Rule 3230 regulates how telemarketing calls are made by businesses. On your exam you may see the telemarketing rule tested under the telephone Consumer Protection Act of 1991, FINRA Rule 3230, or as telemarketing rules. Telemarketing calls that are designed to have consumers invest in or purchase goods, services, or property must adhere to the strict guidelines. All firms must:

- Call only between the hours of 8 a.m. and 9 p.m. in the customer's time zone.

- Maintain a do not call list. Individuals placed on the do not call list may not be contacted by anyone at the firm for 5 years.

- Give the prospect the firm's name, address, and phone number. Caller ID must display firm name and phone number. Caller ID blocking may not be used.

- Maintain adequate policies and procedures to maintain a firm specific do not call list.

- Maintain adequate policies and procedures to ensure numbers called do not appear on the national do not call list.

- Train representatives on calling policies and use of the do not call list.

- Ensure that any fax solicitations have the firm's name, address, and phone number.

 TAKENOTE!

An interesting situation can arise when a customer of the firm who maintains an account with the firm is on the firm-specific do not call list. In these cases, the representative may not contact the customer unless it is to verify account information such as the mailing address. The customer may not be contacted to discuss holdings in the account or to make a recommendation.

DO NOT CALL LIST EXEMPTIONS

The following are exempt from the prohibited calls listed above:

- Calls to existing customers who have executed a transaction or who have had an account containing cash or securities on deposit within the last 18 months or to a person who has contacted the member within the last 3 months

- Calls to a person where the caller has a personal relationship with the recipient

- Calls to a person who has given written permission to be contacted by the firm and the number where the person may be contacted

- Inadvertent calls to a number that currently appears on the national do not call list but was not included on the do not call list used by the member, so long as that list was not more than 31 days old

THE PENNY STOCK COLD CALL RULE

The penny stock cold call rule was enacted in order to ensure that investors do not purchase penny stocks without knowing the risks. A penny stock is an unlisted security that trades below $5 per share. Prior to purchasing a penny stock:

- The agent must make sure that the purchase is suitable.

- The customer must sign a suitability statement.

- The firm must supply a current quote.

- The firm must disclose the amount of commission earned by the firm and the agent.

 TAKENOTE!

Established customers are exempt from the penny stock cold call rule. An established customer is one that has made three transactions in three different penny stocks on three different days. An established customer is also one that has had cash or securities on deposit with the firm during the previous 12 months.

THE ROLE OF THE PRINCIPAL

Prior to any firm being admitted as a FINRA member, it must have at least two principals to supervise the firm's activities. All firms are required to have a written policy and procedures manual to ensure compliance with the firm's rules as well as the rules of the industry. The manual must be updated to reflect the adoption of new policies, a change in personnel, or new industry rules. It is the principal's responsibility to ensure that all rules in the policy and procedure manual are followed by all of the firm's employees. It is the responsibility of the principal to review and approve all of the following:

- New accounts

- Retail communication

- Transactions

VIOLATIONS AND COMPLAINTS

FINRA's code of procedure sets forth guidelines for the investigation of alleged violations and complaints against a member firm or a registered representative. The FINRA staff originates many complaints against member firms and associated persons during their routine examinations of member firms. Complaints and allegations of wrongdoing may also originate from a customer of the member firm or from another member. If a FINRA staff member has received the complaint that alleges a violation of securities regulations, it is up to FINRA to determine if the complaint is meritorious. FINRA will begin an investigation of the complaint by notifying the member and/or the associated person that a complaint has been received and will request the member or an associated person to respond in writing. All requests for information must be met within 25 days from the day that the request was made.

RESOLUTION OF ALLEGATIONS

Should FINRA find that the allegations are baseless, it may dismiss it without action. However, if FINRA finds that the allegation has merit, it may be resolved through summary complaint procedure or through a formal hearing process.

MINOR RULE VIOLATION

A minor rule violation letter is traditionally used in cases that involve only small violations. FINRA has outlined a number of rule violations that qualify to be resolved using a minor rule violation (MRV) procedure. This is offered to respondents in an effort to avoid a costly hearing. Under MRV procedure, the maximum penalty is a censure and a $2,500 fine. If the MRV procedure is offered, the member or associated person has 10 business days to accept it. By signing the MRV letter, the respondent does not admit or deny the allegations and gives up his or her right to appeal the decision. Should the offer of MRV procedure not be accepted, the Department of Enforcement will proceed with a formal hearing to determine if a violation has occurred. Possible penalties after having been found to have violated one or more of the association's rules include:

- Censure

- Suspension for up to 1 year

- Expulsion for up to 10 years

- Barred for life

- Fined any amount

- Any other penalty deemed appropriate, such as restitution

Decisions of the Department of Enforcement may be appealed within 15 days to the National Adjudicatory Counsel (NAC). If no action is taken, the decision of the Department of Enforcement becomes final in 45 days. Should the NAC determine that the appeal is meritorious, it must start a review within a 45-day period. The decision of the NAC may be appealed to the SEC and finally to the court system. Upon final determination, all fines, penalties, and costs must be paid promptly.

CODE OF ARBITRATION

FINRA's arbitration procedure provides parties with a forum to resolve disputes. All industry participants who have submitted a U4 are required to resolve disputes through FINRA's arbitration process. Most claims submitted to arbitration are financial in nature, although other claims may be submitted. Sexual harassment and discrimination claims are not required to be resolved in arbitration unless both parties specifically agree to arbitrate. Class action claims are also not resolved in arbitration. Class action status is awarded by the court system. Arbitration provides a cost-effective alternative to dispute resolution, and many disputes are resolved much sooner than they otherwise may have been in court. All industry members are required to settle all disputes through arbitration. A public customer, however, must agree in writing to settle any dispute through arbitration. When a customer opens an account with a broker dealer, the broker dealer will often have the customer sign a customer agreement, although this is not required by industry standards. The customer agreement usually contains a predispute arbitration cause where the customer agrees to settle any dispute that may arise in arbitration rather than court. Should the customer request a copy of the predispute arbitration clause the member has 10 business days to provide it to the customer.

THE ARBITRATION PROCESS

Arbitration begins when an aggrieved party, known as the claimant, files a statement of claim, along with a submission agreement and payment for the arbitration fee, with FINRA. The party alleged to have caused the claimant harm (known as the respondent), must respond to the statement of claim within 45 calendar days. The response is sent to both the arbitration director and the claimant, and the claimant then has 10 calendar days to reply to both the arbitration director and respondent. Dispute resolution through arbitration is available for matters involving:

- Member vs. member

- Bank vs. member

- Member vs. bank

- Member vs. registered representative

- Registered representative vs. member

- Customer vs. member

- Member vs. customer

SIMPLIFIED ARBITRATION

Simplified arbitration is available for disputes involving amounts in dispute of $50,000 or less. Simplified arbitration provides no opportunity for a hearing. Parties submit their case in writing only. One arbitrator reviews the case and renders a decision. For amounts that exceed $50,000, a hearing must be held.

LARGER DISPUTES

Larger disputes are submitted to a panel of up to three arbitrators to render a decision on the matter. A hearing will take place and evidence and testimony will be presented to the panel. The number of arbitrators must always be odd, so the panel is made up of one or three arbitrators from both the public and the industry. An arbitrator is deemed to be a nonpublic or industry arbitrator if the person is or was in the securities industry at any point in the last 5 years. Included in this definition are persons associated with hedge funds and accountants and attorneys whose practice, within the last 2 years, is dedicated at least 20% of the time to industry clients. An accountant or attorney is deemed to be a public arbitrator if 10% or less of the business of such professional was dedicated to industry clients in the last 2 years and the revenue received was less than $50,000.

AWARDS UNDER ARBITRATION

Awards under arbitration are final and binding; there is no appeal. If a monetary payment has been awarded, the party required to pay has 30 days to comply with the decision. A member or a registered representative who fails to pay an award under arbitration is subject to suspension. All pending arbitrations, arbitrations settled prior to final judgement, and arbitrations settled in favor of the customer will be disclosed on BrokerCheck. If an arbitration is settled in favor of the firm or representative it will be removed from BrokerCheck. Any sanction by a regulator which carries a penalty of $15,000 or more will also be disclosed on BrokerCheck.

MEDIATION

Mediation is an informal attempt by two parties to try to resolve a dispute prior to entering into the formal arbitration process. During the mediation process the two parties meet to discuss the contested issue, and the dialog is monitored by a mediator. The mediator is a neutral person with industry knowledge suggested by FINRA who tries to help the parties reach an agreement. If the mediator is not acceptable, the parties may select another mediator from a list of approved mediators or provide their own independent mediator. Prior to entering into the mediation process, both parties must agree to try to resolve the issue in mediation and must split the mediator's fee. The mediation process begins with an initial joint meeting where both parties lay out their claims for the mediator and the other party. During the second phase of the process, each side meets with the mediator individually in meetings known as caucuses. The mediator is a neutral party and will not disclose information provided during the caucus sessions to the opposing side. The mediation process continues until an agreement is reached, the mediator declares an impasse with no possible resolution, or one of the parties or the mediator withdraws from the process in writing. The mediation process may provide a resolution for all or some of the contested issues. Mediation may take place while the parties are moving forward with the arbitration process. Issues that are not resolved in mediation may be resolved through formal arbitration.

The party who served as the mediator may not serve as an arbitrator for the same dispute.

CURRENCY TRANSACTIONS

The Bank Secrecy Act requires all member firms to guard against money laundering. Every member must report any currency receipt of $10,000 or more from any one customer on a single day. The firm must fill out and submit a currency transaction report, also known as Form 4789, to the IRS within 15 days of the receipt of the currency. Multiple deposits that total $10,000 or more also require the firm to file a currency transaction report (CTR). Additionally, the firm is required to maintain a record of all international wire transfers of $3,000 or greater.

THE PATRIOT ACT

The Patriot Act, as part of the Bank Secrecy Act, requires broker dealers to have written policies and procedures designed to detect suspicious activity. The firm must designate a principal to ensure compliance with the firm's policies and to train firm personnel. The firm is required to file a Suspicious Activity Report (SAR) for any transaction of more than $5,000 that appears questionable. The firm must file the report within 30 days of identifying any suspicious activity. Anti-money-laundering rules require that all firms implement a customer identification program to ensure that the firm knows the true identity of its customers. All customers who open an account with the firm, as well as individuals with trading authority, are subject to this rule. The firm must ensure that its customers do not appear on any list of known or suspected terrorists. A firm's anti-money-laundering program must be approved by senior management. Should the approving member of management leave the firm the plan should be reapproved by the new member of senior management.

All records relating to the SAR filing, including a copy of the SAR report, must be maintained by the firm for 5 years. FINRA Rule 3310 requires member firms to identify to FINRA the name of the person in charge of the firm's AML program as well as the name and full contact details of the person(s) who are to oversee the day-to-day operation of the AML program. Any changes to AML persons identified to FINRA must be updated within 30 days. Members must also conduct an annual independent test of the program. The person conducting the test may not perform the daily AML duties at the firm or report to anyone in charge of the program. The person should have substantial knowledge of the Bank Secrecy Act and its related rules and regulations.

The money-laundering process begins with the placement of the funds. This is when the money is deposited in an account with the broker dealer. The second step of the laundering process is known as layering. The layering process consists of multiple deposits in amounts less than $10,000. The funds will often be drawn from different financial institutions, which is known as structuring. The launderers then purchase and sell securities in the account. The integration of the proceeds back into the banking system completes the process. At this point, the launderers may use the money, which now appears to have come from legitimate sources, to purchase goods and services. Firms must also identify the customers who open the account and must make sure that they are not conducting business with anyone on the OFAC list. This list is maintained by the Treasury Department Office of Foreign Assets Control. It consists of known and suspected terrorists, criminals, and members of pariah nations. Individuals and entities who appear on this list are known as Specially Designated Nationals and Blocked Persons. Conducting business with anyone on this list is strictly prohibited. Registered representatives who aid in the laundering of money are subject to prosecution and face up to 20 years in prison and a $500,000 fine per transaction. The representative does not even have to be involved in the scheme or even know about it to be prosecuted.

FinCEN is a bureau of the U.S. Department of the Treasury. FinCEN's mission is to safeguard the financial system and guard against money laundering and promote national security. FinCEN collects, receives, and maintains financial transactions data, analyzes and disseminates that data for law enforcement purposes, and builds global cooperation with counterpart organizations in other countries and with international bodies. FinCEN will e-mail a list of individuals and entities to a designated principal every few weeks. The principal is required to check the list against the firm's customer list. If a match is found the firm must notify FinCEN within 14 calendar days.

U.S. ACCOUNTS

Every member must obtain the following from U.S. customers:

- A social security number/documentation number
- Date of birth

- Address
- Place of business

FOREIGN ACCOUNTS

All non-U.S. customers must provide at least one of the following:

- A passport number and country of issuance.
- An alien ID number.
- A U.S. tax ID number.
- A number from another form of government-issued ID and the name of the issuing country.

ANNUAL COMPLIANCE REVIEW

At least once per year the member must conduct a compliance review of each OSJ, supervising branch office, and each registered representative. Nonsupervising branch offices should be directly reviewed every 3 years. When the member reviews the OSJ, the member is automatically inspecting the activities of the branch offices under the jurisdiction of the OSJ. Each member must designate a principal to test the firm's supervisory and compliance controls. This principal must file a report with senior management detailing the results of these tests. Controls must be in place to provide daily supervision of any producing managers.

BUSINESS CONTINUITY PLAN

One of the regulations developed as a result of the attack on 9/11 is the requirement for FINRA member firms to develop and maintain plans and backup facilities to ensure that the firm can meet its obligations to its customers and counterparties in the event that its main facilities are damaged, destroyed, or inaccessible. The plan must provide for alternative means of communication between the firm, its employees, customers, and regulators as well as a data backup. The plan must provide for data backup in both hard copy and electronic format. The plan must be approved and reviewed annually by a senior member of the firm's management team and ensure that customers have access to their funds. The plan must be provided to FINRA upon request. The plan must identify two members of senior management as emergency contacts, one of whom must be a registered principal with the firm. Should one of the contact people change, FINRA must be notified in 30 days. Customers of the firm must be advised of the business continuity plan at the time the account is opened, and in writing upon request. The plan must also be posted on the firm's website. Small firms with one office should provide a contact number to the clearing firm.

THE UNIFORM SECURITIES ACT

In the early half of the twentieth century, state securities regulators developed their state's rules and regulations for transacting securities business within their state. The result was a nation of states with regulations that varied widely from state to state. The Uniform Securities Act (USA) laid out model legislation for all states in an effort to make each state's rules and regulations more uniform and easier to address. The USA, also known as "The Act," sets minimum qualification standards for each state securities administrator. The state securities administrator is the top securities regulator within the state.

The state securities administrator may be the attorney general of that state or may be an individual appointed specifically to that post.

The USA also:

- Prohibits the state securities administrator from using the post for personal benefit or from disclosing information.

- Gives the state securities administrator authority to enforce the rules of the USA within that state.

- Gives the administrator the ability to set certain registration requirements for broker dealers, agents, and investment advisers.

- Administrators may set fee and testing requirements.

- Administrators may suspend or revoke the state registration of a broker dealer, agent, investment adviser, or a security or a security's exemption from registration.

- The USA also sets civil and criminal penalties for violators.

The state-based laws set forth by the USA are also known as blue-sky laws.

INVESTMENT ADVISERS ACT OF 1940

The Investment Advisers Act of 1940 regulates industry professionals who charge a fee for the advice they offer to clients. The Investment Advisers Act sets forth registration requirements for advisers as well as disclosure requirements relating to the adviser's:

- Methods of recommendations.
- Types of securities recommended.
- Professional background and qualifications.
- Fees to be charged.
- Method for computing and charging fees.
- Types of clients.

The Investment Advisers Act of 1940 prohibits an investment adviser from disclosing client information to a third party without the client's consent unless the adviser is required or compelled to disclose the information by law.

TENDER OFFERS

A tender offer is made by a person or firm who is seeking to purchase all or part of the outstanding securities of an issuer at a specific price. The SEC has issued strict guidelines that must be followed by both the person making the tender and investors who tender their securities. The guidelines to be followed by parties making a tender offer include:

- The offer must be open for 20 business days from the day it is announced.
- If any of the terms of the tender are changed, the tender must remain open for at least 10 business days from the day the change in the terms was announced.

- A party making a tender offer for stock may not buy the stock or the con-vertible securities of the issuer during the term of the tender. However, the party may purchase nonconvertible bonds.

- If the duration of the offer is extended, the announcement extending the offer must be released no later than the opening of the exchange on the business day following the original expiration date for exchange-listed securities. The announcement must include the amount of securities tendered to date.

- If a tender offer is extended for securities that are not listed on an exchange, the announcement must be made no later than 9:00 a.m. EST the business day following the original expiration and must also include the amount of securities tendered to date.

- Shareholders must be notified of the tender offer not later than 10 business days after the tender is announced.

- Management of the company subject to the tender offer must advise shareholders as to management's opinion on the offer (i.e., accept, decline, or neutral).

- A party making a tender offer must pay the price offered for the securities to the extent the offer was made.

Investors may only tender securities that they actually own. An investor may not sell short into a tender, which is known as short tendering. Investors are considered long the security if they have possession of the security or have issued exercise or conversion instructions for an option, warrant, or convertible security. Additionally, investors may only tender their securities to the extent of their net long position. If an investor is short against the box or has written calls with a strike price lower than the tender price, then the investor's net long position will be reduced.

| **EXAMPLE** | If an investor owns 1,000 XYZ and has written 5 XYZ June 40 calls when a tender offer is announced at $42 for XYZ, the investor can only tender 500 shares. |
| | During a partial tender the exact amount of securities to be accepted from all tendering parities is not known. As a result, an investor who has a convertible security may tender an amount equal to the amount to be received upon conversion. If the investor is informed that its tender has been accepted, it must convert the securities and deliver the subject securities. |

STOCKHOLDERS OWNING 5% OF AN ISSUER'S EQUITY SECURITIES

The Securities Exchange Act requires individuals or entities who acquire 5% or more of an issuer's equity securities to file Form 13D with the SEC. Rule 13D requires that the SEC, the exchange where the securities are listed, and the issuer be informed of the size of the investor's holdings and the purpose for the investment. Rule 13D does not require that the stockholders be informed directly by the investor. An entity may acquire more than 5% of the issuer's securities for investment purposes, for control, or for acquisition.

Other entities must also disclose their large holdings in an issuer's securities. Investment companies who acquire 5% or more of an issuer file a notice of their ownership on Form 13G. Investment advisers who have discretion over $100 million or more in assets must disclose their holding within 45 days of the end of each calendar quarter on Form 13F.

FINANCIAL EXPLOITATION OF SENIORS

While many people are living active and productive lives well into their eighties and beyond, FINRA has enacted rules designed to protect the financial interests' seniors who are 65 or older. FINRA is particularly concerned about clients being taken advantage of by unscrupulous or otherwise self-serving people. Registered representatives should have a clear understanding of the financial needs, resources, and behavior of their clients. This is specifically important when dealing with older clients who may require the assets to meet their current financial needs, and who can fall victim to bad actors. Registered representatives should be particularly concerned with any requests to withdraw money from an account that is outside the normal actions of the client.

EXAMPLE Sally is a retired school administrator who is 83 years old and is living on her assets. Sally and her late husband had planned well for their retirement. She has the proceeds from her husband's life insurance policy, a significant savings and retirement account, as well as her social security. Sally has been a client of your firm for 10 years and generally moves $1,800–$2,000 per month from her brokerage account to her checking account. Twice per year she travels and moves $5,000 to her checking account to pay her travel expenses. One day Sally calls up and says she needs $35,000 wired to an out-of-state bank account. When the agent inquires what this is for Sally says her friend has told her of an investment opportunity in real estate that she would like to take advantage of. When the agent inquires about the opportunity, the details she provides do not sound right to the agent.

ANALYSIS

This is a serious red flag, and in this situation the agent has a significant conflict. On the one hand, the agent is required to do as the client requests. On the other, the agent feels a duty to protect the client and senses that his or her client may be the victim of senior exploitation. Even discussing the matter with a principal of the firm is not enough to determine if the client is being taken advantage of.

FINRA's rules allow broker dealers to withhold distributions to senior clients in cases of suspected financial exploitation for 15 business days. During this time the broker dealer should investigate the client's request and obtain as much information regarding the receiving party as it can. To further protect seniors, broker dealers should obtain the name and contact information of a "trusted contact" for senior clients. The firm in very limited circumstances may contact the trusted contact to inquire about requests to withdraw money when financial exploitation is suspected. The firm may also contact the person to inquire as to the welfare of the client and to inquire as to the identity of any individual who may hold power of attorney or who may be named as executor of the client's will. If the firm at the end of 15 business days has gathered information relating to the request that indicates that this is a case of financial exploitation, the firm may withhold the funds for another 10 business days. The firm should share its findings with the center for elder abuse as well as with law enforcement.

Pretest

COMMUNICATIONS WITH THE PUBLIC, DISPUTE RESOLUTION, INSIDER TRADING, SIPC, AND AML

la.finra.comm.res.sipc.001_1811

1. A firm has been taken to arbitration by a customer. The disputed amount is $47,400. Which of the following is true?

    a. There will be a hearing, and the decision may be appealed.

    b. There will not be a hearing, and the decision may not be appealed.

    c. There will be a hearing, and the arbitrator's decision is final.

    d. There will be a hearing with up to three arbitrators.

la.finra.comm.res.sipc.002_1811

2. FINRA considers which of the following to be classified as retail communication?

    I. Video displays.
    II. Listings in phone directories.
    III. Circulars.
    VI. Telemarketing scripts.

    a. II and III.

    b. I and II.

    c. I, II, III, and IV.

    d. I and III.

la.finra.comm.res.sipc.003_1811

3. Your brokerage firm has placed an ad in the local newspaper, advertising its new line of services being offered to investors. The firm must maintain the ad for how long?

   a. 24 months.

   b. 36 months.

   c. 12 months.

   d. 18 months.

sa.finra.comm.res.sipc.001_1811

4. A testimonial by a compensated expert, citing the results she realized following a member's recommendations, must include which of the following?

   I. A statement detailing the expert's credentials.
   II. A statement that past performance is not a guarantee of future performance.
   III. A statement that the individual is a compensated spokesperson.
   IV. The name of the principal who approved the ad.

   a. I, II, and III.

   b. II and IV.

   c. I and II.

   d. I, II, III, and IV.

sa.finra.comm.res.sipc.002_1811

5. According to Rule 135, as it relates to generic advertising, which of the following is NOT true?

   a. The ad may contain information about the services a company offers.

   b. The ad may describe the nature of the investment company's business.

   c. The ad may contain information about exchange privileges.

   d. The ad may contain information about the performance of past recommendations.

Answer Keys

EQUITY AND DEBT SECURITIES

INTRODUCTION TO EQUITY SECURITIES

1. (b) Authorized stock is all of the answers listed, except the number of authorized shares may be changed by a vote of the shareholders.
2. (d) Common stockholders do not have voting power in the matter of bankruptcy.
3. (a) In addition to maintaining control, a company may want to increase its earnings per share, fund employee stock option plans, or use shares to pay for a merger or acquisition.
4. (d) As a common stock holder, you will have the right to receive your percentage of any residual assets.
5. (b) A stockholder does not get to vote directly for executive compensation.

WHY DO PEOPLE BUY STOCK?

1. (c) The yield on the stock will have gone up as the price has fallen because the dividend has remained constant.
2. (d) The investor will receive $8 per share × 100 shares: $800 plus $1 per share because it is participating, so $800 + $100 = $900.
3. (c) The investor who buys a 7% preferred stock is entitled to $7 per year or $3.50 every six months.
4. (c) A holder of a cumulative preferred has all the rights listed, except the right to convert the preferred into common stock.

5. (b) The current yield is found by using the following formula: annual income / current market price of $10 / $110 = 9.1%.

6. (c) First you must determine the number of shares. Par / conversion price = 100 / 20 = 5, multiplied by the number of preferred shares: 5 × 100 = 500.

DIVIDENDS, RIGHTS, WARRANTS, AND ADRs

1. (d) All choices listed are ways that a company can pay a dividend.

2. (d) All qualified dividends received by ordinary income earners are taxed at a rate of 15% for the year in which they were received.

3. (b) Each ADR represents between one to 10 shares, and ADR holders have the right to vote and receive dividends. Foreign governments put restrictions on the foreign ownership of stock from time to time.

4. (c) 800 shares × 5% = 40 shares.

5. (b) An ADR may represent more than one share of the company's common stock and may be exchanged for the ordinary common shares. The dividend, however, is paid in the foreign currency and is received by the investor in U.S. dollars; as a result, the investor is subject to currency risk.

6. (d) Dividend yield (or current yield) is found by dividing the annual income by the current market price.

INTRODUCTION TO DEBT SECURITIES

1. (c) An investor who has purchased an 8% corporate bond will receive the principal payment plus the last semiannual interest payment at maturity for a total of $1,040.

2. (a) The current yield is found by dividing the annual income by the current market price. In this case $100 / $1,200 = 8.33%

3. (a) An investor would expect to realize the largest gain by purchasing bonds when rates are high. The bond with the longest time left to maturity will become worth the most as interest rates fall.

4. (a) One bond point is worth $10.00; 1.25 points, therefore, is worth: $12.50 × 10 bonds = $125.

5. (a) The real interest rate will determine the return after inflation.

TYPES OF CORPORATE BONDS

1. (d) Bonds registered as to principal only will still require the investor to clip coupons.

2. (b) A mortgage bond is secured by real estate.

3. (d) Collateral trust certificates have pledged securities, which they own, issued by another company as collateral for the issue.

4. (b) The parity price of the stock is found by using the following formulas: no. of shares = PAR / CVP, 1,000 / 20 = 50, parity price = CMV of bond / no. of shares = 1,100 / 50 = 22.

5. (c) The parity price is found by determining the number of shares that can be received upon conversion par / conversion price = 1,000 / 25 = 40 shares. Then the parity price equals the current market value of the convertible / no. of shares, 1,200 / 40 = $30.

6. (d) Bearer bonds are issued without a name on them, meaning that whoever has possession of the bond may clip the coupons and claim the interest.

7. (c) All of the choices listed are reasons a corporation would attach warrants to their bonds, except to increase the number of shares outstanding.

MUNICIPAL BONDS

1. (d) Bonds issued by a turnpike authority to improve roads would be revenue bonds and the debt service would be supported through the collection of tolls. If the collection of tolls were not sufficient to cover the bond interest, the issuing state or county may cover the shortfall out of the general revenue. Of the choices listed, the bond is the most likely to have two sources of revenue backing the payments.

2. (a) General obligation bonds are subject to a statutory debt limit and voter approval. Revenue bonds do not draw on tax revenue and are not subject to voter approval or debt limits.

3. (c) Of all the choices listed, only an industrial revenue bond pays interest; all of the other choices are issued at a discount.

4. (d) When comparing a corporate bond and a municipal bond of the same quality and maturity, the corporate bond would have a higher coupon rate. Interest earned on municipal bonds is free from federal

income taxes and, as such, the coupon rate is lower than equal quality corporate bonds, which are subject to taxation.

5. (d) An industrial revenue bond is a private purpose municipal bond that is used to finance a facility leased to a corporation. The corporation rents the facility from the municipal government and the lease payments are used to pay the interest and principal payments. High income earners may have the interest income subject to tax.

GOVERNMENT AND GOVERNMENT AGENCY ISSUES

1. (a) EE savings bonds are sold at a discount and at maturity are redeemed at face value, which includes the interest income.

2. (b) Interest earned by investors on FNMA securities is taxable at all levels: federal, state, and local.

3. (c) The investor purchased the Treasury bond at 95.03 or 95-3/32% of $1,000 = $950.9375

4. (a) The minimum dollar amount to purchase a GNMA pass-through certificate is $1,000.

5. (c) T-bonds are quoted as a percentage of par to 32nds of 1%. A quote of 103.16 = 103

$$16/32\% \times 1,000 = \$1,035$$

THE MONEY MARKET

1. (b) The money market is a place where issuers go solely for short-term financing, typically under a year.

2. (d) A high-quality debt instrument with less than one year to maturity, regardless of its original maturity, may trade in the money market.

3. (d) Only bankers' acceptances have an original maturity of less than a year.

4. (d) The maximum duration for a piece of commercial paper is 9 months, or 270 days.

5. (a) A bank may borrow money from another bank to meet their reserve requirement and consequently pay the other bank the federal funds rate.

6. (b) Treasury bills are government money market instruments, not corporate money market instruments.

7. (c) The short-term maturity and the fact that the issuers have solid credit ratings make money market instruments very safe.

ECONOMICS, CORPORATE FUNDAMENTALS, ISSUING, AND TRADING SECURITIES

AN INTRODUCTION TO ECONOMICS AND CORPORATE FUNDAMENTALS

1. (b) The main theory of economics is one of supply and demand; if the supply outpaces the demand, the price of the goods will fall.

2. (d) The discount rate is the rate that is actually controlled by the Federal Reserve Board. All of the other rates are adjusted in the marketplace by the lenders as a result of a change in the discount rate.

3. (c) Falling inventories are a sign of a pickup in the economy.

4. (a) The two tools of the government are monetary policy, which is controlled by the Federal Reserve Board and controls the money supply, and fiscal policy, which is determined by the president and Congress and controls government spending and taxation.

5. (d) Fiscal policy is controlled by the president and Congress.

6. (c) The Federal Reserve sets all of those except government spending.

7. (a) A decline in the gross domestic product must last at least two quarters or 6 months to be considered a recession.

8. (c) During an inflationary period, the price of a Treasury bond will fall the most. The fixed-income security with the longest maturity will change the most in price as interest rates change.

9. (d) Rising interest rates are bearish for the stock market.

ISSUING AND OFFERING CORPORATE SECURITIES

1. (d) All of the items listed must appear in the tombstone ad.

2. (d) All of the parties listed may be held liable to the purchasers of the new issue.

3. (a) A corporation must issue common stock before it issues any preferred stock.

4. (c) Anytime the SEC wants more information, it would most likely issue a deficiency letter.

5. (a) Primary commitment is not a type of underwriting commitment.

6. (b) Purchasers of stock that has just gone public must get a prospectus for 25 days if the stock is Nasdaq listed.

7. (d) A company doing a rights offering will use a standby underwriting agreement whereby the underwriter will "standby" ready to purchase any shares not purchased by shareholders.

8. (a) All of the answers listed will appear in the preliminary prospectus, except the offering price and the proceeds to the company.

THE UNDERWRITING SYNDICATE AND EXEMPT TRANSACTIONS

1. (a) All of the choices listed are types of offerings except for Rule 149.

2. (d) Under Rule 147, 100% of the purchasers must be in the state. The issuer must meet one of the doing-business standards as listed in the other choices.

3. (c) A greenshoe provision allows the syndicate to purchase up to an additional 15% of the offering from the issuer.

4. (b) A business must first hire an underwriter to advise the issuer about the types of securities to issue.

5. (c) The number of nonaccredited investors is limited to 35 in any 12-month period.

6. (c) A Regulation A offering covers an offering of $50,000,000 or less in a 12-month period.

7. (c) An insider may sell securities under Rule 144 for 90 days.

8. (b) A syndicate may only enter a stabilizing bid at or below the offering price.

9. (b) Rule 145 covers mergers involving a stock swap or offer of another company's securities in exchange for its current stock.

ISSUING MUNICIPAL SECURITIES

1. (d) The debt service for general obligation bonds issued by the state is supported by revenue received at the state level. This revenue includes sales taxes and income taxes.

2. (b) General obligation bonds will be advertised in the daily bond buyer and the official notice of sale will provide details on the bidding procedure.

3. (c) This is a very small bond issue. As such it would not make sense in many cases to pay substantial legal fees to obtain a legal opinion. These bonds are said to be ex-legal because no legal opinion was ever obtained.

4. (b) Revenue bonds are issued through a negotiated underwriting process. The issuer will select the underwriter they would like to have offer the bonds and negotiate the terms with the underwriter directly.

TRADING SECURITIES IN THE SECONDARY MARKET

1. (d) An allied member may not trade on the floor. He is only allowed to call himself a member and have electronic access to the exchange.

2. (d) Mini/maxi and best efforts are types of underwriting commitments, not types of orders.

3. (c) A technical analyst would want to buy the stock when it breaks through resistance.

4. (a) The inside market is the highest bid and the lowest offer.

5. (a) Specialists on the NYSE work for themselves or for a specialist firm.

6. (b) The order has been elected because the stock has traded through the stop price. The order has now become a limit order to sell the stock at 160.

7. (a) Selling stock short will expose an investor to unlimited risk because there is no limit as to how high a stock price can go.

8. (c) An investor who is bullish would most likely enter a buy stop above the market.

THE ROLE OF BROKER DEALERS AND NASDAQ

1. (a) When acting as a market maker, the firm is trading for its own account and is acting as a dealer.

2. (c) Firms that act as market makers in Nasdaq securities are trying to make the spread, which is the difference between the bid and the ask.

OPTIONS, INVESTMENT COMPANIES, VARIABLE ANNUITIES, AND RETIREMENT PLANS

OPTION BASICS

1. (d) I is incorrect in that an option is a contract between two parties, which determines the time and price at which a security may be bought or sold.

2. (b) Option trades settle the next day.

3. (b) The OCC or Options Clearing Corporation issues all standardized options.

4. (c) Call sellers and put buyers are both bearish. They want the value of the stock to fall.

5. (a) The Options Clearing Corporation issues all option contracts and guarantees their performance.

USING OPTIONS TO HEDGE A POSITION AND EXERCISING OPTIONS

1. (b) To gain some protection and take in premium income, you would sell 100 XYZ Oct 45 calls.

2. (d) Buying puts will give the investor the most protection from a fall in the stock price. The investor will have set the minimum sales price for the stock as the strike price of the put.

3. (b) The investor is long the stock and wants to protect his position. The key to the question is that he does not want to spend any additional money. In this case he must sell a call. He will receive partial protection in the amount of the premium received.

INVESTMENT COMPANIES AND MUTUAL FUNDS

1. (c) An investor in a mutual fund portfolio has an undivided interest in that portfolio and is not an investor or stockholder in the fund company itself.

2. (d) The ex-dividend date is set by the NYSE/FINRA for a closed-end fund just like for a stock

3. (c) A mutual fund calling itself a diversified fund is limited to owning no more than 10% of any one company.

4. (c) New shares will be created for the investor as soon as the mutual fund company receives the money. The investor becomes an owner of record on that day.

5. (c) A mutual fund's custodian maintains books and records for accumulation plans.

6. (a) A fund with a portfolio turnover ratio of 25% replaces its portfolio every 4 years.

MUTUAL FUND INVESTMENT OBJECTIVES, VALUATION, AND SALES CHARGES

1. (b) A letter of intent is good for 13 months and may be backdated by the purchaser for 3 months. The 13-month window starts at the back date.

2. (a) A 12B-1 fee may be up to ¼ of 1% of the NAV.

3. (a) A 12b-1 fee is assessed by the mutual fund to cover printing of prospectuses and other promotional materials. It also covers other distribution expenses. It is an annual fee charged quarterly to the shares.

4. (b) A fund that charges a front-end load will be offered to the public at a price that is higher than its net asset value. The price known as the public offering price or POP contains the sales charge.

VARIABLE ANNUITIES

1. (b) A fixed annuity does not provide protection from inflation. If inflation rises, the holder of a fixed annuity may end up worse off due to the loss of value of the dollar.

INDIVIDUAL AND CORPORATE RETIREMENT PLANS

1. (c) The investor may contribute to both a traditional and Roth IRA in the same year. However, the amount contributed to both accounts may not exceed the annual contribution limit.

2. (c) Nonqualified accounts do not require that the owner take minimum distributions. A Roth IRA, variable annuity, and joint account do not allow owners to deduct contributions from their income. As such, the accounts are not required to take minimum distributions.

3. (d) An investor may always make a contribution to his IRA as long as he has earned income.

4. (d) The maximum amount that a couple may contribute to their IRAs at any one time is $22,000. Between January 1 and April 15, a contribution may be made for the prior year, the current year, or both: $5,500 \times 2 \times 2 = $22,000.

5. (c) The retirement account is qualified, which means the investor has deposited the money pretax, therefore, all of the money is taxed when it is withdrawn.

6. (a) A 529 plan would allow the investor to make a lump sum deposit.

7. (d) The maximum contribution for a SEP IRA is the lesser of 25% of the post contribution income or $57,000.

8. (c) This is a nonqualified plan, meaning the money is deposited after taxes so the retiree will only pay taxes on the growth.

9. (a) The money has been deposited in a Roth IRA after taxes. It is allowed to grow tax deferred. If you are over 59.5 and the money has been in the IRA for at least 5 years, then it may all be withdrawn without paying taxes on the growth.

CUSTOMER ACCOUNTS, CLIENT RECOMMENDATIONS, PROFESSIONAL CONDUCT, AND INDUSTRY REGULATIONS

CUSTOMER ACCOUNTS, UGMAS, ACCOUNTS FOR EMPLOYEES OF BROKER DEALERS, AND CUSTOMER PRIVACY

1. (a) In a custodial account, the custodian is the nominal owner of the account and carries on all transactions for the minor, the real beneficial owner of the account.

2. (d) An adult may never have a joint account with a minor.

3. (a) The assets of the decedent will be distributed according to the decedent's will.

4. (c) An account set up by a guardian must be accompanied by declaration papers.

5. (b) In a fiduciary account, the trustee enters all orders for the owners of the account.

6. (d) There is no limit to the size of the gift that may be given to anyone, but $15,000 per year is the tax-free limit.

7. (a) The nominal owner of an UGMA account is the custodian.

8. (b) A representative may borrow from a client if the client is in the business of making loans (i.e., a bank or credit union).

9. (c) The customer is not required to sign anything when opening a new account.

10. (d) The rule is one custodian and one minor for each UGMA account. There is not a rule regarding who must be custodian.

11. (a) A client may have a numbered account if his signature as owner is on file; broker dealers may give gifts to the employees of other broker dealers with certain restrictions. To obtain outside employment, a representative must first obtain approval from the member firm where he works.

12. (c) The customer's educational information is not required on the new account form.

13. (a) This is a joint account with rights of survivorship. All assets become the property of the surviving party.

14. (a) Before opening a new account for any customer, a registered representative must fill out and sign a new account form, which does not require the signature of the customer.

15. (c) A registered representative may only accept orders from the client.

16. (b) Although the minor's social security number is listed on the account, it does not appear in the account title.

EMPLOYEE CONDUCT AND REPORTABLE EVENTS

1. (b) This is known as painting the tape, matched purchases, or matched sales.

2. (d) Showing a client the past performance for a mutual fund that has only been around for 3 years is in line with the regulations. All of the other choices are violations.

3. (a) The investor has a large position in a thinly traded stock; as a result, the investor is subject to a large amount of liquidity risk.

4. (b) This is a violation known as trading ahead.

CUSTOMER RECOMMENDATIONS, PROFESSIONAL CONDUCT, AND TAXATION

1. (d) An industrial revenue bond may subject some wealthy investors to the alternative minimum tax.

2. (b) Of all the investments listed, only the Ginnie Mae pass-through certificate will provide income. Ginnie Mae pass-through certificates pay monthly interest and principal payments.

3. (b) An investor who is concerned with changes in interest rates would be least likely to purchase long-term bonds. As interest rates change, the price of the long-term bonds will fluctuate the most.

4. (b) Bankers' acceptances are money market instruments and are short term; series HH government bonds can only be exchanged for mature series EE; and convertible preferred stock is a security with risk. A 90-day T-bill is considered a risk-free investment.

5. (d) Using the pending dividend to create an urgency on the part of the investor to purchase this stock is a perfect example of this violation, and the results are listed in the first three answers.

6. (d) An investor in a low tax bracket seeking current income would be best suited for a corporate bond fund.

7. (d) An investor seeking protection from interest rate risk will most likely be best suited for a portfolio of Treasury bills. As the bills mature, the investor can roll over the position into newly issued bills with new interest rates.

8. (c) Treasury STRIPS are government-issued zero-coupon bonds. They are issued at a discount and mature at par, or $1,000. For the exam, they are the best answer for college expense planning if the question is asking for an investment recommendation, not the type of account that it is deposited into.

9. (c) A money market fund is the best recommendation for investors who will need access to their funds in the next few years.

10. (a) If an investor may lose part or all of his capital, it is called capital risk.

11. (d) This client is concerned about legislative risk, which is the risk that the government will do something that adversely affects an investment.

SECURITIES INDUSTRY RULES AND REGULATIONS

1. (d) The Securities Exchange Act of 1934 regulates the secondary market.

2. (d) The Uniform Practice Code regulates the way members conduct business with other members.

3. (d) The Maloney Act of 1938 was an amendment to the Securities Exchange Act of 1934 and established the NASD (now part of FINRA) as the self-regulatory organization for the over-the-counter market.

4. (a) A member firm may charge a customer a larger than ordinary commission for the execution of a specific order so long as it is disclosed to the customer. A member firm must always execute a customer's order.

5. (c) The SEC is the ultimate industry authority in regulating conduct.

REGISTRATION OF AGENTS AND CONTINUING EDUCATION

1. (a) The representative would have to notify her employer before working outside the office in any capacity.

2. (b) The part-time sales assistant who takes orders from customers must be registered because she is taking orders.

3. (c) When submitting the U4 an individual is required to provide all residence information for the last 5 years. Educational background is not required. The divorce would not be reported. However, if the person changed their name as a result of the divorce, the name change would be reported.

4. (d) All of the choices listed are associated people.

COMMUNICATIONS WITH THE PUBLIC, DISPUTE RESOLUTION, INSIDER TRADING, SIPC, AND AML

1. (b) There will be no hearing unless specifically requested by a public customer, and the decision of the arbitrator is final and binding. Claims under $50,000 will be resolved in simplified arbitration.

2. (c) All of the choices listed would be considered retail communication, if any part of the communications listed could be seen by an individual investor.

3. (b) Brokerage firms must maintain their advertising for at least 3 years.

4. (a) All of the choices listed must be included, except for the name of the principal who approved the ad for use.

5. (d) Generic advertising may not contain information about past recommendations.

Redeem Your 50% Coupon for the Securities Industry Essentials (SIE) Exam Review Course + eBook

ONLINE

✔ Bite-sized lessons to help you learn faster and retain more
✔ Dashboards & performance metrics
✔ Prepare alongside The Securities Institute of America, Inc.

Visit
efficientlearning.com/securities/products/ securities-industry-essentials-sie/

Enter Code: **SIE50**

This code is limited to the first 500 customers

For customer support, please visit: **efficientlearning.com/contact-us**

Visit efficientlearning.com/securities

WILEY